Pushkin's Historical Imagination

Russian Literature and Thought

Gary Saul Morson, Series Editor

PUSHKIN'S

Historical Imagination

Svetlana Evdokimova

Yale University Press New Haven and London

Chapter 7 is a slightly modified version of an article
published in *Russian Literature* 28 entitled "Медный
Всадник: история как миф," pp. 441–60, 1990,
with permission from Elsevier Science.

Library of Congress Cataloging-in-Publication Data
Evdokimova, Svetlana.
Pushkin's historical imagination / Svetlana
Evdokimova.
p.   cm. — (Russian literature and thought)
Includes bibliographical references and index.
ISBN 0-300-07023-3 (cloth: alk. paper)
1. Pushkin, Aleksandr Sergeyevich, 1799–1837 —
Knowledge — History.   2. History in literature. —
I. Title.   II. Series.
PG3358.H45E94   1998   98-9228
891.71'3 — dc21   CIP

Printed in the United States of America by
BookCrafters, Inc., Chelsea, Michigan.
A catalogue record for this book is available from the
British Library.

The paper in this book meets the guidelines for
permanence and durability of the Committee on
Production Guidelines for Book Longevity of the
Council on Library Resources.

10 9 8 7 6 5 4 3 2 1

For my mother, Kseniia Vogak,
and in memory of my aunt Eugenia

contents

preface

Only the fool does not change, for time does not
bring him any development, and experience does not
exist for him.

—Alexander Pushkin

During his short but tempestuous life, Pushkin fought many
duels. His most persistent and never-ending duel, however, was
not with his enemies, slanderers, and offenders but with the
past, time, and history. Pushkin was the first major Russian
poet after Karamzin who devoted himself both to fiction and to
history proper. Spurred by the defeat of Napoleon in 1812 and
the shock of the abortive Decembrist revolt in 1825, Pushkin's
interest in history developed into a lifetime quest.

In October of 1830, during the famous Boldino autumn, at
the crucial moment in his literary career and his personal life,
Pushkin set down a poem emblematic of his incessant search
for the enigma of time and history. While contemplating the
clockwise motion and striking of the clock, the lyrical persona
of "The Verses Composed at Night During Insomnia" ("Stikhi,
sochinennye noch'iu, vo vremia bessonnitsy") questions the
meaning of time and of the present that inevitably and relent-
lessly slips away into the past:

> Что тревожишь ты меня?
> Что ты значишь, скучный шепот?
> Укоризна, или ропот
> Мной утраченного дня?

От меня чего ты хочешь?
Ты зовешь или пророчишь?
Я понять тебя хочу,
Смысла я в тебе ищу . . . (III: I, 250)

Why do you disturb me?
What is your significance, wearisome whisper?
A reproach or a complaint
Of a bygone day?
What do you wish from me?
Do you call or prophesy?
I want to comprehend you,
I seek your meaning . . .

The poet faces the eternal symbol of time, a clock, as his adversary. Significantly, his addressee is not the clock, but the motion of time or of history itself. More importantly, Pushkin frames the relationship between the poet and time as a reciprocal one, as a mutual challenge: *ty khochesh'—ia khochu; ty trevozhish', ty zoviosh'—ia ishchu*. Challenged by time (*ty zoviosh' ili prorochish'*), the poet in turn responds to time with emphatic questions (five interrogative sentences). The poem thus marks a communicative event, a sort of a contest between the poet and time or history, but offers no resolution. The ellipsis at the end underscores the unfinalizability of the historical quest in which each answer generates only new questions.

In this contest with the past, present, and future, Pushkin alternately and sometimes simultaneously experienced moments of triumph, frustration, bewilderment, defeat, and reconciliation. However, after each encounter with history (history as narrative or history as immediate life experience), the poet would approach a new barrier with renewed energies and perseverance.

Pushkin was challenged not only by history, which he himself challenged, but he emerged also as a challenge *to* Russian history and to Russian literary criticism. Pushkin's role in formulating and stimulating modern debates on Russian history could hardly be overestimated. The poet's preoccupation with Peter the Great and his epoch made him the progenitor of a Russian national mythology that shaped the historical discourse of generations of Russian writers and intellectuals. His provocative statements about the nature of Russian history laid the groundwork for subsequent historical and literary debates—continuing to this day—between the "Slavophiles" and "Westernizers." The ensuing scholarship on the subject of Pushkin and history is extensive and continues to proliferate.

Although both Russian and American scholars have furnished several stimulating analyses of Pushkin's individual narratives dealing with historical subjects, surprisingly few attempts have been made to consider Pushkin's historical writings as a group.[1] In fact, a study addressing directly Pushkin's historical imagination still represents a distinct gap in North American scholarship.[2]

This monograph delineates Pushkin's fascination with history as a set of historical encounters. Each encounter represents his need to comprehend history and at the same time reflects Pushkin's awareness of history's insolubility and the impossibility of its completeness. This study aims to delineate the poet's continuously shifting perspectives on specific historical events and on the nature of historical process. What characterizes Pushkin's historical quest is not an attempt to create a system, a philosophy, a theory that would cohere, but rather a desire to remain an observer and persistently to challenge established historical "formulas," including his own. This explains why again and again Pushkin rewrites not only his predecessors' texts but also his own, returns to the same historical figures and epochs in various genres, and considers them from different points of view and within new contexts. He wrote a history of the Pugachev rebellion in Russia, *History of Pugachev*, at the same time as he composed a historical novel, *The Captain's Daughter*, one which portrays Pugachev as one of the protagonists. He created his famous imaginative narratives in different genres on the theme of Peter the Great—*The Blackamoor of Peter the Great, Poltava, The Bronze Horseman*—and simultaneously set about a scholarly history of Peter the Great. One can clearly discern artistic and conceptual motivation behind Pushkin's "multi-perspectival" approach to art and history.[3]

In her pivotal study of *Boris Godunov*, Caryl Emerson shows how Pushkin offers the reader "an assemblage of glimpses drawn from different perspectives," rather than "a series of interlocking and exemplary life situations" (Emerson 1986, 97). To further elaborate on her observation, one might say that Pushkin's "multi-perspectival" approach manifests itself not only in a seemingly random arrangement of the scenes within a single text but also in self-conscious experimentation with different narratives focusing on the same historical phenomenon. The creative impulse behind this experimentation is rooted in Pushkin's commitment to such concepts as change, relativity, context, and complementarity in the study of events.

If Pushkin's views may appear or are indeed inconsistent, they are so not because of the poet's fault, but because of his perspectival approach. Each context generates different generic expectations and presupposes different goals. Looking at the same phenomenon from different perspectives, both diachronically and synchronically, Pushkin creates multiple self-enclosed universes, each governed by its own inner consistency.

The most productive critical approach, then, to Pushkin lies in focusing on each individual text rather than trying to deduce universal conclusions from his heterogeneous oeuvre. With the exception of the Introduction, which provides a theoretical framework for this study, and Chapter 1, this book relies almost exclusively on close analysis of Pushkin's imaginative writings of various genres.

Part I examines Pushkin's attempts to establish the connection between historical development and national identity. Pushkin assesses various historical institutions and events and explores the role of historiographical categories comparatively and circumstantially, always trying to relate them to a specific historical context. Thus, he addresses the role of chance and necessity not in terms of invariable historiographic categories, but as notions whose meanings change in diverse political contexts.

Part II further develops the notion of national and cultural context as a dominant element in Pushkin's historical and artistic vision. Contextualism emerges as a principal method of historical inquiry adopted by Pushkin in order to better comprehend historical processes in general, and the Russian situation in particular. The contextualist approach is revealed in the poet's dealing with each specific situation, his avoidance of generalizations, and his attempt to see the relative nature of events. Pushkin sought to demonstrate how a single phenomenon might have different meaning in different historical circumstances. "What London needs," Pushkin cautions the reader, "is too early for Moscow."

Part III explores a typically Pushkinian approach to history, the one consisting of multiple complementary perspectives on the same historical phenomenon. These are Pushkin's Peter the Great narratives.

Clearly, Pushkin had a predilection toward the periods of political turbulence including the critical moments of modern Western civilization, such as the American and the French revolutions, and the advent of Napoleon. Likewise, he turned his attention to the periods of Russian history marked by turmoil and drastic change: the reign of Boris Godunov and the emergence of Russian impostors, the reforms of Peter the Great, the peasant riots of Razin and Pugachev. Yet there is no historical character that would figure more prominently in his works than Peter the Great. Several lyric poems and three major fictional works of Pushkin—*Poltava, The Blackamoor of Peter the Great, The Bronze Horseman,* and his uncompleted historical project, *A History of Peter*—emerged from his fascination with the first Russian emperor.

It is hardly surprising that the reign of Peter the Great—

the most eventful and controversial period of Russian history—
attracted Pushkin to the point that it became a center for his
historico-philosophical and literary inquiries. For it is Peter the
Great who was and still remains a stumbling-block—a *Lapis offe-
sionis et Petra scandali*—of Russian history and of all Russian historical debates. Few figures in nineteenth century Russia achieved
historical and symbolic status comparable to that of Peter the
Great. In search of the historical periods that would hold the key
to solving the Russian predicament, and provide the clue to the
elusive and fragile Russian identity, Russian intellectuals incessantly turned to Petrine reforms. Both those who eulogized Peter
for introducing Westernization to the old Muscovy and those who
blamed him for breaking with tradition and inflicting the un-
bridgeable gap between the educated upper classes and the common people, considered Peter *the* hero of Russian history.

The riddle of Peter the Great haunts Russian imagination to
this day. Suffice it to mention the fierce polemic concerning the
installation of the monument of Peter in St. Petersburg, by the
Russian émigré artist Mikhail Shemiakin. For what is at issue now
(as it has been for 150 years) is a problem of national identity
that is closely intertwined with the way Russians perceive Peter
the Great and his role in Russian history. In their historical bewilderment, Russians still look at Peter in a way reminiscent of
Pushkin's Tatiana's view of Onegin:

Кто ты, мой ангел ли хранитель,
Или коварный искуситель:
Мои сомненья разреши (VI, 67).

But who are you:
the guardian angel of tradition,
or some vile agent of perdition
sent to seduce? (*Eugene Onegin*, 101)

Pushkin's Peter the Great narratives, however, suggest no an-
swers but only generate further questions—similar to those for-

mulated in his Boldino poem about the enigma of time: *Ia poniat'* *tebia khochu,* / *Smysla ia v tebe ishchu.* . . . Whether by chance, fate, or intention, Pushkin did not complete his monumental work *A History of Peter the Great,* one of the most symbolic ellipses in his writing, an ellipsis signifying the incompleteness of history itself.

This analysis of Pushkin's historical and metahistorical texts should extend our understanding of the poet's infinitely varied perceptions of history. If there is anything that unites them, it is Pushkin's believing in, and striving for, the complementarity of multiple truths.

A Note to the Reader

Unless otherwise noted, all quotations from Pushkin's works are cited by volume (Roman numbers) and page number (Arabic) in his *Polnoe sobranie sochinenii,* Moscow: Akademiia Nauk, 1937–58, 17 vols. When there are two sub-volumes, the volume number is followed by a colon and the number indicating the part. For example, "IX: I, 37" refers to vol. 9, sub-volume 1, p. 37.

When citing from another edition of Pushkin's collected works, I include additional information. For example, "Pushkin 1962–66: VIII, 145" refers to Pushkin's *Polnoe sobranie sochinenii,* ed. by B. V. Tomashevskii, Moscow: Nauka, 1962–66, 10 vols.

I have used a modified Library of Congress system of transliterating Russian, except for names whose Anglicized spelling is more familiar to readers (e.g., Belinsky, Dostoevsky, Tolstoy, Tertz). In quotations, I preserve the original spelling of the names, which may deviate from my own.

I have used ellipses with square brackets around them to indicate my omissions to portions of the original text; ellipses without brackets are in the original. Except where noted, all italics are in the original.

All translations are mine unless otherwise specified.

acknowledgments

I would like to acknowledge my debt to a number of people who have responded to this book during various stages of its evolution. My first thoughts on this project came while I was a graduate student in the Department of Slavic Languages and Literatures at Yale University. First and foremost, my sincere gratitude and thanks are to Robert Louis Jackson, who has been my reader since the book's inception, who has provided me with invaluable commentary on successive drafts, and who has inspired me with his own love and appreciation of Russian literature, history, and culture. Several people, most notably Tomas Venclova, Victor Erlich, and Gary Saul Morson, made comments on the whole or parts of the earlier versions of this study, which have been indispensable in shaping this book. I owe a very special debt to Caryl Emerson for her meticulous reading of the entire manuscript and for her wise comments, advice, and encouragement, as well as for her own exemplary Pushkin scholarship, which served as a model for me. Paul Debreczeny's detailed and scrupulous criticism of this book's final drafts not only led me to many corrections and improvements, but made me rethink certain parts of this study and modify the book's structure. I benefited greatly from Richard Gustafson's generously extensive and profound comments on the final manuscript and his always useful suggestions for modifications of formulations of my ideas.

An earlier version of Chapter 7 appeared as "Mednyi Vsadnik: istoriia kak mif," in *Russian Literature*, 28 (1990). I thank the journal for permission to use this material. In addition, I have given a talk on what constitutes the core of Chapter 4 and part of Chapter 3 at a dozen conferences and institutions in the United States and in Russia during the past seven years. Critical responses of those who listened to these sections of my book helped me to sharpen the issues laid out in those earlier versions of the argument and to avoid many dangerous misconceptions. Chapter 4 in particular benefited greatly from Elizabeth Allen's many useful stylistic suggestions and from Snejana Tempest's expertise in finding the right words in some of my translations. I am also grateful to Molly Kertzer and Ashley Minihan for looking for typos and syntactical lapses. I alone of course am responsible for any errors that may remain in the text despite all the advice and scrutiny my book received.

A grant from the International Research and Exchanges Board, with funds provided by the U.S. Department of State and the National Endowment for the Humanities, permitted me to consult with Russian colleagues and to browse through Russia's extensive library resources. I am especially grateful to the Academy of Sciences' Institute of Russian Literature (Pushkinskii Dom) for its hospitality, intellectual generosity, and the expertise of its scholars.

A fellowship from the National Endowment for the Humanities (Spring 1995) and sabbatical leave from Brown University (Fall 1994) enabled me to complete this project. None of these organizations is responsible for the views expressed in this study.

I am also indebted to my colleagues at Brown University, Alexander Levitsky, Patricia Arant, and Robert Mathiesen for their encouragement at times when I needed it most. At the university administration level, Dean of the Faculty Kathryn Spoehr kindly subsidized a portion of the costs of manuscript preparation.

My editor at Yale University Press, Jonathan Brent, resolved a variety of expected and unexpected technical problems with inimitable courtesy and professionalism. It was a particular joy to work with Gary Saul Morson, general editor of the Russian Literature and Thought Series, and the staff of Yale University Press, Margaret Otzel and Cynthia Wells. I am immensely grateful to them for their editorial expertise and patience.

Finally, Vladimir Golstein, my husband and colleague, has provided moral and intellectual support in the dreariest moments of doubt and demonstrated unfailing patience in dealing with my obstinacy during our literary debates.

introduction   History, Fiction, and the
Complementarity of Narrative Representations

The analysis of the relationship between history and fiction—a
problem that has stimulated European thought since the time
of Aristotle, was developed by Vico, and then elaborated in
structural and post-structural theory—has special relevance in
the Russian context in general and for the study of Pushkin
in particular. The beginning of the nineteenth century was a
turning point in the development of both Russian literary and
historical imagination. This was the time of artistic experimentation, when old genres were rethought and new ones prolifer-
ated. The Romanticist interest in history generated an intense
growth in historical fiction and history proper. This further
stimulated generic awareness among Russian writers.

It has often been observed that the conflation of history and
imaginative literature was particularly typical of Russian literary and historical traditions. Russia, with its peculiar development and separation from the rest of Europe, had no formal
historiography, nor did it have fully developed traditions of
formal theology and philosophy until the beginning of the nineteenth century. Literature came to fulfill those functions that
were divided in the West among various disciplines and areas of
human knowledge such as philosophy, theology, history, ethics,
aesthetics, law, and political science. The particular characteristics of European Romantic historiography—a desire to supplement the traditional skills of the neoclassical historian, such
as erudition and critical judgment, with creative mythmaking
and poetic insight—were deeply rooted in Russian cultural tradition. The European Romantics at the beginning of the nineteenth century advanced the figure of the poet-historian, one

that Nietzsche later conjured up in reaction to positivist science and conventional historical thought. In Russia, however, the figure of the poet-historian represents a continuous tradition and remains unchallenged to the present day. The following passage from *Russian Nights* (*Russkie nochi*, 1844), a work by an influential Romantic writer, Vladimir Odoevsky, illustrates this peculiarity of the Russian cultural tradition:

> Everywhere in the world, scholarly research preceded the poetic approach to history. In Russia, on the contrary, poetic *insight* anticipated actual investigation . . . Pushkin (in *Boris Godunov*) divined the character of the Russian chronicler, although our chronicles were not scrutinized by centuries of historical criticism and the chroniclers themselves are still a sort of myth in the historical sense. [. . .] Lazhechnikov (in *The Infidel*) reproduced an even more complex character, a character of the Old Russian young woman, while the significance of women in Russian society which predates Peter the Great still remains a real puzzle in the *scholarly sense*. Now look at these characters in the historical monuments which are just being published, and you will be struck by the truthfulness of these ghosts, conjured up by the magic power of poets (I: 244).

It is not surprising, then, that Pushkin had a greater impact on Russian political thought as a poet and mythmaker than as a historian. In its popularity both among the common reader and scholars, Pushkin's *History of Pugachev* (*Istoriia Pugacheva*) could never compete with his historical novel on the same subject, *The Captain's Daughter* (*Kapitanskaia dochka*). The fate of his unfinished *History of Peter the Great* (*Istoriia Petra*) is even more symbolic. While his celebrated poetical works dedicated to Peter the Great were memorized by generations of Russians, the manuscript of his *History* was lost because of his relatives' and friends' neglect and was recovered only by chance in 1917. It was first published in 1938—a century after the poet's death!

Pushkin was rarely explicit about the problem of the relationship between history and imaginative literature. Yet he treated the same historical themes, periods, and figures in both fiction and non-fiction. His reflections on the nature of history and fiction, or in his own terms between *istoriia* and *vymysel* ("fiction," "imagination," "invention"), are scattered throughout his letters and are often incorporated in both his fictional and non-fictional writings. As opposed to the dominant Russian trend and the general Romanticist tendency to merge history and fiction, Pushkin had a measured and considered approach to the problem of history and imaginative literature. He wanted to be both poet and historian and strove for complementarity of history and fiction as two distinct modes of historical representation that can and, indeed, must coexist.

Literary and historical theorists (Foucault, Lévi-Strauss, Barthes, White, Gearhart, among others) have often emphasized the elusive boundary between history and fiction. Hayden White, for example, treats historians like any other narrators; they are distinguished by their modes of speech. Similarly, Suzanne Gearhart postulates an "open boundary of history and fiction," one that is open "in a more radical sense, for the very domains it is supposed to separate and delimit continually cross over it also" (4). It is more and more frequently stressed that there is no significant difference between historical and fictional narratives, that in histories proper historians use literary devices and techniques of selection and organization not too different from those of a historical novel and ultimately create narratives that appear as linguistic constructs similar to any other genre of writing (see Hutcheon). As a result, very different works are reduced to sets of the same structural principles and often used to lead the reader to essentially the same conclusion, one postulated from the outset: history's claim to be a science is wrong, there can be no objective historiography, and, therefore, a mythic or poetic consciousness lies behind all representations of reality. Eventually such a view leads to a further reduction of the poetic, or mythic consciousness, to a limited number of available mythic and literary patterns, as demonstrated by Northrop Frye[1] or White's tropology.

Moreover, as the notion of objective truth has been shaken and the status of historical fact problematized, history's empiricist and positivist claims encounter ever-growing skepticism, and the nineteenth century epistemology is viewed with persistent distrust. While structuralist and formalist approaches to historical writings may be useful for our understanding of both history and fiction and the critics' Kantian questioning of the objective "reality" fully valid, it is clear that postmodernist literary criticism tends to obscure some significant differences between the two modes of writing for the sake of promoting its own dominant ideology, that of suspicion and ultimately denial of any objective truth. The problem, however, is that this negation of objective truth often is not viewed historically, that is, as a manifestation of a specific historical phase, and results, therefore, in a contradiction, for it emerges as a new version of an absolute truth. It is necessary, therefore, to place these important postmodernist insights in a proper historical and philosophical perspective.

First, one should acknowledge that the notion of the artificiality of the barriers separating history from fiction is not a particularly original discovery of the twentieth-century theoreticians. The sharp distinction between historiography and fiction that has come to characterize later eighteenth-century historiography and post-Romantic historicism was vital only for a relatively short period of time. The classical Greek view regularly conflated history and myth without insistence on strict chronological and temporal fidelity (see Weinstein). As Herbert Lindenberger says in his study *History in Literature: On Value, Genre, Institutions,* in earlier centuries "what separated historical narrative from other forms such as epic and tragedy was largely a matter of generic classification. By the nineteenth century, however, literature had come to occupy its own realm, a realm that defined itself as art and that literature came to share with painting and music. Whereas letters could once accommodate such diverse genres as historical narrative, biography, and scientific treatise, that new art-oriented classification called literature could absorb history only when the latter was subsumed within one of the reigning literary genres" (Lindenberger 1990, 7–8). Moreover, the rhetorical implications of historical writing were recognized and accepted at least since Cicero's *De legibus*. Thus, it seems that when post-Nietzschean Western European and American thinkers such as Heidegger, Sartre, Bakhtin, Auerbach, Lévi-Strauss, Foucault, Gallie, and White, among many others, questioned the very notion of "scientific" history by stressing the fictive character of historical reconstructions, they articulated views not too different in this respect from pre-eighteenth-century notions of history and fiction. Moreover, the nineteenth-century Romantics already sought to mediate between empirical historicism and creative mythmaking.[2] For many Romantics, works of the literary artist and those of the historian were virtually indistinguishable.

It is important to point out here that the very concepts of history and fiction are not static, and therefore, the affinities and distinctions between the two forms of writing are fluid as well (cf. Hutcheon, 55; Gearhart, 11). The way history is understood in the eighteenth century, for example, is radically different from the view of history as science, which gradually establishes itself in the nineteenth century. Just as nineteenth century progressively strove to delineate the boundary separating history from fiction, so the twentieth century theoreticians (and practicians) seem to focus on what connects them. With our changing notions of the distinctions between history and fiction, the specific realizations of historical and fictional discourses also change. Thus, whatever we say about the differences and similarities between history and fiction may be true only for the history and fiction as defined in a specific age.

It is no coincidence that along with the historians' mixing fiction, fact, and legend in their historiographical practice, there was a tendency to delineate history's and fiction's different tasks.

The problem, however, is that this difference was often located in the wrong place, that is, in the accuracy of the represented events. Even Aristotle who seems to differentiate between different *functions* of history and poetry, formulates the main distinction between the two modes of writing in terms of their adherence to historical fact: history speaks of what has happened, whereas poetry preoccupies itself with what could or might happen. Aristotle acknowledges that poetry may include events that really happened. Nevertheless, he insists that these events represent universals rather than the particulars of history and ultimately places poetry above history as being more philosophical.

The distinction between history and fiction as outlined above certainly does not apply to any history and any fiction. A student of Tolstoy, for example, would remember that Tolstoy attempts to reverse the Aristotelian dichotomy of poetry and fiction by claiming that it is a historian who represents the general while the poet is capable of capturing and depicting the particular (see Morson, 144–7; Gifford 1984, 124). Moreover, not only the theory but the art of postmodernism obliterate the notion that fiction is based on plausibility or probability whereas history deals with verification (see Hutcheon, 61). As Linda Hutcheon says, "It is part of the postmodernist stand to confront the paradoxes of fictive vs. historical representation, the particular vs. the general, and the present vs. the past" (56). Both Tolstoy's distrust of historical knowledge and the postmodernist skepticism about the possibility of factual representation reflect the crisis of the positivist and empiricist approach to history and science. It is clear, therefore, that one cannot make any absolute theoretical conclusion about the relationship between history and fiction, since this relationship changes depending on the governing ideologies of the time: what may be true for one age turns out to be completely inadequate for another historical era. Rather one could make an attempt to delineate this relationship for a particular age based on this age's dominant ideology and theoretical assumptions.

Secondly, the postmodernist emphasis on the fictive nature of history is undoubtedly indebted to Kant's concern with the mind's capacity to perceive and, therefore, shape reality. Philosophically, one cannot deny the fact, formulated by Kant, that our knowledge of objects is first given to us in the form of a concept. As Gossman points out, this postulation leads to the conclusion that "knowledge of phenomena (such as philology and history aspire to) and knowledge of ideas (philosophy) are not therefore completely distinct, but complementary and inseparable from each other" (Gossman, 277–8). What follows, then, I believe, from the connection Kant makes between perception, conceptualization, and the effects these conceptualizations might have on human understanding and actions is that one has to take seriously the author's initial choice of a particular narrative form — fictional or non-fictional — to represent historical data. Ultimately, it is inevitable that the choice of fiction over history with their respective generic assumptions should affect the final outcome of one's intellectual activity and will result in distinctly different types of narrative. In other words, we need to observe the observer and to explore the author's shaping mind in order to better understand any text we read.

I contend, therefore, that a fruitful, although also a limited way to evaluate the distinctions between history and fiction is to focus on the underlying principles of both modes of writing during a particular age, that is, to consider the initial assumptions of a historian and a poet rather than the degree of factual accuracy in either type of narrative. The writer's intent was unjustifiably dismissed by many critics at least since the emergence of formalism and New Criticism. Yet if the author's conceptual and aesthetic orientation is not to be understood crudely as a preconceived plan but rather as a general thrust of thought or initial mental set, then the consideration of the author's primary "hypothesis" or assumptions may have great heuristic value as demonstrated most vividly by E. H. Gombrich in his consistently Kantian analysis of the psychology of perception, of the viewer's involvement with a work of art and the way observation both affects representation and depends on the degree of our knowledge. "All culture and all communication," Gombrich maintains in *Art and Illusion*, "depend on the interplay between expectation and observation, the waves of fulfillment, disappointment, right guesses, and wrong moves that make up our daily life. [. . .] The experience of art is not exempt from this general rule. A style, like a culture or climate opinion, sets up a horizon of expectation, a mental set, which registers deviations and modifications with exaggerated sensitivity" (60).

The difference between historical and fictional accounts of reality results, therefore, in part from different sets of expectations that underline the work of a historian and of a fiction writer. I contend, therefore, that whether de facto the dichotomy between history and imaginative literature is true or false is not important for the understanding of the nature of history and fiction. The point is that, no matter what it is called (a different genre or a different type of cognitive inquiry), the *function* of history in historical works is substantially different not only from the role history plays in fiction in general, but from the role it plays in historical fiction in particular.[3] What is significant is that, once the specific assumptions about the nature of history and fiction exist in the minds of fiction and history writers, they have to lead them to specifically different modes of constructing their narratives and ultimately to different conclusions.

As is established now in contemporary science, more specifically in microphysics, there is no method of observation that would not interact with the observed object. My approach to the relationship between history and fiction in the nineteenth century and to Pushkin as a historian and as a fiction writer specifically, therefore, is based on an analogy borrowed from physics. Such an analogy — which was successfully used in the discussion of Shakespeare's ambivalences — facilitates an understanding of the relationship between Pushkin's historical and fictional renderings of the same historical material and helps us to differentiate between history and fiction in general.[4]

This analogy is related to the concept of complementarity in quantum theory. This concept was stimulated by Heisenberg's discovery of the uncertainty principle and developed by Niels Bohr. Heisenberg's uncertainty principle, or the principle of indeterminacy relations of mechanical quantities, states that we cannot know *both* the position and the momentum of a particle with absolute precision. This discovery gave Bohr a clue to the analysis of this particular relationship in terms of complementarity. When we are dealing with atomic systems, Bohr pointed out, the fundamental concepts of physics, such as waves and particles, for instance, have to be applied and restricted in the peculiar manner defined by indeterminant relations. In other words, even though the concepts of waves and particles are thought to be equally essential parts of a full understanding of the phenomena, they still exist in a relationship of mutual exclusiveness. Heisenberg, speaking about the two ways of looking at the phenomena—"the wave picture" and "the particle picture"—summarizes this point as follows: "Bohr advocated the use of both pictures, which he called 'complementary' to each other. The two pictures are of course mutually exclusive, because a certain thing cannot at the same time be a particle (i.e., substance confined to a very small volume) and a wave (i.e., a field spread out over a larger space), but the two complement each other. By playing with both pictures, by going from the one picture to the other and back again, we finally get the right impression of the strange kind of reality behind our atomic experiments" (Heisenberg, 49).

The dualism between two different descriptions of the same reality in history and fiction is analogous to the dualism between the two complementary pictures—waves and particles. As in physics, the result of certain experiments dealing with light depends on the goals of the observer, one could say that the choice of one genre over another depends on the goal of the writer. However, the distinctions between various fictional genres and history differ qualitatively. The goal of all fictional genres (no matter how different they are among themselves and what is the degree of their historicity) is based on similar assumptions and on the same premise. This assumption in most basic terms is as follows: all fiction is fiction, that is, it is based on or includes "invention" (Russian *vymysel*, that is, "invention," "imagination," "fancy"). Invention, as opposed to evidence, is of the nature of the plausible, not the factual. As a result, the notion of truth in fiction is specifically fictional. Or, the writer even in the case where he or she incorporates a great deal of factual information in the narrative—sometimes even strict historical data—nevertheless bases his or her narrative on the premise that it represents *invention*. The artist, in other words, achieves a result, or "truth(s)," derived from his or her perception of reality with the intention of writing fiction.

History, by contrast, is constructed according to a completely different premise, that is, on the assumption that it is based on evidence, research, and verification. History specifically denies *invention*, even though, in fact, it might include various degrees of fiction. History, therefore, presupposes a different notion of truth as well. The historian's result, or "truth(s)" that he or she derives from writing a historical narrative, is deduced on the basis of the premise that the historian deals with evidence. We may conclude then that historical and fictional narratives are different in nature and could not be reduced to merely generic distinctions.

Both a historian and a fiction writer interpret reality and often employ similar methods. But since history and fiction have different goals, they arrive at different results that are true within their own systems. All genres based on the notion of fiction may yield different conclusions of a specific nature (like the differences between a historical play and a historical novel). Yet all the multifarious truths they will arrive at will be truths based primarily on *invention*, or fiction. Likewise, historians may construct their nar-

ratives according to various principles (and here the patterns introduced by White may be very useful); they may draw different conclusions, but all their truths would be based primarily on evidence.

In physical experiments, an observer conceiving a photon as a
wave and an observer conceiving a photon as a particle both deal
with photons but come up with different results. As Gaston Bachelard observes in his book *The New Scientific Spirit*, the images of
waves and particles "do not fit together in any simple way. Each
is clear only when considered apart from the other. In short, both
are condemned to remain mere images; neither can claim to represent the deep, underlying reality. [. . .] Both have proven themselves: the particle theory in mechanics, the wave theory in physical optics" (Bachelard, 92–93). Similar to researchers in physics,
both historian and fiction writers occupy themselves with reality,
and use similar tools and methods; nevertheless they produce different types of narratives and different results depending on the
set of their expectations. History and fiction are mutually exclusive in so far as no matter how much fiction strives to be historical,
the actual fusion of history and fiction is impossible—it remains
fiction. Likewise history, if it wants to remain history, is subject to
the "uncertainty principle," that is, if it strives to absolute factual
precision it must ignore fictional insights.

The "principle of complementarity" should not be confused
with a classical notion of *coincidentia oppositorum*. What Nicholas
of Cusa called the *coincidentia oppositorum* presupposes the union
of contraries, that is, first of all the existence of opposites. The
concept of complementarity, by contrast, does not deal with opposites or any kind of oppositions at all. Waves and particles cannot
be viewed as opposites or contraries, for they are completely distinct realities. Moreover, the *coincidentia oppositorum* implies the
simultaneous coexistence of contraries and the union of opposites
in God. It asserts an idea of the two in the one, that is, a notion
defined by the formula "both . . . and." In physics, however, one
cannot speak about a photon as being simultaneously a wave and

a particle, but either one or the other depending on the context of the experiment and on the observer. For in physics the choice is required, and this choice can be expressed only diachronically in terms of "either . . . or."

It is much harder to define the relation between the principle of complementarity and Bakhtin's dialogism. Bakhtin briefly uses the term "complementarity" (*dopolnitel'nost'*) in his article "Toward a Methodology of Humanities" ("K metodologii gumanitarnykh nauk"). Criticizing the formalization and depersonalization typical of the structuralist method, Bakhtin advances his own view: "As far as I am concerned, I hear *voices* and dialogical relations among them everywhere. I perceive dialogically the principle of complementarity as well" (Bakhtin, 393). Bakhtin does not elaborate, however, upon the notion of complementarity as applied to studies of culture. Rather it seems that he reinterprets complementarity in terms of his own principle of dialogism.

To be sure, concepts similar to that of complementarity understood in the most general terms rather than in its specific meaning as used in hard sciences were part of our philosophical heritage long before the discoveries of Heisenberg and Bohr. A good example of an experiment with complementary interpretations of some pictorial representations can be found in the often-discussed trick drawing that could be seen either as a rabbit or a duck, depending on the focus of the observer. As it is brilliantly argued by Gombrich, the alternative readings of this drawing result from the fact that it is impossible to see the shape apart from its interpretation (Gombrich, 5). Moreover, although we may switch our interpretations and our point of view, "we cannot experience alternative readings at the same time" (5).

The notion of complementarity, however, provides a much more sophisticated and terminologically apt way to account for connections between the goal of the observer and the final outcome of the experiment or any creative process. This is why I believe that the term "complementarity," which, in fact, has been invoked a number of times in literary discussions, could be legitimately borrowed from hard sciences by any layman in the field as a useful metaphor to describe the complex relations between history and fiction, as well as among different genres.

Finally, I include a brief note on the relation of my ideas of the "complementarity" of history and fiction, which were, in fact, formulated earlier in my 1991 dissertation on Pushkin, to Andrew Wachtel's notion of the "intergeneric dialogue" in his book *An Obsession with History: Russian Writers Confront the Past* (1994). Although Wachtel's interest in Russian writers' multiple ways (both fictional and non-fictional) to represent the past may seem to some extent similar to mine, his central claim that these multiple ways to narrate historical events should be viewed in terms of "intergeneric dialogue" is, in fact, quite different from what I suggest in this monograph and discussed earlier in my dissertation. Wachtel's emphasis on the "intergeneric dialogue," perhaps inadvertently, implies that each individual work is somewhat inadequate in its own terms but gains its full significance only when it enters into dialogue with some other texts. While suggesting that the intergeneric approach constitutes a peculiar Russian tradition, which is fundamentally different from Western European literary and historical practices, Wachtel insists that "in this tradition, then, there is an implicit recognition that historical truth cannot be achieved through any one perspective, no matter how convincingly presented. Instead, whatever truth can be achieved emerges from the uneasy coexistence of multiple ways of seeing and narrating the past" (12). Thus, although on the surface the author seems to call for multiple perspectives, in reality he reduces the meaning of different works and different genres to one perspective, the principle of intergeneric dialogue, and one Truth which could only be constituted through this principle. The contingency of truth upon the dialogic relation between multiple texts reminds one of the ubiquitous quest for synthesis—a philosophical position that no longer can be taken for granted. Whether we agree or disagree with Wachtel's assertion that "historical truth cannot be achieved through any one perspective," there is no reason to believe that it may be achieved through multiple perspectives either. Nor is there reason to suppose that Russian writers shared this view.

What I suggest instead in my monograph is that Pushkin was able to combine multiple perspectives and autonomous truths without committing himself to a banal and often easy way to resolve oppositions through synthesis. This is why I introduce the notion of complementarity, which, in my opinion, illustrates very well both Pushkin's natural penchant for multiple perspectives and his suspicion of synthesis or any final truth. Moreover, the principle of complementarity carries with itself the notion of point of view and of the goal of the observer/writer, a key concept for my discussion of the relation between history and fiction. The important point is not that Pushkin simply believed in the heuristic value of multiple perspectives and multiple genres, but how he conceived of their coexistence. Pushkin, I claim, did not believe in Truth, but in truths. Even if both Wachtel and I recognize that each particular work does not contain the Truth, Wachtel suggests that the Truth could be obtained through an intergeneric dialogue, while I maintain that Pushkin made no attempt to find nor suggested that the Truth could be discovered anywhere. Each genre and each work carries its own truth, which emerges contextually, depending on a particular point of view and which may be true only within a specific context. Pushkin's view of the relation between history and fiction does not suggest mediation or any sort of interplay between different genres or between history and fiction, but a fully independent coexistence of sometimes mutually exclusive approaches and views. This is precisely where the notion of complementarity comes in especially useful.

While dedicating himself to alternative representations of historical reality, Pushkin, to use Heisenberg's expression, was "playing with both pictures" of reality, and was "going from the one picture to the other and back again." Lotman was probably first to recognize this unique feature of Pushkin's artistic vision when he concluded his article "*The Queen of Spades* and the Theme of Cards and Card Games in Russian Literature of the Beginning of the Nineteenth Century" (" 'Pikovaiia dama' i tema kart i kartochnoi igry v russkoi literature nachala XIX veka") with the following observation: "One could compare the artistic discoveries of the later Pushkin with the principle of complementarity of Niels Bohr. The fact that the very same symbol (that of a card game, for example), while being filled with opposite meanings, can represent the incompatible as aspects of the whole, make Pushkin's works not only a phenomenon of art history, but also a new stage in the development of human thought" (Lotman 1992: I, 415).

I will further develop the notion of truth in history and fiction and the concept of complementarity as applied to Pushkin's vision of the relationship between history and fiction in Chapter 4 in my analysis of Pushkin's "The Hero" ("Geroi"), a poem that captures this relationship most vividly. Before engaging in a more detailed textual analysis, however, I briefly outline the significance of the debate over history and fiction in Russian cultural tradition and its relevance for Pushkin specifically.

Much ink has been spilled over the problem of the relationship between Pushkin's historical writings and his historical fiction. Most critics, however, perhaps following the lead of Marina Tsvetaeva's essay "Pushkin and Pugachev" (1937), focus primarily on the two texts which became a classic case study of the problem: *A History of Pugachev* and *The Captain's Daughter* (see Oksman; Petrunina; Mikkelson 1982, 1973; Gifford 1984; Wachtel). The simultaneity and completeness of *A History of Pugachev* and *The Captain's Daughter* tempted some scholars to treat these two texts as interdependent. The fact that Pushkin undertook an idealized portrayal of Pugachev in his novel *after* he completed his *History* and learned the historical "truth" about the rebel puzzled many readers and prompted them to consider the opposition between the historical truth and the fictional one. The consensus is that history's aim is a quest for knowledge, whereas fiction's is reconciliation. Fiction offers a sort of self-consolation or an "elevating illusion," a notion that is defined differently by various critics, but consistently points to an idealizing function of art (see especially Tsvetaeva). Andrew Wachtel pushes the interdependence of the two texts still further by insisting that the two works "are meant to be read in tandem," that "ultimately neither of them can be read adequately without a knowledge of its twin" and that "historical truth is seen as dialogic, and is to be found in the interaction of these (and, potentially, other) perspectives" (83, 66, 78).

Neither of these interpretations seems fully convincing. I believe that the so called "idealization" of Pugachev in *The Captain's Daughter* is a myth that obscures the fact that Pugachev is represented through the eyes of the fictitious narrator, Piotr Grinev, and that his relations with Pugachev and his impressions of the peasant leader should not, therefore, be confused with the historical interpretation Pushkin wants to project in his novel. Moreover, the portrayal of Pugachev is clearly subordinated to the constraints of the genre of the Walter Scottian historical novel that often not only depicts the middle of the road hero's split loyalties and his mediating role in the struggle between the two antagonistic camps but provides a sub-plot that could be characterized as a duel of honor. For Scott's characters, the code of honor serves often as a primary motivation for their decisions and actions regardless of their personal political views. The same dynamic is unmistakably present in *The Captain's Daughter* in which both Grinev and Pugachev engage in the contest of generosity that is necessary for maintaining the development of the plot. Finally, although the representation of Pugachev may appear less violent in the novel as compared to the *History,* this does not affect the overall *historical* concept of the novel. The softening of the rebel's portrayal could be dictated by aesthetic considerations, and one should remember that in the novel, Pugachev appears both as a private and a historical personage. As I will show in Chapter 2, it is important to consider the way certain actions or events affect differently history and private life.

It is equally difficult to share Wachtel's extreme position, which ultimately implies that each individual work is somewhat inadequate in its own terms. If the *History of Pugachev* were lost and never published as was, for example, the case with parts of *History of Peter the Great,* would this mean that Pushkin's novel *The Captain's Daughter* would become fatally incomplete without its non-fictional "counterpart"? To be sure, the success of all historical fiction depends, to an extent, on the audience's knowledge of historical events as argued convincingly by Herbert Lindenberger in his discussion of historical drama. Yet nothing suggests that the audience or the reader are expected to acquire a specialized knowledge of the historical past, including reference to specific historical texts, in order to properly comprehend the works of historical fiction. Moreover, if we postulate the concept of "dialogue" between the two texts, then the relationship between the *History* and the novel should be reciprocal. In other words, history should illuminate fiction, and fiction should provide a possibility to interpret history differently. But how does *The Captain's Daughter* help us to better understand Pushkin's *History?*

One should admit nevertheless that the comparative study of *The Captain's Daughter* and *A History of Pugachev* seems to have an obvious advantage over the contrastive analysis of Pushkin's Peter the Great narratives: *A History of Pugachev* and *The Captain's Daughter* were written almost simultaneously, and Pushkin successfully completed both texts. By contrast, the three major Peter the Great imaginative narratives date from 1827 to 1833, whereas his work on his historical project, *History of Peter the Great,* continues to Pushkin's last days. *History of Peter* remains incomplete, as does, for example, the novelistic fragment *The Blackamoor of Peter the Great;* it stays, for the most part, merely drafted. This fact presents an obvious methodological problem for a student of *History of Peter,* for this text lacks a plot and as such precludes any definitive judgment concerning its formal aspects and the concept of causality which it projects.

It is not surprising then, that considered as a group, the Peter the Great narratives do not yield the kind of facile conclusions critics tend to draw from the comparative analysis of *The Captain's Daughter* and *A History of Pugachev*. One could hardly see a dialogue or even interaction between *The Blackamoor of Peter the Great*, *Poltava*, *The Bronze Horseman*, and the incomplete *History of Peter*. Although written by the same author and dealing with the same historical figure, these texts do not allude to each other, but they offer instead self-sufficient and discrete glimpses into the vast field of historical reality, which constitutes the Peter the Great epoch. Furthermore, this time Pushkin undertakes to write his *History* after creating several versions of Peter the Great in fiction. Even after completing *The Bronze Horseman*, a text that both questions and calls for a reconciliation with the past, Pushkin does not reject the idea to write *A History of Peter*. On the contrary, it is in 1834 that Pushkin engages in studying Peter the Great with renewed intensity and dedication. In a letter to Mikhail Pogodin of April 7, 1834 he confesses: "I approach Peter with fear and trepidation, as you approach your historical podium" (XV, 124). Clearly, the knowledge vs. reconciliation formula does not easily apply to the Petrine texts.

The two "truths"—the truth of history and the truth of fiction —do not fit together in any simple way and emerge only when considered apart from each other. If we compare the drafts of Pushkin's fictional representations of Peter the Great to his preliminary notes for *History of Peter*, the difference in basic orientation toward "invention" or fact accumulation becomes immediately visible. In January 1837, three weeks before his death, Pushkin confided in D. E. Keller about the progress of his work on *History of Peter the Great:* "I still have not written anything yet, I was solely preoccupied with collecting the material: I want to conceive an idea about the whole study first, then I will write *History of Peter* in a year or in

half a year and will start correcting it according to the documents"
(Pushkin 1962–66: IX, 546). Although this plan was unrealized,
Pushkin's statement speaks eloquently of the poet's eagerness to
become a historiographer of Peter the Great. Moreover, it reveals
four important elements of methodology that Pushkin envisions
for his historical monograph: the accumulation of facts, the development of the general concept of the work, emplotting the narrative, and the verification of the narrative according to available
documents. In other words, Pushkin wishes to cast his *History* as
both a story and a study. Yet it is the evidence that, in Pushkin's
view, is the alpha and omega of historical inquiry. The creative
process generating *History*, therefore, is conceived as a movement
from evidence to interpretation and back to evidence.

Pushkin, thus, seems to recognize that historical data may
serve as an initial impulse for both history and historical fiction
and that both history and fiction depend on the work of imagination for the formation of the concept, or hypothesis. He is fully
aware of the importance of inspiration, or poetic insight, for both
science and art: "Inspiration is the disposition of the soul to the
most lively reception of impressions and to the consideration of
concepts, and consequently, to their explanation. Inspiration is
needed in geometry just as it is needed in poetry" (II, 54). Imagination, inspiration, and invention are the indispensable components of any intellectual endeavor, whether a scientific inquiry, a
work of art, or any non-fictional narrative. What the postmodernist thinkers, White, for example, advance as a concept that needs
to be argued and defended, that is, the claim that poetic insights
precede particular theories incorporated in historical accounts, is
perceived by Pushkin and, perhaps, by most scientists and writers
of all ages as a given fact. Thus, in his "History of the Village of
Goriukhino" ("Istoriia Sela Goriukhino"), Pushkin parodies Belkin's failure "to compose something" in imaginative genres as well
as in non-fictional ones, such as history, precisely because Belkin
lacks imagination, which would enable him to develop a concept

or connect phenomena in any rational way. A mere desire to become a writer and a historian or even certain technical skills do not
guarantee, Pushkin suggests, a successful authorship. Belkin embarks on his literary enterprises by first choosing a genre (an epic
poem, a tragedy, a ballad, etc.). But he fails to complete his undertakings precisely because it is the insight, or concept, that determines the choice of the genre and not the other way around. The
lack of imagination and invention equally harms Belkin's literary
and historical exercises. It reduces his "history" to an indiscrimi-
nate accumulation of absurd and irrelevant details, just as his wish
to set down isolated thoughts and maxims results in platitudes.
A good example of one follows: "A man who disobeys the laws
of reason and is accustomed to following the inducements of his
passions, often errs and subjects himself to belated repentance"
(VIII: I, 132). Working on "The Excerpts from Letters, Thoughts
and Observations," Pushkin drafted a mock scene that parodies
the aphorisms of his uncle Vasilii L'vovich Pushkin and illustrates
the preeminence of poetic insight and invention for a successful
fictional or nonfictional narrative:

> Once my uncle fell ill. A friend visited him. "I am bored,"
> said the uncle, "I would like to write, but I do not know
> about what." "Write about anything you wish," his friend
> responded, "put down your thoughts, literary and politi-
> cal observations, satirical portraits, and the like. This is
> very simple: it is the way Seneka and Montaigne used to
> write." His acquaintance left, and my uncle followed his
> advice. In the morning, they brewed bad coffee for him,
> and this irritated him. Now he philosophically reasoned
> that he was upset by a trifle and wrote down the follow-
> ing: sometimes we get upset by real trifles (XI, 59).

The uncle's inability to select among the raw material of life and
to derive an original concept from it makes a travesty of a literary
process and its final outcome. The simpleminded maxims of Bel-

kin and Pushkin's uncle, which contain no "invention" but merely record immediate perceptions of reality, fail to stimulate the workings of the mind.

Pushkin seems to acknowledge that certain grounding in reality, poetical invention, and dependence on language are necessary for both fiction and nonfiction. Yet, although the creative processes generating history and fiction may coincide to a certain point (this includes collecting facts, invention, or development of a concept, and emplotment of the material according to some formal and rhetorical structures), fiction and history part ways when it comes to the fourth stage of the creative process, as implicitly suggested by Pushkin, namely the verification of the narrative according to available documents. Or, to put it differently, history and fiction differ fundamentally in their various methods of what Charles Peirce identified as the "fixation of belief."

Peirce's ideas on the method of scientific investigation have direct bearing on understanding the differences between history and fiction in the nineteenth century. The purpose of any inquiry, Peirce maintains, is the transition from a state of doubt to that of belief, so that "the settlement of opinion is the sole end of inquiry" (11). By distinguishing and contrasting the four methods of "fixing belief" (the method of tenacy, the method of authority, the a priori method, and the scientific method), Peirce insists that the scientific method is the only one which "presents any distinction of a right and a wrong way" (19). The scientific belief is of a kind that it is not determined by any circumstance extraneous to the facts, but "by some external permanency — by something upon which our thinking has no effect" (18). Pushkin shares this view about the nature of scientific historical investigation.

In his draft letter to Benkendorf (6 December 1833) Pushkin maintains: "I put aside fiction and wrote *The History of the Pugachev Rebellion*. [. . .] I do not know whether it will be possible for me to publish it, but at least I honestly fulfilled the duty of a historian: I searched for truth zealously and narrated it without duplicity, making no attempt to flatter either power or fashionable way of thinking" (XV, 226). Clearly, Pushkin juxtaposes here history and fiction (*vymysel*) and seems to believe in the possibility of the representation of history "as it really was" (to use Ranke's famous phrase). Even though in his historical fiction Pushkin wanted to remain true to history (and he claimed that he did so in *Poltava* and *The Captain's Daughter*), he still referred to his historical fiction as *vymysel*. For fiction allows for imagination and is oriented not to the recording of facts but to the artistic recreation of the past. In his definition of the task of the historian, on the other hand, he stresses research (*izyskival istinu*) and truthful, relatively inartistic narration of the facts (*izlagal bez krivodushiia*). Pushkin links, therefore, fiction with *thought* (the etymology of the word *vymysel* suggests this connection), whereas history is associated with the disinterested *research* of the historian (*izyskival*) and his simple *putting down* the facts (*izlagal*). Significantly, as an honest historian, Pushkin claims that he sought to avoid flattering the "fashionable way of thinking." A similar definition of the historian's task could be found in the calm impartiality of Pimen from *Boris Godunov*. This is how Grigorii describes Pimen's work: "He looks calmly at innocent and guilty, / Dispassionately listening to good and evil, / Knowing neither pity nor wrath" (VII, 18). Pimen's advice to Grigorii is also unambiguous: "Describe, without philosophizing slyly, / All that you will witness in your life" (VII, 23).

Pushkin often counterpoises *vymysel* and myth to historical research. His unfortunate historiographer, Belkin, clearly associates fiction with myth when he confesses that "his name [that of Kurganov] seemed to me invented and the legend about him merely an empty myth, awaiting the research of a new Niebuhr" (VIII: I, 127). Here again *vymysel* (*vymyshlennym*) and myth are joined and opposed to the historian's research (*izyskaniia*). Within the dichotomy "myth/*vymysel*—history," history is linked to rational fact-finding, whereas myth occupies the territory history seems to

disdain (*pustaia mifa*). Pushkin most often connects or even identifies *vymysel* with poetry or fiction. Hence Pushkin's famous lines
from his "Elegy" (1830): "At times I will revel in a harmony / And
shed my tears upon an illusion" ("Poroi opiat' garmoniei up'ius', /
Nad vymyslom slezami obol'ius'," III: I, 228). Likewise, in a letter
to P. A. Pletnev of 14 April 1831, Pushkin recommends Russian
legends to Zhukovsky as a true source of *vymysel* or poetry: "In the
poetry of the fantastic, Russian legends yield nothing to those of
Ireland and Germany. If he [Zhukovsky] is still being carried away
by inspiration advise him to read the *Menologion*, particularly the
legends of the Kievan miracle-workers; they are gems of simplicity
and invention!" (XIV, 163). Fiction, according to Pushkin, cannot
be fiction without *vymysel*. While criticizing Kiukhelbeker, Pushkin points out that his literary works do not display enough of
vymysel.[5]

The oppositions of *istoriia* and *vymysel* are scattered throughout
Pushkin's oeuvre and are, in fact, as typical of the Romantic age
as they are of the late Enlightenment. In his Foreword to *History
of the Russian State* (*Istoriia gosudarstva Rossiiskogo*), Karamzin
clearly juxtaposes history to fiction by identifying the latter with
"invention" (*vymysel*) and the former with the truthful representation of reality. "History is not the novel," cautions Karamzin,
"history portrays the real world" (x). Karamzin specifically alludes
to the new type of historical writing, but formulates these new assumptions about the nature of historical investigation in terms of a
rather naively understood Aristotelian dichotomy between history
and poetry: "New achievements of reason have given us a clearer
notion about history's nature and its aims; sober taste has established fixed rules and has forever separated historical chronicles
from poetry, from flower gardens of eloquence. It has left to history the role of being a true mirror of the past . . . Like natural
history, human history does not tolerate fictions and presents only
what is or was, but not what *might have been*" (xii). Faddei Bul-
garin, Ivan Lazhechnikov, Mikhail Zagoskin, and many other Rus-

sian Romantic writers invoke a similar opposition between history
(*istoriia*) and fiction (*vymysel*), following undoubtedly the established European practice. The tension between history and poetry,
which gradually evolves into the acceptance of the two truths (the
truth of fiction and the truth of history) is at the center of Russian
as well as German, English, French, or Italian Romantic writers,
from Friedrich Schiller to Alfred de Vigny and Alessandro Manzoni, to name a few. The notion of truth in history rests primarily
on verifiable evidence, whereas the notion of truth in historical fiction, regardless of the degree of historical authenticity, is based
on probability and, therefore, on "invention." Characteristically,
similar to Pushkin, both Schiller and Manzoni practiced the two
vocations of historian and fiction writer.[6]

If Pushkin and most other writers of the Romantic age believed that historical fiction inevitably mixes history and invention,
whereas history proper deals more straightforwardly with facts,
how do these sorts of claims and assumptions about the two modes
of writing determine and affect the shape of narrative? Is the distinction between poetry and history characterized by external features?

I believe that one could answer the question affirmatively. There
is a definite correlation between the author's generic assumptions
and the outcome of the creative process that generates a particular text. In the writings of history based on typically nineteenth
century expectations as described above, some new data derived
from experience may completely reverse the set of beliefs underlying a particular scientific investigation. But with art the case is
different. Even though in the process of creating a work of art
an artist may change his concept, this change will not depend on
the acquisition of new factual information extraneous to his own
thinking but on some imperceptible changes within the creation
of his or her own mind. If we, for example, consider the evolution
of *Poltava* through Pushkin's drafts and various versions, we will
see that no extraneous facts affect the initial narrative; the changes

that Pushkin introduces are not dictated by new information, but by his struggle to convey his a priori concept and images with more precision. When Pushkin decides to change the final cheer of the people in *Boris Godunov* with people's silence, he is guided by artistic considerations rather than by new historical data about people's behavior.

By contrast, what strikes the reader of *A History of Peter the Great* is an enormous amount of painstakingly collected facts. Clearly, Pushkin strove to incorporate the maximum of data available for each year of Peter's career. The quantity of historical material surpasses by far the amount of historical data included in any of his fictional works. In other words, even though Pushkin the historian and Pushkin the fiction writer are both forced to make choices in their presentations of historical events, the degree of their selectivity is dramatically different. The difference between historical discourse, novel, drama, or narrative poem, therefore, is, among other things, a difference in scope. The sector of historical events treated in fiction, both poetry and prose, is, as a rule, narrower than in history. Thus, for example, analyzing the Pugachev rebellion in historical discourse Pushkin starts with the prehistory of the event, whereas in *The Captain's Daughter* he portrays Pugachev as an already acting leader and begins his narrative in *media res*. *The Blackamoor of Peter the Great* as well as *The Captain's Daughter* cover a relatively short historical period, without overviewing the reign of Peter or Catherine or the emergence of Pugachev. The genre of the long narrative poem, which allows for more distance than the novel, permits high-magnitude views and attempts a more conclusive and all-embracing representation, but is, nevertheless, also more limited in scope than history.

Since Pushkin and the authors of his time, who write fiction, are forced, in most cases, to be more selective in their choice of historical events and details, the specific weight, or gravity, of each detail is of graver import in fiction than in history. This is why details in their fictional narratives are endowed with significance in regard to the future of past events and have been often interpreted by scholars symbolically or emblematically (cf., for example, Richard Gustafson's term "emblematic realism" as applied to the works of Tolstoy). For the assumption is that in fiction, details function within a rather tight structure and are subordinated to the general concept of the work. By contrast, Pushkin's history, which abounds in details and facts, may include a greater number of details that do not necessarily fit into a general design, for the meaning in history, according to the dominant assumptions of the time, is generated by emplotment (as any other narrative, both fictional and non-fictional), and by fact accumulation and continuous verification by evidence. To be sure, the historical "quality" of this kind of history is not merely the result of the Hegelian transition from quantity into quality. But it is more dependent on quantity than fiction, which seems to disregard the quantity of facts in favor of single details, often reinforced by means of repetition. A higher degree of selectivity of details, which is characteristic of Pushkin's fiction, is also central to myth. This is why my analyses of Pushkin's fictional renderings of the events set during the Peter the Great epoch in Part 3 of this book focus primarily on Pushkin's strategies of mythologization of the past and on the close connection between representations of history in fiction and myth. Since the function of myth is to explain and to cohere the chaos of history, myth—like fiction—selects only those details which create a true and coherent "story" that could be properly used by the community. (Cf. Hans Blumenberg's theories of myth and natural selection).[7]

To be sure, as specific sets of expectations associated with history and fiction change, so the respective forms of history and imaginative literature also transform. Once again, it may be useful to recall Tolstoy's iconoclastic attitude toward both traditional nineteenth-century historiography and fiction writing. Tolstoy criticized historians for what traditionally was attributed to fiction writers: for the historians' fact manipulation, for their inability to focus on what is located in the immediate proximity, on the minute and specific details of everyday life. It is fiction, rather than history, Tolstoy proclaimed, that may better represent historical reality as an endless continuum of microscopic incidents and interactions between tiny units of historical reality. One can never, however, completely account for the infinite number of microscopic elements that comprise this reality.

Thus, in his study of Tolstoy's *War and Peace*, Gary Saul Morson refuses to endorse the idea of the relevance of all the details and incidents in Tolstoy's novels. On the contrary, Morson maintains, Tolstoy's novels display the accumulation of arbitrary details that are not subordinated to any pre-existing plan and do not shape themselves into a coherent plot. If Morson is right, then Tolstoy completely reverses the nineteenth-century concepts of history and fiction. Not only does Tolstoy's fiction become as large in scope as traditional history (the scope being reflected among other things in length), but the principle of selectivity is also reversed. These are historians who are selective and who emplot the events into a coherent story, whereas Tolstoy the writer attempts to render life in all its plotlessness.

If Tolstoy seems to shatter the conventions of nineteenth-century fiction and to allow certain elements in his historical novel that are characteristic of history, Pushkin is more traditional and more Aristotelian in his perception of the relation of fiction to non-fiction. Pushkin emerges as a perfect representative of the nineteenth century, embracing the prevailing assumptions about the relations between art and science. Moreover, Pushkin does not privilege one kind of writing over the other, the trap that most theoreticians of both history and fiction rarely manage to avoid. Neither poet nor historian, according to Pushkin, can portray the way things really happened. If the writer's ambition is to reconstruct the whole truth, then any interpretation of historical processes would inevitably result in misinterpretation. The reconstruction of the whole truth requires the omniscience that neither the artist nor historian can achieve (Pushkin and Tolstoy undoubtedly agree on this point). Since representation is always inseparable from context and point of view, the tension between generalities and particulars can never be resolved in any one genre. The infinite multiplicity of contexts defies the possibility of any final representation of reality and presupposes the necessity of the choice of the vantage point from which the events are evaluated. Each genre, therefore, establishes the limits of context. The past then emerges in its infinitely various complementary shapes.

part I History and National Identity

one   The Impediments of Russian History

Russia is a European Empire.

— *Instructions* of Her Majesty the Empress Catherine II

Ivan Kireevskii, a contemporary of Alexander Pushkin and one of Russia's most brilliant literary critics, wrote in 1830: "History in our time is at the center of all intellectual quests and is the most important of all sciences; it is the indispensable condition for all development; historicism embraces *everything*" (44). Indeed, the whole pleiad of Russian intellectuals in the first half of the nineteenth century exhibited a near obsession with history. They delved not only into the history of Russia but also into the nature of history *per se*. Yet they were not engaged in a purely scholarly endeavor; their preoccupation with history was, above all, a deliberate effort to awaken national self-awareness and establish a national identity.

This persistent preoccupation with history, spurred by the Napoleonic wars, was a part of a general European concern with national past and national consciousness and characterized both Russian and European Romanticism. In Russia, however, the problems of national identity were discussed with particular fervor. As late as the nineteenth century, Russia still had difficulty in regarding herself as a legitimate member of the European community. Neither did the Europeans consider Russia a part of their historical and cultural heritage. Characteristically, Jean-Jacques Rousseau claimed that Russian people were unsusceptible to culture and "not ripe for laws." In *The Social Contract*, criticizing Peter the Great's policy of what he considers to be premature Westernization, Rousseau maintains that

Peter "set out to produce Germans and Englishmen—when he should have made it his first task to produce Russians. He kept his subjects from becoming what they might have been—by persuading them that they were what they were not" (Rousseau, 65–6). In his Introduction to *The Philosophy of History,* Hegel insisted that Russia (and Siberia, which, according to Hegel, "must be eliminated" from "the pale of History"), along with Poland and the Slavonic Kingdoms, "came only late into the series of historical States" (Hegel, 100, 102). Likewise, the Russian philosopher, Peter Chaadaev, complained that Russia had no history and no past: "We belong to none of the great families of mankind; we are neither of the West nor of the East, and we possess the traditions of neither. [. . .] Historical experience does not exist for us. [. . .] Isolated in the world, we have given nothing to the world, we have taken nothing from the world; we have not added a single idea to the mass of human ideas; we have contributed nothing to the progress of the human spirit" (Chaadaev, 34, 41).

It is not surprising, then, that Russian writers and thinkers of the first third of the nineteenth century suffered a severe crisis of identity as they reflected on their cultural and historical past. To preserve its sense of identity and national pride, a country with allegedly no history of its own vacillated between two extremes: on the one hand, it strove to proclaim itself unique and independent from the dominant patterns of Western European development; on the other, it compulsively (by way of decrees!) claimed its membership in the European community. Russian historians and writers sought both to evaluate the extent of Russia's debt to European history and culture, and at the same time to disclose Russia's unique historical role, its distinct cultural traditions, and its ineluctable destiny. When in 1830 Alexander Pushkin declared that "Russia never had anything in common with the rest of Europe," he only expressed a characteristic Russian sentiment well in tune with a common European outlook. Yet Pushkin's position vis-à-vis the "accursed" questions of Russia's relation to the West and its literary and historical tradition was a far cry from both the crude messianism of the Slavophiles and the outright condemnation of Russian backwardness by the Westernizers.

In his treatment of historical subjects, Pushkin was guided both by Russian tradition as represented by Karamzin and by the literary and scholarly achievements of European thought. Pushkin shared many of his historical views and perceptions with contemporary historians and writers; in particular, the French school of liberal historiography, represented by Augustin Thierry, François Guizot, and Prosper de Barante; Walter Scott's historical fiction became a main source of inspiration and polemic to him.

**Liberal Historiography of the Beginning
of the Nineteenth Century**

An all-absorbing interest in history coincided in Europe with the flourishing of Romanticism. Reinterpreting and rewriting the past as a commentary on the present and prophecy for the future became a common practice among Romantic writers. In their reaction against the empirical historiography of the Enlightenment, Romantic artists sought to mediate between empirical historicism and creative mythmaking. As a result, Romantics put forward a figure of the poet-historian who possesses a special insight into the past and is not constrained by strict chronological and temporal authenticity. The task of the Romantic historian—similar to that of the Romantic poet—is to unveil the remote past and the continuity between the past and the present. As Lionel Gossman points out in his study *Between History and Literature*, "It was almost universally agreed that in order to write the new history, the traditional skills of the neoclassical historian—erudition, critical judgment, and rhetorical facility—had to be supplemented by unusual powers of divination. At this point Humboldt, Niebuhr, and Michelet were at one" (Gossman, 261).

The liberal historians of the generation of 1789 shared this Romantic belief in insight. These historians felt the need not merely to retell the stories as chroniclers, but to recover the *meaning* of old documents, to discern what had been veiled to their predecessors. To accomplish this task, the historian had to not only carefully establish, seek out, and study new sources but to use the power of imagination to discern general connections between the events. That is why Walter Scott, who studied new sources, including legends and old documents, and was a master of historical divination, or insight, appeared to Thierry and to other Romantic historians as a great authority in the area of historical writing. Thierry maintains that "there is more true history in his novels of England and Scotland than in many compilations that still go by the name of histories" (Gossman, 95).

In their desire to recover the *meaning* of the past age and to discern the laws governing European history, these historians tended to overestimate the role of patterns of historical development. According to George P. Gooch, a distinguished scholar of nineteenth-century historiography, this school of French historians included "a group of writers whose object was rather to explain than to narrate, to teach than to paint, for whom the individual was of less interest than the State, the anatomy and physiology of history of greater importance than its outward form and color. Among its main interests were the structure of society, the evolution of forms of government and the relation of states to one another. Its ideal was to apply the methods of science to history" (Gooch, 186).

Indeed, both Thierry and Guizot stressed the role of institutions and class structure in their historical narratives. Thierry considered the bourgeoisie a leading force of historical development. He insisted: "Bourgeois historiography is truth, not ideology, and it is so because the triumph of the bourgeoisie is the fulfillment of reason, of the universal, in history" (Thierry, 11). For Guizot too, the dominant theme of European history was the development of representative institutions through the agency of the middle class that he considered the chief carrier of the liberal tradition. Furthermore, while analyzing the institutions of England and France, the historians of this school tended to proclaim the formulas they asserted to be the universal laws of history; in his "Introduction" to the *Histoire de la conquête de l'Angleterre par les Normands* (1825), Thierry claimed that his history of the Norman Conquest was a model of all the histories of the European countries. Likewise, Guizot made it clear that in studying France one studied in microcosm larger European phenomena: "I have used the term European civilization, because it is evident that there is a European civilization; that a certain unity pervades the civilization of the various European states; that, notwithstanding infinite diversities of time, place and circumstance, this civilization takes its first rise in facts almost wholly similar, proceeds everywhere upon the same principles, and tends to produce well nigh everywhere analogous results" (Guizot 1878, 2). Guizot believed that his knowledge as a contemporary of the French Revolution allowed him to understand previous epochs as well, and to explain all other revolutions that he considered positive and prepared by the course of the history. Nothing, he maintained, is purely accidental; all historical events can be understood as historical incarnations of universal human principles.

The overdeterministic "formulas" of Guizot were consonant with the philosophy of history dominant in his time, one which was based on faith in progress. Even in the beginning of the nineteenth century, French historians could scarcely think of the universe except in terms of orderly design. The idea that mankind progresses steadily to a final goal had been suggested earlier by Herder and Hegel in their philosophies of history. This philosophy grew out of the eighteenth-century notion of continuity in the rational development of mankind. The generation of French scholars contemporary with the Revolution easily interpreted their own time as a final realization of the historical goal and their historiography as an absolute paradigm of universal history. As a result, the histories of Barante, Thierry, and Guizot acquired a distinct providential character. Guizot's philosophy of history was based on an unshakable belief in Providence and certitude that Providence might be eventually explained: "The march of Providence is not restricted to narrow limits [. . .] The consequences will come in due course, when the hour for them has arrived, perhaps not till hundreds of years have passed away; though its reasoning may appear to us slow, its logic is nonetheless true and sound. To Providence, time is as nothing; it strides through time as the gods of Homer through space: it makes but one step, and ages have vanished behind it" (Guizot, 1878, 14).[1] For the bourgeois historians of early nineteenth-century France, it was the French Revolution that appeared as the true culmination of this providential development. As Gossman observes, "the Revolution illuminated all previous history and made it possible to totalize and thus decipher it. [. . .] Only after the Revolution was it possible to construct French history as a genuine narrative 'because before 1789,' according to Henri Martin, 'History could [. . .] have no plan, since it did not yet have a conclusion' " (Gossman, 282).

It is not surprising, then, that this historical school was widely criticized for its overdeterministic nature, disregard of the influence of individuals on history, and underestimation of the role of chance. As George P. Gooch points out, in Guizot's histories "the epochs dovetail too neatly into one another, and the design of the mosaic is suspiciously correct" (189). "The most penetrating criticism of this intellectual habit," he continues, "came from Sainte-Beuve. 'Guizot's writings form a chain from which you cannot remove a link. His aim is to rule and organize the past as well as the present. [. . .] History seen from a distance undergoes a singular metamorphosis; it produces the illusion—the most dangerous of all—that it is rational. The follies, the ambitions, the thousand strange accidents which compose it, all these disappear. Every accident becomes a necessity, Guizot's history is far too logical to be true' " (190–91).

**Pushkin's Response to the French Liberal Historians
and His Polemic with Polevoi**

Pushkin shared the Romanticist belief in the principle of historical imagination and insight and praised Walter Scott for the same
reasons as did Thierry. He also shared the idea of resurrection of
the past by the act of divination. In his essay "On National Drama
and on 'Marfa Posadnitsa' " ("O narodnoi drame i drame 'Marfa
Posednika,' " 1830), Pushkin insists that a writer treating historical themes should "resurrect the past age in all its truth" (XI, 181).
But since it is not an easy task to resurrect the past age, the writer
should possess a gift of special insight. Significantly, Pushkin uses
the same word "divination," when he praises Zagoskin: "Our good
common folk, boyars, Cossacks, monks, riotous vagabonds—*all of
them are divined* [emphasis added], all of them act and feel as they
must have acted and felt during the troubled times of Minin and
Avraam Palitsyn" (XI, 92). In other words, for Pushkin, as for
the Romantics, history is a riddle that has to be deciphered. Pushkin believed in the special role of the genius who would be able to
penetrate the truth. In a letter to Karl Tol' of 26 January 1837, he
discusses the role of Mikhelson in history and thanks Tol' for his
approval of *A History of Pugachev (Istoriia Pugacheva)*. He complains that writers often distort the true picture of the events out
of prejudice. He writes: "No matter how strong the preconception
of ignorance is, how greedily one accepts calumny, a single word,
spoken by such a person as you, destroys them forever. Genius un-
covers the truth at first sight, and, as the Holy Writ says, *truth is
stronger than the tsar*" (XVI, 224). In other words, the genius has
insight and is able to recover the truth.

However, while the Romantics and the French historians of the
"providential" school believed they could know Providence and
interpret the modern history of France as a prophecy of a new
social order, Pushkin objected to this prophetic or, as he called it,
algebraic approach to history. According to Pushkin, insight, or
ugadyvanie, is an important method accessible to a historian, but

the full truth can never be known. As he states in his review of Nikolai Polevoi's *History of the Russian People* ("Istoriia Russkogo naroda," 1830), "Providence is not algebra. The human mind, to use an expression taken from common parlance, is not a prophet, but a conjecturer; it can see a general course of things" (XI, 127). (The Russian folk saying says: "Man assumes, but God determines.")

In his fiction Pushkin was close to the Romantics' method of "divination." However, Pushkin objected to this method as a guiding historiographical principle. Seduced by their method of historical insight and the temptation to make broad generalizations, the French historians derived conclusions that were not applicable to Russian history. Such was their conclusion about the universal prophetic role of the French revolution and of the *tiers état*. Pushkin felt that this "formula" did not apply to Russian history, for Russia never had a strong middle class. Moreover, as Pushkin pointed out on several occasions, in Russia, due to its specific development, the government was often "ahead of people," whereas in the Western Europe, he thought, it was the other way around. It was on these grounds that Pushkin parted ways with these historians whom he criticized for the rigidity of their awe-inspiring schemes. Instead he turned to the Russian past in search of another "formula" of Russian history, to the Russian *dvorianstvo* as a leading force in its historical development and to the Russian revolution—that of Peter the Great.

In Guizot and the French school of historians, Pushkin found manifestations of their own subjective ideals and personal sympathies, as well as attempts to equate one's own history with a universal one. The realization that Russian reality offered different conclusions inspired Pushkin to review the French historians' philosophy of history based on their belief in Providence and underestimation of the accidental in history. Pushkin apparently never denied the existence of Providence, but suggested that it could not be known, and was therefore irrelevant to historical inquiry. His criticism and internal polemic with the French historians thus acquired two main aspects: an attempt to trace the specifics of Russian historical development and a theoretical disagreement concerning the role of chance in history.

Some Peculiarities of Russian Historical Development

When Pushkin polemicized with Polevoi for his uncritical imitation of Barante, Thierry, and Guizot and his "desire to apply the system of the recent historians to Russia as well" (XI, 126), he argued that their conclusions did not fit Russian history. Guizot transformed his belief in the middle class as the chief carrier of European tradition into a universal principle. Pushkin, on the other hand, insisted on the crucial role of the gentry in Russian historical development. He maintained that "aristocracy cannot be equated with feudalism, and it is aristocracy, not a feudalism that never existed, that awaits a Russian historian" (XI, 126). Finally, he concludes: "We never had feudalism; so much the worse" (XI, 127).

Pushkin realized that in the West, the aristocracy was shaken by the strong middle class that grew as a consequence of the feudal development of cities. In the West, the feudal lords struggled against the kings, whose autocratic power was limited from the start, for the kings possessed unlimited power only in their own domains. The kings often used the support of the people in order to suppress the rebellious attitudes of the feudal lords. As Pushkin points out in his article "On the French Revolution" ("O frantsuz-'.oi revoliutsii"), a set of agreements was established in France between the feudal lords and the vassals, and "the spirit of independence was preserved among the common people" (XI, 202). As a result of the gradually emerging communes and the former vassals' participation in the legislative institutions—encouraged by the kings themselves who struggled against the feudal lords—the aristocracy had to face a new opposition in the tiers état. The continuously growing independence of the citizens limited the power of both the sovereigns and the feudal lords.

In Russia, according to Pushkin, the situation was quite different: there were no independent feudal lords, but only one family that ruled the country: "We had no feudalism. One family, that of the Varangians, ruled independently, striving for the great principality" (XI, 126). Russian aristocrats, as opposed to the feudals, created no opposition to the ruling family: "The boyars lived in the cities at the courts of the princes, without making strongholds out of their estates, without concentrating in a small family, without struggling against the kings and selling their help to the cities" (XI, 126). The Russian people also remained politically passive, for Russian princes had no need to ally themselves with the people against the aristocracy. Aristocracy, Pushkin deplores, did not evolve to feudalism as a first step of independence: "Finally, feudalism could emerge as a first step in the institutionalization of independence (with communes as the second), but it did not have enough time to succeed. It developed during the Tartar yoke and was suppressed by Ivan III, then persecuted and obliterated by Ivan IV; it began to develop during the interregnum, was gradually eliminated by the skills of the Romanovs, and finally was destroyed once and for all by Peter and Anna Ivanovna (who abolished the ukaz of Peter by the ukaz of the year 31)" (XI, 377). Although Pushkin approved of monarchy, he differentiated between autocracy and despotism and believed that a strong nobility could prevent the institution of monarchy from slipping into boundless tyranny and despotism.[2] In Russia, however, the might of the ancient nobility (aristocracy) was replaced by a "smaller gentry" (*men'shoe dvorianstvo*) that could not have any political power. "It is not Feodor, but Iazykov, that is, a smaller gentry, that destroyed localism and a boyar class, if we take this word not in the sense of a court rank, but in the sense of an aristocracy" (XI, 127). According to Pushkin, in Russia, only the independence and power of an aristocracy could limit the absolute despotism of the tsars. In his excellent discussion of Pushkin's aristocratism, Sam Driver makes this point clear: Pushkin was an ardent defender of his own class of nobility primarily because he viewed it as the only legal opposition to autocracy, on the one hand, and the only class who could protect the peasantry, on the other.[3] Indeed, in his outline of an article, later entitled by critics "On the Nobility" ("O dvorianstve"), Pushkin writes: "La haute-noblesse n'étant pas héréditaire (de fait) elle est donc *noblesse à vie;* moyen d'entourer le despotisme de stipendiaires dévoués et d'étouffer toute opposition et toute indépendance. L'hérédité de haute-noblesse est une garantie de son indépendence—le contraire est nécessairement moyen de tyrannie, ou plutôt d'un despotisme lâche et mou" (Without being hereditary, aristocracy [*la haute-noblesse*] [de facto] is thus aristocracy that is granted for life [*noblesse à vie*]. This is a means for despotism to surround itself with devoted mercenaries and to stifle all opposition and all independence. The heredity of the aristocracy guarantees its independence—the contrary is necessarily a purveyor of tyranny, or rather of a cowardly and weak despotism [Pushkin 1962–66: VIII, 146]).

And indeed, the consequence of this historical development was a strong autocratic power with no serious opposition from any class. An obvious historical implication of such a political system was the minor role of the common people or any other class in the historical process as opposed to the larger role of autocrats and individuals. According to Pushkin, this is precisely what defines the character of Russian history—autocracy as a fundamental principle of its governmental system, and a lack of a serious opposition, such as a bourgeoisie. The individual will of the monarchs under such a régime turns out to be more crucial than institutions: "Catherine the Great accomplished much for history, but the Academy did nothing. That is proof that our government always is a step ahead" (Pushkin 1962–66: VIII, 145). Furthermore, if all the changes come from the top, then historical development must be marked by the intrusion of chance and arbitrariness: "Il fallait ajouter (non comme concession, mais comme vérité) que le gouvernement est encore le seul Européen de la Russie, [et que malgré tout ce qu'il a de lourd et de pénible et de cynique] et que tout brutal [et cynique] qu'il est, il ne tiendrait qu'à lui de l'être cent fois plus. Personne n'y ferait la moindre attention" (One must add [not as a concession, but as the truth], that the government is still the only European in Russia, [and despite all that is crude and painful and cynical] and as brutal [and cynical] as it is, it might have been one hundred times more so. No one would have noticed in the least. XVI, 261)

These pecularities of Russian historical development, which Pushkin registers though does not endorse, determine the task and the approach of a historian. Rather than trying to discern the general laws governing the historical process in Russia, one should pay more attention to the turning points of Russian history, marked by the unique influence of strong individuals. To be sure, Pushkin never intimated that history is entirely governed by strong personalities, but he insisted on the augmented role of the individual within the structure of autocracy. Hence Pushkin's interest in the Russian Impostor, Grishka Otrep'ev, and in the figures of Peter the Great and Pugachev. The titles of his major historical works (as he originally conceived them) are revealing: *History of Pugachev* and *History of Peter I* (Cf., for example, the titles of Guizot's works: *Histoire des Origines du Gouvernement Représentatif; Histoire de la Révolution d'Angleterre depuis Charles I à Charles II; Histoire de la Civilization en Europe; Histoire de la Civilization en France.* Or Thierry's works: *Histoire de la Conquête de l'Angleterre par les Normans; Recueil des Monuments Inédits de l'Histoire du Tiers Etat*). In Pushkin's attention to revolutions (the French revolution, the Decembrist revolt, etc.) and in his interest in great historical figures there is an element of polemic not only with the French liberal historians, but with Karamzin as well. Unlike Karamzin, for whom historical heroes, such as the tsars, symbolically reveal the significance of the historical process but are unable either to influence this process or be influenced by it, Pushkin focuses on the dynamic relationship between the individual and the flux of history. Moreover, Pushkin's continued interest in Peter the Great and his "revolution" is clearly opposed to Karamzin's concept of Russian history based on a cyclical notion of historical process.[4] *The History of the Russian State* contains no periods of drastic changes. By contrast, although Pushkin personally had a negative attitude toward revolutions and conspiracies (cf. his letter to Prince Piotr Viazemskii of 10 July 1826): "It is true that I have never liked revolt and revolution" (XIII, 286), he never excluded them from his philosophy of history.

Pushkin concentrates, therefore, on the great historical figures that signify the turning points in Russian history, and specifically on Peter the Great. In his letter to Piotr Chaadaev (19 October 1836), he writes: "Quant à notre nullité historique, décidément je ne puis être de votre avis. [. . .] Et Pierre le Grand qui est à lui seul une histoire universelle!" (As for our historic non-entity, I decidedly cannot share your opinion. [. . .] And Peter the Great who is in himself alone a universal history!" XVI, 172) Incidentally, Aleksandra O. Smirnova recalls Pushkin saying: "I maintain that Peter was an arch-Russian, although he shaved off his beard and put on Dutch clothes. Khomiakov is wrong when he says that Peter thought like a German. I asked him recently why he had decided that the Byzantine ideas of the Muscovite state are more national than the ideas of Peter."[5]

The First Russian Revolution: Peter the Great, or *la Révolution incarnée*

Peter represents for Pushkin the whole of Russian history not only because of his powerful personality, but also because he exemplifies the essence of the Russian historical process—its potential for drastic changes. According to Pushkin, it is Peter who fulfilled the historical mission of bridging the gap between Russia and Europe and who represents in this sense the culmination of Russian history:

> An overthrowing of the yoke, the conflicts of the great
> princedom with local principalities, of autocracy with
> the sovereignties of the cities, of autocracy with the bo-
> yars and of the conquering with national identity were
> not conducive to the free development of enlightenment.
> [. . .] But in the epoch of upheavals and turning-points,
> tsars and boyars agreed on one thing: on the necessity of
> efforts to bring Russia closer to Europe. From this follows
> the contacts of Ivan Vasil'evich with England, the corre-
> spondences between Gudunov and Denmark, the condi-
> tions presented to the Polish prince by the aristocracy in
> the 17th century, emissaries of Alexei Mikhailovich. . . .
> Finally Peter appeared (XI, 268–9).

Significantly, while acknowledging Peter's crucial role in shaping the course of modern Russian history, Pushkin does not oversimplify the historical process by suggesting that Peter created a new, westernized, Russia from scratch, but rather stresses the teleological aspect of his reforms. Peter's reforms become for Pushkin a culminating point of Russian history, a Russian counterpart to the French Revolution.

Addressing the problem of the first Russian revolution, many scholars refer to the Decembrist revolt. The title of Anatole G. Mazour's book on this subject, *The First Russian Revolution, 1825,* is revealing. Efim Etkind joins this view and calls the Decembrist uprising "la première révolution avortée" (Etkind, 131). By contrast, Pushkin, clearly, placed the first Russian revolution at the time of Peter the Great. In his article "On the Nobility" he declares: "Pierre I est tout à la fois Robespierre et Napoléon (La Révolution incarnée)" (Peter I is both Robespierre and Napoleon combined [The Revolution incarnated]. Pushkin 1962–66: VIII, 146) Indeed, for Pushkin, the epoch of Peter the Great represents a Russian analogue to the French Revolution in terms of its historical significance and moral ambiguity. Robespierre, the "sentimental tiger" as Pushkin names him in his article on Radishchev, destroyed the ideals of the Revolution by violence, cruelty, and disregard of the law. However, by calling Peter the Great "Robespierre," Pushkin implied what makes him similar to the famous Jacobinic leader is not only Peter the Great's contempt for law and the terror of his *dubinka*, but also Peter's reforms directed against Russian nobility that represented, in Pushkin's opinion, the only force that could constitute opposition to the absolute monarchy. In his draft letter to Chaadaev (19 October 1836) he further elucidates this thought: "Pierre le Grand dompta la noblesse en publiant la Табель о рангах, le clergé—en abolissant le patriarchat (NB Napoléon disait à Alexandre: vous êtes *pope* chez vous; ce n'est pas si bête). Mais autre chose est de faire une révolution, autre chose est d'en consacrer les résultats. Jusqu'à Catherine II on a continué chez nous la révolution de Pierre au lieu de la consolider. Catherine II craignait encore l'Aristocratie; Alexandre était jacobin lui-même" (Peter the Great tamed the nobility by publishing the *Table of Ranks*, and clergy—by abolishing the patriarchate [NB Napoleon said to Alexander: you are the *pope* in your country; this is not so stupid]. But it is one thing to do a revolution, it is another to consolidate its results. Until Catherine II we continued Peter's revolution instead of consolidating it. Catherine II still feared the Aristocracy; Alexander was himself a Jacobin. XVI, 260) Considered in the light of Peter's humiliation of the hereditary nobility, the Decembrist revolt becomes merely a logical consequence of, and a counter-revolution to, Peter's fundamental revolution. Moreover, any attempt to support and guarantee the traditional rights of the nobility might be viewed as a "counter-revolution to the revolution of Peter." Pushkin intimates this idea in his letter to Viazemskii of 16 March 1830: "Before his departure, the sovereign left in Moscow a project of the new organization, a counter-revolution to the revolution of Peter. Here is an opportunity for you to write a

political pamphlet and even to publish it, for the government acts
or intends to act in the sense of European enlightenment. Protection of the nobility, suppression of the officialdom, new rights
of the petty bourgeoisie and of the serfs—these are lofty topics"
(XIV, 69).

The "Jacobinic" nature of "Peter's revolution," in other words,
manifested itself in his subversion of both nobility and clergy and
his institutionalization of ranks open to all classes. It is in this sense
—the limitation of the rights of the Russian hereditary nobility—
that Alexander I was called a "Jacobin" as well. So much was Pushkin convinced of the intrinsic "Jacobinic" nature of all attacks on
the old Russian nobility that, so Pushkin's diary suggests, he did
not hesitate to share this view with the Grand Duke Michael during their personal audience. "All you Romanovs," he announced,
"are levelers and revolutionaries" (Pushkin 1962–66: VIII, 60).
According to Pushkin, however, limitation of the nobility's rights
could not lead to the people's freedom, but rather to its enslave-
ment. As he said in "Notes on Russian History of the Eighteenth
Century ("Zametki po Russkoi istorii XVIII veka"): "Our political freedom is now inseparable from freeing the serfs" (XI, 15).
This is why, being a committed oligarch and a supporter of aristocratic government that would limit autocracy, Pushkin was so
wary of democracy and all "democratic" institutions. In the same
draft letter to Chaadaev he continues: "Voila déjà 140 ans que la
Табель о рангах balaye la noblesse; et c'est l'empereur actuel, qui
le premier a posé une digue (bien faible encore) contre le déborde-
ment d'une démocratie, pire que celle de l'Amérique (avez-vous lu
Tocqueville? je suis encore tout chaud et tout effrayé de son livre)"
(*The Table of Ranks* has already been brushing the nobility aside
for one hundred forty years; and it is the current emperor himself
who is the first to place a dike [still rather weak] against the over-
flow of a democracy worse than that of America [have you read
Tocqueville? I am still all hot and frightened from his book] XVI,
260–61).[6]

Napoleon, on the other hand, was the one who consolidated the results of the revolution by establishing permanent institutions. He built up a new nobility and created a nationalistic empire. In this sense Peter the Great could definitely be compared to Napoleon. Both declared themselves emperors. Moreover, like Napoleon, Peter was perceived as a morally and politically ambiguous figure, both a hero and a tyrant. As early as in 1822 Pushkin links Peter to Napoleon: "Peter I was not afraid of the people's Freedom, an inevitable consequence of the enlightenment, for he had confidence in his power and despised mankind maybe even more than Napoleon did" (XI, 14). Similar to Napoleon, whom Pushkin deems "an heir and a murderer of the rebellious freedom" in his poem of 1824, Peter both brings enlightenment and destroys it by his tyrannical rule. Thus in a paradoxical twist, Pushkin not only calls the actions of the Nicholas I government that are directed in support of the nobility a "counter-revolution to the revolution of Peter," but also deems them the acts of the European Enlightenment. Peter, who supposedly broke the window to Europe through which the European Enlightenment filtered into Russia, turns out to be the obstacle to this very enlightenment.

In his unfinished *History of Peter I*, Pushkin strives to preserve the dualism of his portrayal of Peter the Great, emblematized in his comparison of Peter with both Robespierre and Napoleon in his notes "On the Nobility." Thus in the passage related to 1721 he concludes: "The difference between Peter's state institutions and his temporary ukases is astonishing. The first are fruits of a broad mind, informed by good will and wisdom; the second are *often cruel, self-willed, and seem to be written by a knout.* The first were intended for eternity, or at least for the future,—the second slipped from the tongue of an impatient and despotic landowner" (X, 256). It is clear that Pushkin considers Peter's revolution ultimately a positive event, but in the course of his narrative he demonstrates Peter's cruelty and arbitrariness. Indeed, Peter's "revolution" disclosed the nature of Russian history and revealed its fundamental characteristic, namely its dependence on those at the top of the hierarchical social structure. If the revolution of the French was a manifestation of the French spirit and was performed through the medium of the masses, Russian history and Peter's "revolution" were performed by the few and were marked by the strong impact of powerful historical personalities such as Peter the Great.

French liberal historians of the beginning of the nineteenth century sought their historical "formula" in the Revolution. Pushkin searched for the Russian "formula" in the revolution of Peter the Great. He realized that the Russian revolution was different from both the English and French ones and that knowledge of European history could not fully explain the Russian situation. However, in his interpretation of the epoch of Peter the Great and its significance, Pushkin was not so far from the French historians' interpretations of the French Revolution. For them, the Revolution was a culmination and clarification of history and its direction. For Pushkin, it was Peter who determined the development of modern Russian history and elucidated its historical potential.

t w o   Chance and Historical Necessity

For myself, I am of the opinion that, at all times,
one great portion of the events of this world are
attributable to very general facts and another to special influences. These two kinds of cause are always
in operation; only their proportion varies. General
facts serve to explain more things in democratic
than in aristocratic ages, and fewer things are then
assignable to individual influences. During periods of
aristocracy the reverse takes place: special influences
are stronger, general causes weaker; unless, indeed,
we consider as a general cause the fact itself of the
inequality of condition, which allows individuals to
baffle the natural tendencies of all the rest.

—Alexis de Tocqueville, *Democracy in America*

Chance and Context

In different social structures chance plays different roles. If a
society has a pyramidal structure, much is determined by what
occurs at the top. The balance and stability of the pyramid
completely depend on the stability of its summit. According to
scientific observations, in a pyramid made of sand, one piece of
sand may change the entire configuration with unpredictable results. The structure of democracies, by contrast, is not pyramidal, but corresponds to flat and even surfaces. But if we consider

flat surfaces, we will see that the role of the accidental configurations of tiny grains of sand is almost of no importance there. In other words, hierarchical social structures are characterized by a higher degree of unpredictability and indeterminacy as compared to democracies, just as the accidental shifts of single grains of sand affect more a sand pyramid than even surfaces.

The idea that haphazard events have different impacts in different historical situations and that the role of the accidental in Russian history plays a greater role than in other European countries was indirectly formulated by Voltaire in a book that was familiar to Pushkin—*Russia Under Peter the Great*. Analyzing the battle of Poltava, Voltaire writes:

> The risk run by the two rivals was not equal. If Charles lost a life so often jeopardized, it would be, after all, only one hero the less. The Ukrainian provinces, the Lithuanian and Russian frontiers would no longer be devastated; Poland would resume her tranquillity together with her lawful king, who was already reconciled with his benefactor the czar; and, lastly, Sweden, drained of men and money, would be able to find grounds for consolation. But if the czar perished, tremendous labors beneficial to the entire human race would be buried with him, and the vastest empire in the world would fall back into the chaos from which it had barely emerged (Voltaire, 139).

It is no coincidence that Voltaire uses the word "chaos" here to describe Russian history prior to Peter the Great. Russian history, indeed, demonstrated a desperate attempt to find structure and order, which it finally obtained (or had an illusion of obtaining) through Peter the Great. As discussed in Chapter 1, due to its specific development, much in Russian history depended on the individuals in power. Pushkin frequently emphasized the extent to which Russian history was influenced by the very top of the social hierarchy. He sadly observed the peculiar nature of social change in Russia that was characterized by the relatively active role of the government as compared to all other Russian institutions and the passivity of the masses. Once again the idea that special influence of the few plays a crucial role in Russian history is suggested in *A Journey from Moscow to Petersburg* by Pushkin's fictitious narrator: "I cannot help but note that since the time of the Romanovs' rise to the throne, the government in our country is always ahead in the field of education and enlightenment. The people follow the government always lazily, and sometimes unwillingly" (XI, 244). To be sure, it would be completely false to interpret Pushkin's statements of this sort as praise or approval of the government. One need not cite his negative remarks about Russian emperors to demonstrate that he was critical of not only Peter I and Catherine the Great, but of all the Romanovs. Moreover, he sincerely deplored the sad situation of contemporary Russia with its "absence of any public opinion, its indifference to any form of duty, justice or truth" (XVI, 172). What Pushkin is saying is that under conditions of absolute monarchy, much depends on the government, and by implication, on chance. Pushkin ascertained that the intrusion of the accidental and arbitrary in Russian history is a consequence of its political situation. As early as in his *Notes on Russian History of the Eighteenth Century* (1822), he observes with his typical irony that even during the seemingly enlightened times the system of autocracy is doomed to be "tempered" by chance: "The reign of Paul proves one thing: that Caligulas might be born even during enlightened times. Russian defenders of autocracy disagree and accept the glorious joke of Mme. de Staël as the foundation of our constitution: *En Russie le gouvernement est un despotisme mitigé par la strangulation*" (XI, 17). In an autocratic society no change may occur except from the top. In 1836, Pushkin could find confirmation of the idea about the relative balance between historical laws and special influences during periods of aristocracy and in democracies in Alexis de Tocqueville's *Democracy in America*, a book that he carefully read and much admired.[1] But the general connection between absolutism and the role of chance in history was widely discussed in the eighteenth- and nineteenth-century French historiography and was familiar to him through the works of such writers as Voltaire, Pierre-Édouard Lémontey, or Barante (Cf. Kibal'nik 1993, 134). In his own writings, Pushkin had consistently insisted on a close connection between the method and the type of history analyzed.[2] He professed his historical and methodological contextualism most explicitly in his criticism of the French "providential" school of historiography and of its Russian followers in his comments on the second volume of Polevoi's *History of the Russian People.*

In his essay on Polevoi, Pushkin expresses his attitudes toward the French historian Guizot and his explanatory method and criticizes him for avoiding all that is "distanced, alien, accidental" in history. As brief as most of Pushkin's historical remarks are, these notes (also referred to in Chapter 1) illuminate Pushkin's own perception of history.

Guizot has explained one of the events of Christian history: the *European Enlightenment.* He discerns its germination, describes its gradual development, and, setting aside all that is distant, alien or *accidental,* he carries it to us through dark, bloody, rebellious and, finally, flourishing centuries. You understood the great merit of the French historian. You should understand too that Russia never had anything in common with the rest of Europe; its history demands a different thought, a different formula than the thoughts and formulas deduced by Guizot from the history of the Christian West. Do not say: *It could not have been otherwise.* If that were true then the historian would be an astronomer, and the events of the life of mankind would be predicted in calendars like solar eclipses. But Providence is not algebra. The human mind, according to a common expression, is not a prophet but a conjecturer, it sees the general course of things and can deduce from it profound suppositions, often justified by time, but it cannot foresee *chance*—that powerful and instantaneous instrument of Providence (XI, 127).

What Pushkin meant by the "formulas deduced by Guizot" cannot be easily resolved, for nowhere does he precisely define either Guizot's "formula" or his own "formula" for understanding Russian history. While admiring the French historian, Pushkin nevertheless acknowledges his weaknesses. According to Pushkin, Guizot invests historical events with too much coherence and too many neat generalizations. Pushkin recognizes that these historians select evidence to conform to their theories, that they create a system, a pattern that could presumably explain everything. In so doing they impose causal patterns on past events that could very easily be false, for they inevitably would "set apart," as Pushkin put it, everything "haphazard," everything that is inconsistent with their general scheme. By excluding everything accidental, the historian turns history into destiny.

Pushkin definitely objects to the French Romanticist historians' obsession with systems. He does not, however, directly criticize Guizot's method, but suggests that Russian history does not fit Guizot's orderly paradigm and requires a different approach. Although Pushkin was personally committed to the Enlightenment's ideas about human progress, the role of education, and evolution, he could not fail to realize that the theory of progress and the form it acquired in the "providential" school of French historians was based on the limited experience of recent European civilizations. Russian history, by contrast, demonstrated anything but progressive development; instead it displayed centuries of regression, such as the Tartar yoke or the monstrous despotism of Ivan the Terrible. As Karamzin eloquently put it in his *History of the Russian State*, "granted the Batyi's yoke did humiliate the Russian spirit, there is no doubt that the reign of Ivan IV did not elevate it either" (IX, 260). After the publication of Karamzin's *History of the Russian State,* the Russian reading public had difficulty viewing Russian history in terms of evolution. Ivan IV emerged as a highly ambiguous figure. Although Ivan IV achieved the consolidation of the Russian state, this did not lead the nation to prosperity and progress: his rule signified a terrifying and demoralizing abuse of power.

Were these events fully governed by historical laws and necessity? What, if any, is the role of chance and human personality in Russian history? With these questions at the center of intellectual debates of the time, chance becomes one of the most important subjects of eighteenth- and early nineteenth-century literature (Lotman 1992, 398–412; Toibin 1980, 15–19). In his article *"The Queen of Spades* and the Theme of Cards and Card Games in Russian Literature of the Beginning of the Nineteenth Century"* ("'Pikovaia dama' i tema kart i kartochnoi igry v russkoi literature nachala XIX veka"), Iurii Lotman points out that the eighteenth-century favoritism augmented the general atmosphere of chaos and unpredictability in Russian aristocratic society. Specific sociopolitical reasons emerged for a particularly Russian perception of the historical process as a play of haphazard events:

> Beginning with the Petrine reforms, the life of Russian educated society developed on two realms: the intellectual and philosophical development followed the path and tempo of the European movement, whereas the sociopolitical foundation of the society changed at reduced pace and in accordance with other laws of development. This led to a dramatic increase of chance in historical movement. Each single factor within one level was inconsequential and accidental when considered from the point of view of the other level; whereas a continuous mutual intrusion of the phenomena of these levels resulted in the kind of erratic pattern and a seeming inconsequentiality of events that forced contemporaries to declare entire as-

pects of Russian life to be "inorganic," illusory, or non-existent (Lotman 1992, 398).

Since Russian history appeared to be more haphazard and amorphous than its Western counterparts, its historiography, according to Pushkin, should also have developed a new explanatory approach that would consider the role of chance in history and avoid overly symmetrical and rational formulations. Pushkin felt that although Western history may fit the formula of progress and rational development of human relations marked by a direct connection between causes and effects, Russian history could not be described according to the same explanatory principles. Pushkin criticized the French scholars for their "eurocentrism" and insistence on the universal nature of the historical laws that they attributed to their histories. It is important to note that Pushkin did not simply condemn the French historians' explanatory principles as false, but dismissed them as irrelevant for the understanding of Russian history.

The lack of easily definable linear development in Russian history, Russia's autocratic form of government with its inherent tendency toward arbitrariness, and a general post-Napoléonic and post-Decembrist interest in the accidental—all these factors stimulated Pushkin's profound concern with chance. Pushkin was incessantly preoccupied with the role chance plays in history and the way it should be incorporated in the accounts of the past. Shortly after Pushkin launched his attack on Polevoi, he wrote a parody of contemporary historiography, "History of the Village Goriukhino" (1830). Whether the target of Pushkin's parody here is Karamzin, Mikhail Kachenovsky, Mikhail Pogodin, or Polevoi, it is clear that Pushkin mocks in this tale the same historiographical principles he attacks in his article on Polevoi. The unfortunate historian, Belkin, cherishes the ambition to be "a judge, a witness and a prophet of the centuries and nations," that is, he takes pride in exactly those qualities that Pushkin deems inappropriate for a historian (VIII: I, 132). In their article "The [Hi]story of the Village Gorjuxino: In Praise of Pushkin's Folly" David Bethea and Sergei Davydov demonstrate that Belkin, trying to imitate the principles of modern historiography, "commits precisely those mistakes he most wants to avoid, namely the historiographic fallacies. From a contiguous (hence accidental) connection between weather and calendar events [. . .] Belkin extrapolates a causal connection." As a result, the authors conclude, "under Belkin's unruly pen these precautionary devices become absurd" (301).

Pushkin develops his most intense interest in chance in the 1830s when he writes *The Tales of Belkin* (*Povesti Belkina*) and *The Queen of Spades* (*Pikovaia dama*). His historical imagination, however, as well as his ideas about chance, fate, necessity, and causality, began to crystallize as early as 1824–25, while working on his first historical project, *Boris Godunov*.

The Invisible Duel: Chance and Certainty in *Boris Godunov*

Pushkin's *Boris Godunov* explores the tension between the elements of determinacy and indeterminacy in history. Tsar Boris and the Pretender exemplify two radically different attitudes toward the historical process. Boris's notion of history excludes everything accidental. Grigorii, by contrast, makes chance his true companion. The two main characters of the play, who never meet on stage, engage, nevertheless, in an invisible duel that becomes not only a contest for the Russian throne but represents a clash of two antagonistic concepts of history. Pushkin's play, however, promulgates no winners in this duel. On the one hand, chance seems to rupture all cause-effect relations that Boris is trying to create.[3] On the other hand, the Pretender's disregard for historical laws and causality, his reliance on chance and good luck condition both his short triumph and his impending doom as foreshadowed in Grigorii's dream:

Мне снилося, что лестница крутая
Меня вела на башню; с высоты

Мне виделась Москва, что муравейник;
Внизу народ на площади кипел
И на меня указывал со смехом,
И стыдно мне и страшно становилось —
И, падая стремглав, я пробуждался . . . (VII, 19)

I would dream that stiff steps
Led me to a tower; from atop
I could see Moscow as an ant hill;
Below on the square people swarmed
And pointed at me with laughter,
I felt both frightened and ashamed —
And while falling down headlong, I would wake up . . .

Godunov rationalizes, calculates, but fails to achieve his goal precisely because he is unprepared to cope with the unpredictable, with the emergence of the Pretender who appears to him as chance incarnate, as "an empty name, a shade" (VII, 49). In his search for certainty Boris anticipates Hermann from *The Queen of Spades*. Like Hermann, who had "little true faith" but "many prejudices" (VIII: I, 246), Boris seeks the company of fortune-tellers, sorcerers, and magicians; he wants to *know* his destiny. Similar to Pushkin's other tragic rationalist, Salieri, who "verified harmony with algebra" and who "dissected music like a corpse" (VII, 123), Boris attempts to overstep one corpse, that of tsarevich Dmitri, in order to turn history into algebra. But he stumbles, as stumble Aleko, Salieri, Hermann, and all Pushkin's characters who strive to manipulate chance and Providence. For as we have seen, Pushkin warns us that "Providence is not algebra." Similar to the jealous composer, Boris laments his vain achievements and cannot reconcile himself with the power of the irrational. His famous first soliloquy, "I have attained the highest power" (*Dostig ia vysshei vlasti*), echoes Salieri's complaints about the unjust correlation between the efforts and the reward: "Finally in boundless art / I have attained a high degree" (*Ia nakonets v iskusstve bezgranichnom / Dostignul stepeni vysokoi*) (VII, 124). This reward, which Salieri envisions as "immortal genius" (*bessmertnyi genii*) and which Tsar Boris perceives as the people's love, is distributed irrationally and causes deep anxiety to both achievers.[4] No credit is granted for their apparently righteous endeavors; with all their gifts and accomplishments, the tragic ruler and the tormented musician lack something that lies beyond their control—God's grace. Godunov's efforts, his political and his private undertakings appear to be disrupted by chance:

> Я выстроил им новые жилища.
> Они ж меня пожаром упрекали!
> Вот черни суд: ищи ее любви.
> В семье моей я мнил найти отраду,
> Я дочь мою мнил осчастливить браком—
> Как буря, смерть уносит жениха ... (VII, 26)

> I built new dwellings for them.
> But they had blamed me for fire!
> That is the judgment of the mob: just seek its love!
> I longed to find solace in my family,
> I longed to marry off my daughter happily,
> But as a storm, death took her groom away ...

Regardless of his actual guilt or innocence, Godunov is endangered by the mob's judgment (*cherni sud*), by the whimsical, often apparently irrational and volatile opinion of the people.[5] People's transient love or hatred emerges as a stumbling block in Boris's otherwise rationalistic system; it introduces an element of the unpredictability that Boris cannot fully control or manipulate, and which threatens, therefore, the coherence of his rational universe. Godunov's secret opponent, Afanasii Pushkin, seems to know that the tsar's "Achilles' heel" is hidden in his head. When Prince Shuisky reveals to him important news about the emergence of the Pretender in Poland and warns that his appearance could cause a "storm" among the Russian people, Afanasii Pushkin echoes the manipulative courtier by emphasizing the danger of this news for

Boris. Significantly, he refers to the Tsar's "clever head": "Such a storm, that Tsar Boris will hardly / Keep the crown on his clever head" (VII, 40).

It is precisely, however, the volatility of "people's opinion" by which Boris is victimized and which, in fact, turns out so perilous for the Tsar, that the Pretender welcomes and exploits. Just as Boris appears to be crushed by rumors, so the Pretender feeds on them and finds strength in gossip. Gavrila Pushkin states explicitly that the False Dmitri's power lies in "people's opinion":

> Но знаешь ли чем сильны мы, Басманов?
> Не войском, нет, не польскою подмогой,
> А мнением; да! мнением народным (VII, 93).

> But do you know, Basmanov, where lies our strength?
> We are strong neither in army nor in Polish support
> But in opinion; yes, in popular opinion.

But what does the "people's opinion" mean in the context of the play? From beginning to end Pushkin is careful to demonstrate how "popular opinion" is skillfully manipulated by the few sly courtiers; he depicts the ease with which people shift their sympathies and allegiance. We are forced to learn from the play through the people's own action or rather inaction, as well as through various characteristics of the people provided by the Tsar and his courtiers, that the people's opinion is unreliable and extremely unstable. Prince Shuisky articulates this idea eloquently:

> Но знаешь сам: бессмысленная чернь
> Изменчива, мятежна, суеверна,
> Легко пустой надежде предана,
> Для истины глуха и равнодушна,
> А баснями питается она (VII, 46).

> You know yourself; the senseless mob
> Is fickle, rebellious, superstitious,
> And gives itself up to an empty hope with ease;

It obeys a sudden persuasion,
Is deaf and indifferent to truth,
But it nurtures itself with fables.

The same *narod* who grieves Godunov's indecision and then hails his consent in the beginning, who greets the Pretender in Moscow, and who is silent at the news of Godunov's family's cruel murder in the end of the play will ultimately laugh at Dmitri's fall as anticipated by Grigorii's dream. The Tsar Boris claims that he was elected by the "people's will" (VII, 15), but the preceding scene seems to discredit his assertion as mere self-delusion. Godunov's compulsive need to repeat that he was "elected by the entire nation" (VII, 47) only confirms his inner vulnerability and his vain attempt to replace the irrationality of the grace of God (the gift of inheritance) with the rationality of election. Pushkin's comic depiction of the mass scenes aims to expose the people's political apathy. The disoriented and inert masses obey orders without understanding or questioning their meaning; they listen to the Duma's decrees but remain perplexed about their uncertain future. The remarks of the few anonymous citizens underscore the people's complete withdrawal from political decisions: "Oh, God! Who is going to rule over us?"; "How should we know? the boyars know this, / Not us, simple folk"; "Everybody cries. Friend, let's cry as well" (VII, 10–13). The very ability of the people to form their own conscious "opinion" is, therefore, suspect.

The people's notorious silence (*narod bezmolvstvuet*) at the end of the play further reveals the stunning degree of their ineptitude. To be sure, their silence could mean disapproval and the refusal to endorse the Pretender, as many critics have contended.[6] But depending on the context in which it is observed, silence could mean submission to fate and be, therefore, passive, or it could stand for active accusation. Pushkin's play, however, offers no indication that the people grow in maturity throughout the course of the tragedy; the preceding mass scenes contain no evidence of people's political consciousness. Moreover, only moments before the people grow silent at the horror of the Godunov family's murder, the same *narod* asks for the murder of Boris's son. The intoxicated and confused crowd calls for the elimination of the entire Godunov family: "Let's tie them up! drown them! Long live Dmitri! Death to the family of Boris Godunov!" (VII, 96). As Emerson persuasively puts it, "However generously one approaches the *narod* in this play, it is simply not heroic. Neither here, nor in Pushkin's several poems where a 'crowd' (*tolpa*) or 'mob' (*chern'*) plays a role, is there anything but despair of and contempt for the people's response" (Emerson 1986, 136). Furthermore, the original version of the controversial remark *narod bezmolvstvuet* was much more unambiguously consistent with the general representation of people's servile compliance and political indifference. In the 1825 completed manuscript of the play the final line of text represents the cheer: "Long live Tsar Dmitri Ivanovich!" (VII, 302). Whether Pushkin's replacement of the final phrase in the 1831 printed text was motivated by restrictions of censorship or by purely artistic considerations, it is unlikely that Pushkin intended to completely reverse the meaning of his final stage direction. To read it as an act of resistance, therefore, as did Belinsky and his successors, is to ignore the sequence of the last scene's events as well as the general context of the play. This means that for some unknown reason Pushkin decided in a final stroke to change dramatically his interpretation of the people's political role. Yet, as becomes clear from other texts of Pushkin written in the 1830s, the people's passivity was regarded by the poet as a general and deplorable feature of the Russian political make-up. It might be wise, therefore, to interpret the 1831 *narod bezmolvstvuet* merely as a version of the 1825 final line, that is, to consider the people's silence and the cheer as two sides of the same coin. Whether the play should end with the greeting of the Pretender or with the people's silence, the general meaning of the play's concluding lines would remain intact, conveying the people's confusion and Pushkin's skepticism of popular opinion and the people's political consciousness.

The mob's sympathies appear to be as unstable as the play of dice. Curiously, the people's opinion and fate are inseparable in Grigorii's mind: "Everything lends me support: both people and fate" (VII, 52). The ambitious and intelligent Marina Mnishek knows this well when she warns the False Dmitri about the uncertainty of the people's support: "Dubious rumors are already in the air, / One novelty replaces yet another one" (VII, 60).

Grigorii, however, seems to find his strength in the unpredictability itself. He is open to chance, alert to numerous possibilities that life can offer, and quick to improvise. As opposed to the distrustful and ever doubting Boris, whose actions are dictated by reason and calculation and who wants to usurp God's providence, Grigorii has faith and confidence. He does not seek advice from the astrologers but believes in prophecies of poets and in his fate. "Providence, surely, protects him," one of the Pretender's companions reassures (VII, 85). Yet does the Pretender really emerge victorious in Pushkin's play?

Just as Boris fails when he confronts chance, Grigorii fails when he tries to plan and consider the general causes or possible consequences of the events. He denies laws and seems to rely on chance and his good luck alone. In the garden scene by the fountain he admits his inability to calculate: "But the time has come—and I remember nothing. I cannot find the well-prepared speeches" (VII, 58). When sober and calculative Marina demands that he reveal to her his prospects ("hopes, intentions and even fears"), the Pretender is at a loss, for he has no preconceived, detailed plans and no secrets to share (VII, 59). Moreover, the False Dmitri turns out to be peculiarly inept and near-sighted in his assessment of the general historical development of Russia. He attempts to convince the Polish Jesuit Chernikovky that the Russian people would easily trade their Orthodox faith for Catholicism:

Нет, мой отец, не будет затрудненья;
Я знаю дух народа моего;
В нем набожность не знает исступленья:

Ему свящⸯен пример царя его.
Всегда, к тому ж, терпимость равнодушна.
Ручаюсь я, что прежде двух годов
Весь мой народ, вся северная церковь
Признают власть наместника Петра (VII, 50).

No, my Father, there won't be complications;
I know the spirit of my people;
Their piety knows no frenzy:
Sacred to them is the model of their Tsar.
Moreover, tolerance is always indifferent.
I guarantee that two years won't pass
Before all my people, all the Northern Church
Will accept the power of St. Peter's deputy.

To be sure, this argument might be a good strategy to recruit a Polish ally. But if Pushkin meant his *Boris* to be perceived against the historical background provided in Karamzin's *History*, — as indeed his contemporaries did perceive it—then the reader or the spectator of the drama would know that the Polish-style government will be exactly what will shake the False Dmitri's authority. Although Grigorii appears to be a skillful improviser, able to assume various identities (Emerson 1986, 100), not only his manipulative skills and poetical gifts precipitate his temporary success. Grigorii "succeeds," Emerson maintains, "because he *makes* history, or rather, he makes it up" (Emerson 1986, 100). But then he also fails because history makes him. Grigorii realizes that he is merely a "pretext for feud and warfare" (VII, 65). In *Boris Godunov* Pushkin captures the accident-prone atmosphere of the time, the only atmosphere that could facilitate the False Dmitri's ascent to power, but which also would condition his ultimate fall. The pyramidal structure of the unlimited autocracy is what increases the role of accidental configurations in history. Afanasii Pushkin blames Boris for despotism and complains about the uncertainty and unpredictability of autocratic rule:

Уверены ль мы в бедной жизни нашей?
Нас каждый день опала ожидает,
Тюрьма, Сибирь, клобук иль кандалы. [...]
Зависим мы от первого холопа,
Которого захочем наказать.
Вот—Юрьев день задумал уничтожить.
Не властны мы в поместиях своих (VII, 40–41).

Do we have confidence in our humble life?
Disfavor awaits us every day,
Prison, Siberia, monastic cowl or shackles. [...]
We depend on every servant
Whom we would like to punish.
Here he decided to abolish St. Iurii day.
We have no power over our own estates.

Afanasii Pushkin articulates all the evils of absolutism and clearly indicates that this is the atmosphere that might generate hazardous events: "Let the Pretender only try / To promise them old St. Iurii day / The funmaking would be on its way" (VII, 41).

Grigorii knows that his success lies in chance; in this "game of bloody war" he gambles and is equally ready for triumph and for defeat. He proudly confesses to Marina:

Теперь иду—погибель иль венец
Мою главу в России ожидает,
Найду ли смерть, как воин в битве честной,
Иль как злодей на плахе площадной,
Не будешь ты подругою моею [...] (VII, 64).

Now I am ready to set off. Whether ruin or crown
Awaits my head in Russia,
Whether I find death as a warrior in the honest battle
Or as a scoundrel on the square's execution block,
You won't be my companion. [...]

But if it is indeed "popular opinion" and chance that strengthen the Pretender's position and guarantee his success, then his victory cannot be viewed as a real triumph. As Tolstoy's Kutuzov knows, "it is not difficult to take a fortress but is difficult to win a campaign. For that, one needs no storming and attacking but one needs *time and patience*" (Tolstoy VI, 181). The "popular opinion" and good luck, which seem to commend the Pretender now, will inevitably betray him in the future. Such is the law of the wheel of fortune.

There are no winners in Pushkin's play. History defeats equally those who attempt to calculate it as algebra and those who refuse to see historical patterns in it. Between blind necessity and the chaos of accidental events lies a huge gulf of probability. Pushkin does not deny causality but argues powerfully against determinism by focusing on the dynamics of chance. *Boris Godunov* is the tragedy of Boris, and Boris's tragedy is grounded in the existence of the accidental in history and life, in the presence of chance that he cannot bend to his liking. Moreover, Boris seems to be caught in a contradiction: on the one hand, he attempts to eliminate the accidental by consolidating his power; on the other, it is precisely absolute power that appears to generate the chance-prone atmosphere that will ultimately challenge his authority. The emergence of the Pretender is simultaneously a law-governed event and an accidental phenomenon. Or, in the kind of history that Pushkin presents in his drama, chance becomes law.

Exercises in Counterfactual History: Chance in *Count Nulin*

Chance plays an equally—if not more—significant role in Pushkin's fictional narratives, such as *Count Nulin* (*Graf Nulin*) (1825), "The Snowstorm" ("Metel' ") (1830), "The History of the Village Goriukhino" (1830), and "The Queen of Spades" (1833), which do not openly address historical figures or specific historical events but contain, nevertheless, important insights into Pushkin's philosophy of history. As different as these works may be, they are united by two common elements: concern with chance and parody. In all these works Pushkin's parody goes beyond merely parodying specific themes or genres. As Emerson points out, "One of Pushkin's most sophisticated sorts of parody can be found, it seems, at a level *above* that of specific theme or plot" (1993, 32). The target of Pushkin's parody in these works is a specific world view, a philosophy of history that does not provide for the proper place of chance in history.

Pushkin's mock poem *Count Nulin,* the earliest of the parodies mentioned above, written shortly after Pushkin had completed *Boris Godunov,* is Pushkin's tour de force on the nature of chance in history. Pushkin wrote *Count Nulin* during his stay at Mikhailovskoe, when he was also writing *Boris Godunov* (1824–25) and "Notes on the *Annals* of Tacitus" (Zamechaniia na 'Annaly Tatsita' 1825). Both his work on *Boris Godunov* and his reading of Tacitus stimulated Pushkin's reflections on the nature of chance in history.

Later, in 1830, Pushkin provided a clue to this mock poem in his "Note on *Count Nulin*" ("Zametka o 'Grafe Nuline' "). He pointed to its parodic nature and to its hidden subject matter, the role of chance in history:

> At the end of 1825 I was in the country. While rereading *Lucrece,* a rather weak poem of Shakespeare's, I thought: what if it had occurred to Lucrece to slap Tarquin's face? Maybe it would have cooled his initiative, so that, embarrassed, he would have been forced to retreat. Lucrece would not have stabbed herself, Publicola would not have been enraged, Brutus would not have driven out the kings, and the world and its history would have been different.
>
> And so we owe the republic, the consuls, the dictators, the Catos, and Caesar, to a seductive event similar to one which took place recently in my neighborhood, in the Novorzhev district.
>
> I was struck by the idea of parodying both history and

Shakespeare; I could not resist the double temptation and in two mornings had written this tale. I am accustomed to writing down the year and the date on my papers. *Count Nulin* was written on 13 and 14 December. Strange coincidences do occur (XI, 188).

Most critics who consider the poem in the context of Pushkin's later "Note" agree that the poem has a serious subtext and that the role of the accidental in history represents its deepest subject matter.[7] The sentence "strange coincidences do occur" (*byvaiut strannye sblizheniia*) allegedly refers to the fact of Pushkin's "accidental" non-participation in the Decembrist revolt. An unexpected meeting with a priest or a hare crossing his road stopped Pushkin from leaving Mikhailovskoe and going to Petersburg where he would have joined the Decembrists. Pushkin preferred to interpret this episode as a providential coincidence that protected him from disaster. Another coincidence Pushkin alludes to is that he was writing a tale provoked by the idea of the "accidental" in history exactly on those days (13 and 14 of December), when their last meeting and the Decembrist revolt took place in Petersburg.[8]

Arguing against the determinism of Western thought, Pushkin insists that one should not presume that events must have happened when they might just as well not have happened. As he says in his article on Polevoi: "Don't say it could not have been otherwise."

Pushkin's preoccupation with "what if . . ." reminds one of the well-known argument about the charms of Cleopatra's nose.[9] If Anthony had not been infatuated with Cleopatra, so the argument goes, then the result of the Battle of Actium would have been different. In the 1820s it became fashionable to speak about the consequences of Napoleon's cold and various "what-ifs."[10] Pushkin plays with this "might-have-been" argument in his mock poem and arrives at a rather sophisticated conclusion about the relationship between accidental coincidences and historical laws.[11]

Coming back to Russia from France, the frivolous young Count

Nulin (who is incidentally a reader of Guizot!) stops at the estate of a young, bored, and no less frivolous housewife, Natalia Pavlovna. Moreover, Natalia's husband has just left, assuring his wife that he will not come back that night: "[The husband] hails to his wife: 'Don't wait up for me!' / And rides out onto the road" (V, 3). In a word, everything promises a savory and alluring development of the intrigue. Pushkin entices the reader with playful hints: "In late September / (To speak in humble prose) / The countryside is boring: mud, nasty weather [. . .]" (V, 3); "But what is the wife doing, / Alone in her husband's absence?" (V, 4) And indeed, the readers' expectations—as well as those of Count Nulin—seem close to being fulfilled:

> Проходит вечер неприметно;
> Граф сам не свой. Хозяйки взор
> То выражается приветно,
> То вдруг потуплен безответно . . .
> Глядишь—и полночь вдруг на двор (V, 8).

> The evening passes unnoticed.
> The Count is beyond himself. The hostess's eyes
> Now express sympathy,
> And now are downcast unremittingly . . .
> But look—here's midnight suddenly arriving.

The promise of a romance seems unambiguous: "The prankster—may God forgive her—gently presses the Count's hand" (V, 8). (*Prokaznitsa—prosti ei, Bozhe!—/ Tikhon'ko grafu ruku zhmet.*) The natural succession of events and common sense lead the Count to Natalia's bedroom. But then the unexpected happens: the flirt turns out to be a virtuous wife and slaps "the young Tarquin" in the face: "To the young Tarquin with all her might, / She gives— oh, yes, a slap! A slap, and what a slap!" (V, 11) (*Ona Tarkviniiu s razmakha / Daet—poshchechinu. Da, da! / Poshchechinu, da ved' kakuiu!*) To emphasize the unexpected character of Natalia's behavior and to create suspense, Pushkin employs a dash between the verb and the object (*Daet — poshchechinu*).

One could say that the reader's insight into and "divination" of the development of the events is frustrated by the intervention of the inconsequential and unmotivated. A young, bored, curious, pretty, vain, and idle wife is unlikely to have such stubborn virtue and should yield to the advances of a fashionable dandy. Freedom of will or whim, however, seems to triumph over determinism. Count Nulin, the reader of Guizot, seems to approach life according to the French historian's historical principles, i.e., from the point of view of general laws and "historical necessity." He fails pathetically when confronted with "chance," or an individual case.

Pushkin calls his young Count "Tarquin." The implication is that, were the liaison between the Count and Natalia consummated, this could have had most serious consequences.[12] Pushkin, however, depicts a zero-event, or non-event; all the expectations of the "seductive incident" are canceled and reduced to zero. Significantly, the Count's last name is derived from *nul'*, "zero." Was Pushkin simply replaying here a Tarquin/Lucrece scenario by making chance work differently? Does the poem, as Lotman suggests, reveal Pushkin's belief that "as a result of a series of coincidences, a great event might not take place" (Lotman 1977, 90)? Would Natalia's acceptance of the Count's advances have a major impact on the characters' lives in the poem? What if, to paraphrase Pushkin, "it had occurred to Natalia *not* to slap Count's face"? Would the "world and history" have been different?

In the final lines of his mock poem Pushkin teases the reader once more with an ironic twist. The reader who is about to lose faith in his ability to predict the course of the events has to re-evaluate his views: yes, Natalia does have a lover after all, but it is someone else — her twenty-three-year-old neighbor, Lidin. This final detail escapes the attention of most interpreters, yet it is precisely this playful denouement that is crucial for the understanding of Pushkin's complex and ambiguous attitude toward the problem of historical necessity and chance. Pushkin denies determinism but does not reject causality and laws.

Using Pushkin's own opposition between a prophet (*prorok*) and a conjecturer (*ugadchik*), one could say that the reader too—similar to a historian—may see, or guess, "the general course of things and deduce from it profound suppositions." Indeed, both the reader's and Count Nulin's suppositions about Natalia's virtue prove to be true. They cannot, however, determine who is going to be Natalia's lover and "foresee a chance" that can slightly modify the course of the events. In a truly Shakespearean manner, Pushkin teases the reader twice: first he parodies his readiness to draw global conclusions; then he laughs at the reader's naive inference that chance could dramatically change the course of the events. In one of the earlier versions of Pushkin's "The Note on 'Count Nulin'" the poet makes explicit his attitude toward the problem of "chance vs. necessity": "I repeated in my mind the trivial observation about trite causes of great [events?] consequences" (XI, 431). If determinism proves to be wrong, excessive reliance on chance as an explanatory method is "trivial" and shallow. Pushkin replaces historical determinism with probability.

If chance is considered in relation to historical necessity or certain laws and expectations that we may deduce from the general course of things, then chance plays the role of a modifier; it affects the development of the events but does not completely change their general thrust, or direction. Natalia Pavlovna's slap symbolizes openness to the future and the various possibilities with which any single moment is imbued. Indeed, Pushkin shows that one cannot say that "this could not have been otherwise." Yet this openness to the future is not without bound; it is controlled by certain trends or laws of causality that offer only a limited number of possibilities for accidental developments.

Pushkin's tale, however, reveals yet another dimension if viewed from a different perspective. Similar to famous curiosity drawings that could represent one or another object depending on the point of view, *Count Nulin* yields a different reading if interpreted not from the point of view of the reader's expectations about the characters' psychology, but comparatively, in direct reference to Shakespeare's *Lucrece,* the poem that Pushkin read most likely in French translation. Pushkin twice mentions Tarquin's name in the poem and invites, therefore, comparison with the Roman story of Tarquin's rape of Lucrece. Moreover, several details describing the Count's brooding before he embarks on his risky enterprise recall Shakespeare's depiction of Tarquin. Similar to Tarquin, Count Nulin recalls the lady's kind hospitality and how she presses his hand; after a short indecision, both succumb to temptation and march to the lady's room, Tarquin throwing his mantle and Count Nulin a silk robe over his arm; both abhor the creaking while they steal their way into the hostess's bedroom; and both are compared to cats preying upon a mouse.[13]

Yet apart from these superficial similarities and the same basic situation involving a stranger's lust for the hostess in the absence of her husband, it is hard to imagine anything that would be so remote from Shakespeare's poem as Pushkin's playful verse tale. The difference, to be sure, is not limited to Pushkin's playful and comic tone that sharply contrasts with Shakespeare's tragic and solemn stance. Instead of the noble Roman matron renowned for her chastity and the son of the sovereign Roman king, Pushkin depicts a frivolous provincial lady without even specifying her family name and a count with an inconspicuous last name, Nulin. From the center of the Roman Empire and the noble Roman mansion, the action is moved to the middle of nowhere, to a small God forsaken place in the Russian *glush'.*

Why does Pushkin purposefully lower the social status of his Lucrece and Tarquin and choose to place them in the Russian countryside, far away from all the world's capitals and political events of the time? Pushkin consistently emphasizes the provinciality of Natalia's estate and bombards the reader with an abundance of mundane details underscoring the village's peaceful, monotonous, and boring life, with hunting being its only entertainment. The poet catalogues Natalia's prosaic occupations such as pickling mushroom, feeding geese, ordering meals, reading novels, and contemplating a fight of a goat with a dog. It is hard to imagine anything so dissimilar as the historical context that involves the king and the leading statesmen described by Shakespeare in his poem *Lucrece* and the "genre scenes" so wittingly depicted by Pushkin:

> Меж тем печально, под окном,
> Индейки с криком выступали
> Вослед за мокрым петухом.
> Три утки полоскались в луже,
> Шла баба через грязный двор
> Белье повесить на забор,
> Погода становилась хуже—
> Казалось, снег идти хотел . . . (V, 5)

> Meanwhile by the window
> The turkeys shouted and sadly marched
> After the wet rooster.
> Three ducks splashed in a puddle,
> A peasant woman crossed the dirty yard
> To hang her linen on the fence,
> The weather was getting worse—
> It looked like it was about to snow . . .

The poet depicts life that is monotonous and uneventful. The only "event" in Natalia's estate is the natural course of life: the weather getting better or worse. It is clear that Pushkin's elaborate "Flemish" descriptions transpose the story of Lucrece and Tarquin into the realm of Russian *byt* and deflate Roman tragedy to the level of farce. Pushkin remakes *history* into *story*, transforms the historical into the private.

Would, then, the same act, that of rape or an attempt at rape, lead to similar consequences under so dissimilar circumstances? It is obvious that from the point of view of "history" it matters little who is the happy man: Lidin or Nulin (their very names seem to be interchangeable). Under different circumstances, however, the same event might potentially acquire a totally different significance. As Shakespeare's Lucrece implores Tarquin to abandon his vile intent, she alludes to his princely status as a major reason for the irrevocable consequences of his deed: "O be remember'd, no outrageous thing / From vassal actors can be wip'd away: / Then kings' misdeeds cannot be hid in clay" (96). Shakespeare repeatedly expresses the idea of the relative significance of the same deed in various circumstances:

> The baser is he, coming from a king,
> To shame his hope with deeds degenerate;
> The mightier man the mightier is the thing
> That makes him honour'd or begets him hate,
> For greatest scandal waits on greatest state.
> The moon being clouded presently is miss'd,
> But little stars may hide them when they list.

> 'The crow may bathe his coal-black wings in mire,
> and unperceiv'd fly with the filth away;
> But if the like the snow-white swan desire,
> The stain upon his silver down will stay.
> Poor grooms are sightless night, kings glorious day;
> Gnats are unnoted wheresoe'er they fly,
> But eagles gaz'd upon with every eye (113).

Whether or not Pushkin implies that Count Nulin and Natalia Pavlovna are "gnats," he makes them "unnoted" and annuls the consequences of their acts. If the rape of Lucrece may have important historical consequences, the same event or non-event would yield zero result in a situation that is not historically charged. By

linking *Count Nulin* to the story of Tarquin and Lucrece, Pushkin effectively contrasts the private realm to the historical one and
raises the question of context. The private realm that Pushkin
recreates has a historicity of its own, but it implies a completely
different type of history.[14]

Pushkin's ideas about the role of chance in history as they
are artistically rendered in *Count Nulin* can be traced back to
Boris Godunov. Insofar as it is a "parody of history," Pushkin's
mock poem represents also a parody of *Boris Godunov*. *Count Nulin* recreates a situation that markedly diminishes the historical
role of accidental events, reducing it almost to zero. *Boris Godunov*,
by contrast, presents a highly volatile historical atmosphere—one
that increases the impact of chance and special influences, similar to the episode from Roman history utilized by Shakespeare
in his poem *Lucrece*. In his mock poem and his tragedy Pushkin
experiments with two different contexts—private and historical—
testing the role of chance in history. In *The Captain's Daughter*, a
historical novel that treats history in a "domestic manner," Pushkin strives to combine in one text a historical realm with a private
one in order to reveal the dynamics of chance and necessity both
in history and private life. As Boris Eikhenbaum observed, the
relationship between private life and history becomes one of the
central issues of the literature of the 1830s (1962, 279).

Chance in History and in Private Life:
The Captain's Daughter
The tension between the role of chance in a "private" and in a "historical" life, similar to the one Pushkin alludes to in *Count Nulin*, is
fully embodied in *The Captain's Daughter*. Chance and "strange coincidences" seem to play a major role in Piotr Grinev's life: it is by
accident that Grinev meets Pugachev in the blizzard and rewards
him with his hareskin coat for helping him to find the road to the
inn; it is by chance that Pugachev recognizes and saves his bene-
factor from inevitable execution or rescues Masha Mironova from

Shvabrin; it is by chance that Masha Mironova meets Catherine the Great in the garden without discovering her true identity and convinces the Empress of Grinev's innocence. Indeed, it has been often pointed out that *The Captain's Daughter* focuses on the role of the accidental in history. Abram Tertz, for example, maintains that in *The Captain's Daughter* "everything spins around chance, around a flimsy coat. [. . .] The whole trick is that Grinev's life and his bride are saved not by strength, courage, shrewdness or money, but by a flimsy hareskin coat" (Tertz, 361).[15] In his recent study, *An Obsession With History,* Wachtel maintains that the historical conception of *The Captain's Daughter* completely differs from that of the *History of Pugachev* precisely in that Pushkin's novel "plays up the role of accident and coincidence in history" (73). Indeed, the list of accidents or coincidences which seem to command the universe of *The Captain's Daughter* could be prolonged further. The accidental events may well play a crucial role in the private lives of the protagonists. Their impact on the historical events around them, however, is nil.

In this sense the plot-line of *The Captain's Daughter* displays close affinity with Pushkin's tale "The Snowstorm" (1830). "The Snowstorm" was written during approximately the same time Pushkin drafted his "Note on 'Count Nulin,' " his criticism of Polevoi's *History of Russian People,* an overt parody of modern historiography in his "History of the Village Goriukhino," and another crucial text that confronts the past, the poem "The Genealogy of My Hero" ("Rodoslovnaia moego geroia"). This tale clearly focuses on the thorny problem of chance and providence in human life. All the strange coincidences that have seemed to us so arbitrary and purely accidental in the process of reading—such as the groom being lost in the blizzard on the way to the church, the irrational decision of the unknown young officer to marry the unsuspecting bride in the darkness of the church, the death in the war of the lady's beloved, and finally, the accidental meeting of the young lady with her mysterious wedded husband whom she falls in love with—could be interpreted as the "instrument of Providence" (to use Pushkin's own definition of chance), if we consider the story's final outcome (Cf. Markovich, 73; Kibal'nik, 153). Likewise, in *The Captain's Daughter*, Grinev recognizes the power of Providence that leads him in his accidental adventures: "A strange thought crossed my mind: it seemed to me that Providence, which brought me to Pugachev for the second time, was offering me an opportunity (*sluchai*) to realize my intention" (VIII: I, 348). *Sluchai* here functions as an instrument of Providence. Suddenly, what has appeared to be chaotic acquires coherence. What has seemed to be a set of accidental events disagreeing with individual efforts, emerges ultimately as a working of Providence. "Strange coincidences do occur" Pushkin concludes in his "Note on 'Count Nulin'"—a thought that he seems to artistically embody both in "The Snowstorm" and in *The Captain's Daughter*.

The tale as well as the novel may well play out the role of accident in private life; nothing suggests, however, the central role of chance in *history* as it emerges in *The Captain's Daughter*. Pushkin clearly incorporates a more complex concept of chance into his novel.

The accident-prone plot structure seems to suggest certain assumptions about the central role of chance that governs the novel's philosophy of history. Yet Pushkin also appears to frustrate these assumptions within the same text. In the chapter entitled "Pugachevshchina," which deals with the social and political atmosphere of the time, Grinev suddenly changes his fact-oriented mode of narration and outlines historical circumstances that led to the Pugachev rebellion in terms of cause/effect development. Grinev's use of such words as "cause" and "consequence" betrays his analytical ambitions and his attempt at critical historical narrative: "In 1722 a revolt broke out in their [the Iaik Cossacks'] main town. The *cause* of it was in the strict measures taken by the Major General Traubenberg in order to bring their army to a proper obedience. The *consequences* were the barbarous murder of

Traubenberg, self-willed change in their governance, and finally the suppression of the revolt with grapeshot and cruel punishments [emphasis added]" (VIII: I, 313). In Grinev's account, the rebellion is interpreted as a logical consequence of specific historical circumstances that include the character of the "half savage nations" populating the Orenburg region, the government's negligence and its overtly criminal politics. An atmosphere was created that was ripe for social upheaval: "The authorities trusted too easily the feigned repentance of the sly rebels who secretly bore malice and waited for a convenient occasion [*sluchaia*] to renew their disturbances" (VIII: I, 313). *Sluchai* in this case is not an accident but an opportunity or occasion. The anticipated occasion has an element of unpredictability, but it is conditioned by the general course of events. In other words, in the public realm of the history of Pugachev's rebellion, chance functions as an accelerator and as a modifier of the otherwise almost inevitable events. That it happened to be Pugachev and not someone else who declared himself Peter III and initiated the rebellion may well be the working of chance; his temporary success, however, is far from being accidental. The siege and the quick fall of the Belogorsk fortress whose defense and defeat Grinev calls a "horrible farce" (*uzhasnaia komediia*) illustrate this point eloquently. As Grinev depicts it, there is nothing accidental in Pugachev's triumph: the fortress was ill equipped to retaliate, and the common folk supported Pugachev, meeting the Pretender "with bread and salt." The reader is fully prepared for the fortress's defeat as soon as Grinev provides his comical description of the fort on his arrival: "I was looking in all directions, anticipating to see fearsome bastions, towers, and a rampart; but I saw nothing except a small village surrounded by a wood-log fence. On one side of it there were three or four haystacks, half covered with snow; on the other side a sagging windmill with idly drooping *lubok*-like wings. 'So where is the fortress?' I inquired in amazement. — 'Why, here it is,' answered the driver, pointing at the village; and as he spoke, we had driven in" (VIII: I, 294).

The farcical prosiness of the garrison's unassuming life reminds one of the "genre scenes" Pushkin depicts in *Count Nulin*. The aged hostess of this God-forsaken fort appears dressed in a padded jacket with a scarf over her head and reprimands her subjects for what seems to be the most significant event of the day. According to the sergeant Cossack's report, everything has been peaceful "except that Corporal Prokhorov had a fight in the bathhouse with Ustin'ia Negulina over a tub of hot water" (VIII: I, 296). Grinev sadly observes the rural simplicity and martial unpretentiousness of the fort: "A dull steppe was spreading out before me. A few huts stood across the street; several hens were roaming about the street. An old woman who stood on her porch with a trough in her hands was calling the pigs who responded to her with a friendly grunt" (VIII: I, 296). In Grinev's fresh and unbiased description of the army's drilling, the military prowess of the garrison acquires the vividness of an animated cartoon: "While approaching the commandant's house, we saw on a small square some twenty elderly disabled veterans with long tresses and wearing triangular hats. They were lined up, standing at attention. The commandant, an energetic and tall old man in a nightcap and a cotton dressing gown, stood in front of them" (VIII: I, 297). Not only does Fort Belogorsk frustrate Grinev's expectations of the fortress, but it frustrates the reader's expectations set in the belligerent epigraph selected for this chapter by the fictitious editor of this "family chronicle":

> Мы в фортеции живем,
> Хлеб едим и воду пьем;
> А как лютые враги
> Придут к нам на пироги,
> Зададим гостям пирушку:
> Зарядим картечью пушку (VIII: I, 294).

> We live in the fortress,
> We eat bread and drink water;

But when ferocious enemies visit us for a treat
We will welcome them with a feast:
We will load the cannon with buck-shot.

The soldier's song, which sets the tone for the description of the fort, promises the army's readiness to attack the ferocious enemy and welcome it with buck-shot. The fortress's meager resources, however, reveal to the reader the tragicomic ineptness of the garrison to cope with any military action. During the assault on the fort by Pugachev, the garrison's cannon fired only twice; afterwards the intimidated soldiers retreated, throwing down their weapons. It is left to the reader to deduce the implications of this "old-fashioned" governance and draw broader conclusions about the preparedness of Russian provincial forts to defend themselves and to retaliate against the rebels.

The siege of Orenburg further confirms the non-accidental nature of Pugachev's triumphs. The comic description of the "war council" in Orenburg, which anticipates Tolstoy's celebrated farcical portrayals of the councils of war in *War and Peace*, exposes the city officials' complete incompetence in military affairs. No one among the members of the "council" except the general belongs to the military. Grinev's sensible opinion that "the Pretender had no means to stand up against proper arms" found support only in the general himself (VIII: I, 339). This opinion, the general maintained, "is based on all the rules of sensible tactics, which almost always prefer offensive actions to defensive ones" (VIII: I, 340). The general, however, turned out to be too weak to contradict his opponents and to take on full responsibility for the proper defense of the city. The reasonable strategy, therefore, the one based on experience and proper evaluation of the situation, is dismissed in favor of the ignorant majority of city officials. The outcome of this "memorable council" is predictable. Grinev explicitly blames the local officials for the city's overwhelming misery: "I will not describe the siege of Orenburg, which belongs to history rather than to family chronicle. I will only say briefly that due to the carelessness of the local authorities this siege was ruinous for the citizens, who endured famine and all kinds of other calamities" (VIII: I, 341). Significantly, when we turn from a "family chronicle" to "history," as Grinev advises the reader to do, we find that Pushkin's own explanation of the Orenburg tragedy in his *History of Pugachev* is almost identical to the account provided by Grinev: "In this city, there were up to three thousand troops and seventy cannons. With these resources one could and should have destroyed the rebels. Unfortunately, among the military commanders there was not a single one who knew his business. Frightened from the very beginning, they gave Pugachev time to reinforce himself and in doing so they deprived themselves of all means for offensive actions" (IX: I, 23). Once again, both in *History* and the novel, it is not chance, but the general sluggishness and corruption of the local authorities that play the crucial role in the outcome of the siege of Orenburg. In his explanations of the historical events, Grinev consistently shifts the emphasis from "strange coincidences" and chance, which may well play an important role in his own life, to general causes. "Such was the nature of our military operations! This was what the Orenburg officials called caution and prudence!" bitterly complains the narrator (VIII: I, 341). Pugachev's advantage during the siege of Orenburg is rooted, according to Grinev, in the relative well-being of his army, which is "well-fed, intoxicated and rides good horses," rather than in Pugachev's luck or his particular skills (VIII: I, 341). The city's emaciated cavalry and starving infantry, on the other hand, could hardly compete with the rebels.

Yet just as Pugachev's success could be explained rationally in terms of cause/effect relationships, so his impending doom seems inevitable to Grinev. Grinev has no doubts about the outcome of Pugachev's bold enterprise. As he listens to the sorrowful barge hauler's song—the one Pugachev favors most—he ponders with horror and compassion: "It is impossible to describe what impression this simple folk song about the gallows, sung by the people doomed to the gallows, had upon me" (VIII: I, 331). Moreover, Grinev honestly reveals his thoughts about the nature of Pugachev's endeavor to the rebel. "Whoever you may be, you are playing a dangerous game," he warns the impostor (VIII: I, 332). Indeed, Pugachev seems to realize that his hopes for success lie in his belief in good luck and his daring. On the one hand, he proudly declares that "so far fortune has favored my arms" (VIII: I, 352). On the other, he recognizes that the wheel of fortune might turn against him: "My path is a narrow one; I have little freedom. My fellows are getting too smart. They are thieves. I must keep my ears pricked; with the first failure [literally "bad luck," *neudacha*] they will trade my head for their own necks" (VIII: I, 352). Pugachev understands that "chance" or "luck" could aid him only to a certain extent and tells Grinev a Kalmyk tale about the raven and the eagle. The raven who eats carrion does not take any risks and lives three hundred years. The eagle, by contrast, prefers "to drink live blood if only once" rather than feed on carrion for centuries, and "then what will come will come" (VIII: I, 353). Thus the very nature of the eagle, who refuses to calculate but relies only on his luck, predetermines his shorter lot. Curiously, the Orenburg authorities, who like ravens refused to take any risks, ended up, in fact, eating carrion. The reports of the fugitives, as Pugachev's accomplices declare, indicate that "there is famine and death in Orenburg and that they are feeding on carrion" (VIII: I, 349). Pugachev clearly associates himself with the eagle; his reliance on chance is a covenant of both his success and his doom.

It is no coincidence that Pugachev, who seeks support in chance, good luck, and the notoriously untranslatable *avos'* ("perhaps," "may be," "hopefully"), refers twice to his historical predecessor, Grishka Otrep'ev. During his first interview with Grinev right after the taking of Fort Belogorsk, Pugachev is brooding over his historical model: "Is it not that the dare-devil has good luck? Did not Grishka Otrep'ev reign in olden times?" (VIII: I, 332) Later, during Pugachev's siege of Orenburg, Grinev and the Impostor meet again. Once again Pugachev evokes the example of Grishka Otrep'ev revealing his plans "to march on Moscow": "Who knows? Hopefully, I will succeed! After all Grishka Otrep'ev reigned for a while over Moscow, did he not?" (VIII: I, 353) Pugachev unequivocally points to the reliance on chance and luck as False Dmitri's main strategy and thus links himself with his historical and literary predecessor. Indeed, in Pushkin's *Boris Godunov,* Grigorii clearly anticipates Pugachev's attitude toward the accidental, and the Kalmyk tale about the raven and the eagle, which Pugachev narrates to Grinev, applies to the fate of Grigorii as well. Moreover, the tragic and horrifying fall of False Dmitri, which is merely foreshadowed in *Boris Godunov,* becomes a haunting and ominous reminder to Pugachev in *The Captain's Daughter.* "But do you know how he ended up?" Grinev warns the rebel, "He was thrown out of the window, slaughtered, burned; they loaded a cannon with his ashes and fired them off" (VIII: I, 353).

The relative success of both pretenders is far from being purely accidental, although both seem to rely merely on good luck. Pushkin's historical drama and his historical novel demonstrate that Otrep'ev's and Pugachev's temporary triumphs were rooted in specific historical circumstances that made the phenomenon of pretendership possible.[16] As Grinev's narrative reveals, Pugachev's personality plays only a limited role in the course of the rebellion, and the Pretender himself complains about a lack of freedom. Pugachev's exclusive authority is consistently questioned by his companions who, as Grinev notices, "showed no particular deference to their leader" and "freely disputed Pugachev" (VIII: I, 330). Similar to Grigorii Otrep'ev who understands that he is merely a "pretext for feud and warfare," Pugachev is conscious of his role as a plaything in the hands of the rebellious Cossacks. In this sense Grinev the historian, who is trying to find a rational explanation for the events and systematically employs the rhetorical tools of the explanatory historiography such as "on account of," "because of," "due to," "as a result," is not very much different from Pushkin the historian, the author of *The History of Pugachev*. Both narrators treat Pugachev as an instrument of historical process rather than a single accidental phenomenon; both attempt to identify specific historical patterns and consider the course of the rebellion against the historical background.

The paradoxes of chance in *The Captain's Daughter* lead to several seemingly contradictory conclusions: on the one hand, chance, or "strange coincidences," play an undeniable role in the personal lives of the novel's characters; moreover, these "strange coincidences" may point to the existence of some providential plan behind them. On the other hand, in the realm of history, chance plays only a limited role as the modifier of the otherwise law-governed events. As in *Boris Godunov*, Pushkin focuses in *The Captain's Daughter* not so much on the power and arbitrariness of accidental events, but on chance as part of historical necessity within a specific historical situation. *History*, however, as opposed to the *story* of private life, does not have the finalizability of personal life. If the knowledge of the final outcome of Grinev's and Masha Mironova's adventures may allow us to draw certain conclusions about the providential nature of chance in their lives, it can never be true in the case of history. Since history always remains fragmented and open, there are no historical "outcomes" that would permit the historian to approach history providentially. Characteristically, in his Preface to *The History of Pugachev*, Pushkin refers to his *History* as a "fragment" (*otryvok*) or a "page of history" (*istoricheskaia stranitsa*) to be "corrected and supplemented" by future historians (IX: I, 1). Pushkin's careful differentiation of the role of chance, necessity, and the concept of Providence in a *story* and a *history* explains an apparent contradiction in his thought: his criticism of the "providential" school of historiography, on the one hand, and his personal belief in Providence, on the other.

Indeed, Pushkin seems to both assert and parody providentiality. For Pushkin, certain laws or even divine Providence might exist, but it cannot be fully explained and is, therefore, irrelevant to a historian. On the personal level, as the vast biographical material and providential themes in Pushkin's fiction suggest, Pushkin may well have believed in Providence. It is widely known that Pushkin was superstitious and trusted fortune telling.[17] Reliance on divine Providence and the power of the accidental is one of the dominant themes of his oeuvre (Cf. Lotman 1992, 405–12; Tertz, 355–65; Kibal'nik 1993, 120–65). Yet he emphatically objected to providential schemes in historiography. One could never account for *all* factors in the historical process. Historical process, according to Pushkin, is not a necessity; neither is it a sum of accidental events. History is probability continuously modified by chance, whether it is a "tool of Providence" or a blind accidental force.

Significantly, Pushkin never attempts to write universal histories, but chooses smaller topics and concentrates only on some periods of Russian history, such as the Time of Troubles, Peter the Great's epoch, or Pugachev's rebellion. He realizes that not only could one not predict future events, but one could not even fully explain the past.

part II History and Narrative

t h r e e   The Historian as Contextualist:
Pushkin's Polemic with Radishchev

Fact, Meaning, Context

In his attempt to apply different criteria to analysis of Russian historical reality and to stress that "Russia never had anything in common with the rest of Europe," as expressed in his essay on Polevoi (discussed in chapter 2), Pushkin developed a mode of argument that could be conveniently called "contextualist," to borrow Hayden White's terminology for the possible paradigms of historical explanation.[1]

Contextualism asserts, according to White, the idea that "events can be explained by being set within the 'context' of their occurrence. Why they occurred as they did is to be explained by the revelation of the specific relationships they bore to other events occurring in their circumambient historical space" (17–18). It is this mode of argument, I maintain, that Pushkin most often embraces in his critical and historical writings. Pushkin blames Polevoi precisely for his inability to consider different contexts and for his blind application of the French historians' "formulas" to Russian history. All events, according to Pushkin, have to be discussed in their own context, and the choice of a proper perspective from which given facts are analyzed determines the ultimate outcome of historical inquiry. The contextualist form of arguments undoubtedly reflects Pushkin's philosophical perspectivism, a mental disposition that characterizes his thought and work in general.

Although it remained unfinished, Pushkin's *Journey from Moscow to Petersburg* (*Puteshestvie iz Moskvy v Peterburg*) is a highly original and sophisticated polemic to Radishchev's *Journey from Petersburg to Moscow* (*Puteshestvie iz Peterburga v Moskvu*). It is one of Pushkin's metahistorical works addressing the problem of historical and critical method and of the choice of perspective from which a given historical event must be viewed.[2] Pushkin rereads and rewrites Radishchev's *Journey* from the end to the beginning and discloses his own plan from the start: "In Chernaia Griaz' while they were changing horses I started reading the book at the last chapter and in this way made Radishchev travel with me from Moscow to Petersburg" (XI, 245). Pushkin's *Journey* is not so much a story of traveling from one destination to another, but an account of the narrator's traveling through Radishchev's book. Though dealing with the same facts and events, the traveler's rereading of Radishchev leads to very different conclusions. By setting all evidence and all events described by Radishchev in a different perspective, considering them in different contexts, Pushkin demonstrates how the same facts may be used to compose a different meaning, depending on the intention of the observer.

Traditionally interpreted either as Pushkin's declaration of alliance with the government (Annenskii) — by those who fully identified the narrator with Pushkin himself — or as a work written in Aesopian language and representing a hidden defense of Radishchev (Eremin), *A Journey from Moscow to Petersburg* has been largely considered to be a non-fictional work. As Makogonenko correctly points out, however, the narrator of *A Journey* is fictitious and should not be identified with Pushkin.[3] Indeed, one should not take the pronouncements of Pushkin's narrator at face value. Moreover, the narrator's polemic with Radishchev is preceded by a brief introduction, which further points to the fictional nature of Pushkin's narrative.

Pushkin in this work neither supports the regime nor denounces it; neither does he defend Radishchev nor condemn him. Rather he purposefully chooses a fictitious narrator in order to avoid accusations of loyalty to the government and preserve the illusion of objectivity and impartiality. One should not forget that Pushkin strove to differentiate between personal historical sympathies and moral approval and an analytical, disinterested historical judgment. Such is his portrayal of Pugachev—enticing as an individual, and dangerous and vicious as a historical personage. It is no coincidence that very often in his oeuvre Pushkin employs locutions and phrases indicating that he speaks as an impartial observer, while reserving for himself his personal sympathies: "Quoique personnellement attaché de coeur à l'Empereur, je suis loin d'admirer tout ce que je vois autour de moi" (letter to Chaadaev quoted above). Pushkin repeatedly dissociates the facts as he sees them from what he would like them to be (cf. his "I reluctantly agree" from A Journey from Moscow to Petersburg). Significantly, in his article on Radishchev (1836), Pushkin chooses an epigraph from Karamzin: "Il ne faut pas qu'un honnête homme mérite d'être pendu." These words express the same tension between personal and legal judgments: though subjectively honest, a person might violate certain laws and deserve punishment. Likewise, in A Journey Pushkin clearly wants to reserve his authorial and personal sympathy for Radishchev, while at the same time demonstrating that Radishchev's historical vision is blurred. Pushkin did not share Radishchev's views but did admire him as a human being: "We cannot help but acknowledge him as a felon [prestupnik] with extraordinary spirit; a political fanatic, mistaken, of course, but acting with amazing self-sacrifice and with a kind of chivalrous conscientiousness" (XII, 32–3).

The narrator's intention in A Journey from Moscow to Petersburg is not to refute Radishchev, as some have maintained, or to expose him as a "slanderer of Russia," but to correct his perspective. In other words, like an optician, Pushkin's traveler tries to correct the astigmatism of Radishchev's historical vision. At the same time, Pushkin the author engages in not so much an ideological argument but in an experiment that focuses on different facets of the same historical episode. In most cases, Pushkin does not outrightly deny the facts presented by Radishchev but reemplots them and makes his narrator consider them from a different angle. Pushkin's Journey emerges as a metapoetical work in which the author experiments with consciously constructing a different narrative around the same set of events. And, of course, Pushkin is aware that both narratives—Radishchev's and his own—are fictionalized and subjective.

Pushkin precedes the narrator's backward traveling from Moscow to Petersburg and his rereading of Radishchev's book with a short exposition. His narrator engages in a discussion of the quality of Russian roads. This seemingly apolitical argument turns out to be the pretext for commenting on the nature of Russian government and history. As everything in Russia, the quality of the roads depends on the good will of the governors and those in power. As a result of this dependence on central power, the condition of Russian roads is very often less than satisfactory and worse than it could have been if the roads were left in their natural state. An unconcealed irony of the narrator makes this point clear: "In general the roads in Russia (due to its space) are good and could be even better, if only governors took less care of them" (XI, 243). In fact, if the construction of the roads were decided in accordance with common sense—that is, by the practical sense of the people— and not by the whim of a governor, Russian travelers could have avoided the inconvenience of riding through arable land and fields instead of the highways. The narrator cannot hide his vexation: "Take, for example, any peasant you encounter, who is at least a bit clever, and make him construct a new road: it is likely that he will start with digging two parallel ditches for a rain water drain" (XI, 243). But such enlightened decisions are not easily taken in Russia. For nothing guarantees that the governor would be at least as smart as a "clever peasant." And indeed, the narrator recalls a "wise governor" who "made up parapets instead of ditches, so that the roads turned into containers for mud. [. . .] There are enough such governors in Russia" (XI, 244).

In light of this argument exposing the arbitrariness of the Russian system of government, the next paragraph, which could be interpreted as a praise to the Emperor Alexander and to Russian autocracy in general, acquires a very different meaning: "The construction of the superb Moscow highway is begun under the orders of the emperor Alexander; stage-coaches are introduced by a society of private people. This is how things should be in all respects: the government opens the road, private people find the most convenient means to use it" (XI, 244). Russian travelers may enjoy the "superb Moscow highway" created by the fortunate decision of the tsar. Ideally, this is how the system of autocracy should work in all respects (*Tak dolzhno byt' i vo vsiom*), but unfortunately, reality does not always conform to what "should be" — the examples of bad governors are too telltale to allow the reader to interpret these words as support of the autocratic regime. Pushkin, then, merely states the fact and defines the nature of the Russian system of government as being always ahead of the people in terms of its willingness to implement reforms (XI, 244). As noted earlier, Pushkin expresses the same idea in his 1836 letter to Chaadaev (XVI, 261).

Pushkin must speak about the nature of the Russian political system in order to put the events of Russian history and problems of Russian life in a proper perspective. For the rest of his *Journey* is, in fact, an attempt to interpret Russian history on the basis of the following premise: Russia is characterized by a strong autocratic power and a weak people lacking initiative (cf. in *A Journey to Arzrum* (*Puteshestvie v Arzrum*): "We are lazy and uninquisitive"). His polemic with Radishchev is founded on the principles of relativity and contextualism. In his early poem "An Epistle to the Censor" ("Poslanie tsenzoru," 1822), Pushkin formulated this idea in his typical ironic style:

Не бойся: не хочу, прельщенный мыслью ложной,
Цензуру поносить хулой неосторожной;
Что нужно Лондону, то рано для Москвы (II: I, 267).

Don't be afraid: I do not wish, seduced by a false
    thought,

To vilify censorship with an unwary slur;
What London needs is too early for Moscow.

Pushkin's bitter irony seems to qualify Karamzin's claim that "whatever is good for people, cannot be bad for Russians; whatever Englishmen or Germans have invented for the public well-being and the benefit of humankind, that is *mine*, for *I* am a human being!" (Karamzin 1987, 254).

In *A Journey from Moscow to Petersburg* Pushkin stresses the importance of the context and the point of view from the out-set: "In prison or on a journey any book is like a gift from God; and even one which you could not bring yourself to open on re-turning from the English club or when preparing for a ball will seem to you as entertaining as an Arabian tale, if it falls into your hands in prison or in an express coach" (XI, 244). Pushkin jux-taposes the prison (*tiur'ma, kazemat*) and traveling (*puteshestvie, dilizhans*) to the "English club" or a "ball." Indeed, the perspec-tive of the prison is very important for the understanding of both Radishchev's book and Pushkin's answer to Radishchev. For ac-cording to Pushkin, Radishchev unduly forgot that he was not in the "English club" but in Russia with its severe laws that had not changed since Peter the Great: "If we mentally transport ourselves to 1791, if we imagine the political circumstances of that time, [. . .] then Radishchev's felony will seem to us the act of a mad-man" (XII, 32). The mention of prison is, of course, even more ironic, as the reader is expected to know that Radishchev was sent to Siberia for writing his book, that is, for neglecting to apply a prison perspective to prison reality. Pushkin attempts to restore a more appropriate and realistic perspective. This is precisely why elsewhere Pushkin calls Radishchev's ideas "bitter half-truths" (*gor'kie poluistiny*) (XI, 245). By stating incomplete truths or half-knowledge, Pushkin implies that Radishchev is not completely wrong, but that he considers the facts from the wrong angle and takes them out of context. Reestablishing the context is, indeed, the essence of his "defense" of Russia against Radishchev's harsh criticism. Pushkin never tried to prove that Russian reality was perfect; he saw its flaws. (Cf., for example his letter to Chaadaev or his letter to Viazemsky of 27 May 1826: "To be sure, I despise my fatherland from head to toe—but I am vexed when a foreigner shares with me this sentiment" (XIII, 280). His goal was merely to contextualize a concrete historical situation and thus demonstrate its historical cogency. The narrator continues: "One's notion of boredom is very relative. A boring book can be a very good one" (XI, 244). Thus, the same phenomena might play a different role and have different meaning in different situations; one cannot dismiss them simply as wrong or bad. Without directly identifying Russia with "prison" and the West with the "English club," one might say that Pushkin sets forth an important opposition, which, being located in the beginning of the narrative, might be interpreted as a "thematic clue" of a sort for the entire work. And indeed, comparisons with, and allusions to, England or France are scattered throughout Pushkin's narrative: "*Patronage* is still customary in the English literary scene" (XI, 254); "However, there are some improvements, [. . .]; in general, there is more cleanliness and convenience, what the English call *comfort*" (XI, 256).

The traveler applies the contextualist method from the start. In his polemic over Lomonosov, Pushkin's narrator "redistributes" the facts: he stresses some and undermines others. Radishchev reproaches Lomonosov for flattering those in power. To these accusations the narrator objects that one has to know the historical context of the period: "Now all that has fallen out of custom. The problem is that at that time [Lomonosov's] the distance separating one class from another still existed. Lomonosov, who was born into a lower class, had no intention to elevate himself through impertinence and familiarity with people belonging to an upper class (although he might be their equal in rank)" (XI, 254). Pushkin's narrator insists that one must not apply modern criteria to a past situation, and one should understand the role of classes and institutions. Different periods and cultures exist independently from each other. One cannot understand the other culture and draw appropriate conclusions about the past by merely projecting one's knowledge of the present, without engaging in careful research. In his defense of Lomonosov, Pushkin's narrator demonstrates that, in fact, Lomonosov was courageous enough to defend his own dignity, but that Lomonosov's notion of dignity was obviously different from that of Radishchev. One has only to look for different facts in order to draw this conclusion and to examine the historical situation under which Lomonosov lived. Pushkin's narrator maintains, for example, that Russian writers have no need to search for patronage from those in power; this does not mean, however, that they are more noble than those who looked for financial support under different circumstances: "Our writers cannot seek favors and patronage from men whom they consider as their equals, or to present their writings to a lord or a rich man in the hope of receiving from him 500 rubles or a ring decorated with precious stones. What follows from this? Does this mean that our present-day writers think and feel in a more noble way than did Lomonosov or Kostrov? I must confess, I have my doubts" (XI, 255). In other words, what Pushkin's narrator is saying is that a fact in itself does not have any specific meaning, but takes on some significance only in the context. Facts are subject to the same laws that govern language—only general context can define their meaning. Thus, the narrator concludes: "Be that as it may, I repeat, the outward forms mean nothing; Lomonosov and Krabb deserve respect of all honest people in spite of their humble dedications, and Messrs. NN are nevertheless despicable, in spite of the fact that they preach independence in their books" (XI, 255).

Indeed, the contextualist mode of argument prevails in the narrator's criticism of Radishchev. Speaking about the plight of Russian peasants, he insists on the necessity of a *comparative* analysis: "Fonvizin, who had traveled in France approximately fifteen years before that, says that in all honesty, the lot of the Russian peasant is happier than that of the French tiller of the soil. I believe him.

Let us recall the description of La Bruyère" (XI, 257). Pushkin then provides La Bruyère's gloomy description of French peasantry in a footnote:

> L'on voit certains animaux farouches, des mâles et des femelles, répandus par la campagne, noirs, livides et tout brûlés du soleil, attachés à la terre qu'ils fouillent et qu'ils remuent avec une opiniâtreté invincible; ils ont comme une voix articulée, et quand ils se lèvent sur leurs pieds, ils montrent une face humaine, et en effet ils sont des hommes. Ils se retirent la nuit dans des tannières où ils vivent de pain noir, d'eau et de racines; ils épargnent aux autres hommes la peine de semer, de labourer et de recueillir pour vivre, et méritent ainsi de ne pas manquer de ce pain qu'ils ont semé.
>
> (One sees certain wild animals, male and female, scattered throughout the countryside, black, livid, and completely burned by the sun, attached to the land which they till and plow with invincible stubbornness; their voice seems to be articulate, and when they raise themselves to their feet, they show a human face, and they are in fact human. They retire at night into the dens where they live off black bread, water, and roots; they spare other men the trouble of sowing, laboring, and gathering to survive, and thus deserve to not lack for the bread they have sown. XI, 257).

La Bruyère wrote his "Les caractères ou les moeurs de ce siècle" in 1688, which is a hundred years before Radishchev wrote his *Journey*. Pushkin's narrator, however, justifies this citation by saying that the condition of French peasants has not improved since then and that this is a valuable source of historical information, because all these facts are stated in a matter-of-fact manner, without specific aim to denounce the sad reality. In this way the narrator demonstrates his critical approach in his work with sources, considering their reliability not only in terms of voluntary distortion or accurate presentation of the data but also in terms of underlying implications rooted in the author's specific goal and ideology. This is how he evaluates the testimony of another witness of the severe plight of the French peasant: "Mme de Sevigné's words are even more convincing, for she speaks without indignation and bitterness, but simply narrates what she sees and to which she is accustomed. The lot of the French peasant did not improve during the reign of Louis XV and his successor . . ." (XI, 257).

To push his point further, the traveler indulges in a long and eloquent digression about the terrible plight of English workers and contrasts it with the relative ease of the Russian people's plight. He switches the perspective here from an analysis of Russian historical reality to a comparison of the plight of Russian and other nations' peasants, and in doing so he acknowledges some of the more positive aspects of the Russian social system. He concludes: "In Russia, there is not a man who does not have a dwelling of *his own*. A poor man leaves *his own* hut when he goes wandering around the world. In other countries the situation is different. Everywhere in Europe to own a cow is a sign of luxury; in Russia not to own a cow is a sign of terrible poverty. [. . .] The lot of the peasant improves daily to the extent that enlightenment spreads . . ." (XI, 258). This argument is interesting not so much in what Pushkin or his narrator says about the plight of the Russian peasant, but in the narrator's method of constructing the argument. He insists on the relative perspective that allows him to outbalance and contrast one set of historical evidence with another. Such a contextualist approach implicitly alerts the reader to the conclusion that, however terrible a reality might seem to us, it still might have been good enough or necessary for its own time and place. Furthermore, if this reality appears to be relatively good, then there is no need for drastic changes. And, indeed, this contextualizing leads Pushkin's traveler directly to a recognition of the natural order of things accelerated only by educational progress and moral improvement: "Of course, great changes must still come; but one should not rush the time, which is active enough on its own. The best and most durable changes are those which occur as a result of the improvement of morals alone, without forced political upheavals, so terrible for humanity . . ." (XI, 258). "One should not rush the time" — this is one of the most important of Pushkin's concepts, expressed throughout his oeuvre. (Cf., for example, *The Captain's Daughter*).

Narrative Strategies and Political Implications
In addition to the contextualist mode of argument the traveler employs several other devices in order to undermine his opponent: he discloses the inner contradictions and incongruities of Radishchev's presentation of material or simply shifts the emphasis. In the chapter "The Russian Hut" ("Russkaia izba") the traveler writes: "Clearly, Radishchev sketched a caricature; but he mentions a bathhouse and kvass as necessities of Russian everyday life. That is already a sign of well-being. Of note is also that Radishchev, having made his hostess complain about hunger and the bad harvest, completes his picture of want and poverty with this detail: *and she began to put the loaves of bread into the oven*" (XI, 256–57). Again, what is interesting in this polemic is not the argument itself and whether the traveler or Radishchev is right about the level of poverty of the peasants, but the *method* of the polemic. The narrator does not deny the facts presented by Radishchev; he deconstructs them, reveals their internal contradictions and, therefore, suggests the possibility of a different reading. If Radishchev in his description of the peasant hut stresses "hunger," Pushkin's traveler stresses "loaves of bread."

Even when Pushkin's traveler has nothing to object to and no justification to counterpose, he still evades a full solidarity with Radishchev by changing the accents. It is so, of course, in the case of slavery, when the traveler feels that he is close to Radishchev in his ideological or political views. His response to

Radishchev's indignant condemnation of serfdom, however, is extremely laconic. By minimizing the discussion of slavery, Pushkin again wants to put emphasis elsewhere. In the chapter entitled "Mednoe (Slavery)" ("Mednoe [Rabstvo]") he quotes Radishchev and follows his narrative with only a few lines of his own: "A picture follows that is terrible because it is probable. I am not going to lose myself, following Radishchev, in his pompous but sincere dreams . . . which I share against my will this time . . ." (XI, 263). Indeed, the only thing that the narrator can suggest as a counterargument to Radishchev's bitter truth is: "I am not going to lose myself" (*ne stanu teriat'sia*), that is, silence and evasion. A psychological cause of this evasion is clear: to indulge in and to share Radishchev's *mechtaniia* is to accept their political implication — the need for a radical change. The concept of radical change, however, fully contradicts the narrator's belief in slow and moderate reforms encouraged by the politics of enlightenment.

The position of the narrator, therefore, is that of a conservative intellectual who, while being horrified by the idea of violent revolutionary changes, realizes, nevertheless, that it is precisely inactivity in the present that could provoke the outburst of violence. Thus, he encourages efforts directed toward the gradual improvement in the present. In the last chapter, "Sluices," dedicated to landowners' abuses and serfdom, the narrator indirectly leads the reader to this conclusion. The traveler does not seem to contradict Radishchev's portrayal of discrimination against the peasants by an evil landowner and quotes a long passage from Radishchev's book. The fate of the evil landowner in Radishchev's *Journey* has a "happy" ending: he keeps tyrannizing his victims, increases his wealth and "is well known as a famous landowner." The traveler does not directly comment on Radishchev's description, and instead mentions that he knows a very similar case of abuse. In this story the landlord is a tyrant, as he is in Radishchev's book: "in a word, Radishchev's essay seems to draw the picture of my landowner's household." The ending of the traveler's story, however, is quite different: "What would you think? The tyrant had some philanthropic goals. After making his peasants used to want, patience, and labor, he was planning to enrich them gradually, to return their property, to grant them rights! Fate did not allow him to realize his predestination. He was killed by his peasants during a fire" (XI, 267). The prophecy is ominous. For, indeed, this is what happened to Russia's liberal and philanthropical "landowner"-class, which postponed reforms until it was too late. Pushkin's narrator does not explicitly comment on this story, but the moral is obvious to the reader: one should not imagine improvement in the remote future, but act in the present, before a violent revolution takes place. Radishchev's depiction of the triumph of the evil landowner is an invitation to immediate revolt. Pushkin's portrayal of the tragic fate of "the philanthropist" calls for immediate reforms that could prevent this tragedy.

Pushkin's narrator uses a similar technique in his reinterpretation of conscription (*rekrutstvo*). His polemic is based not so much on an open ideological argument, but on a different narrative strategy. In Radishchev's chapter on the subject, the narrative is constructed as a sentimental fiction that emphasizes social injustice and appeals to the reader's emotions. For Radishchev *rekrutstvo* is cause for weeping. Direct speech of the different characters involved in the situation dominates here, so that the whole scene consists mainly of their voices, whereas the narrator appears only as a terrified spectator of this social injustice. The effect is Radishchev's obvious dramatization of the story.

As a fact of social injustice calling for pity and indignation, *rekrutstvo* cannot be disputed by Pushkin's narrator, and therefore he does not argue with Radishchev on these grounds, forced to admit his moral truth: "Our conscription is hard; there is no need to be hypocritical about it. Suffice it to recall the laws against the peasants disabling themselves in order to avoid the soldierhood" (XI, 260). Pushkin, however, then shifts his argument to the sphere of the philosophy of history and economics and reemplots the subject of *rekrutstvo* in a different way. His narrative is constructed as a philosophical essay appealing to the reader's reason. Pushkin's narrator writes about conscription as an institution necessary to the sociopolitical scene of the time and places it in historical and philosophical perspective. Again, he employs the same tool of contextualism and compares Russian *rekrutstvo* to existing systems of conscription in Europe, stressing that it is an unavoidable institution, one which is organized differently in various countries but which is painful for people everywhere: "The way of recruitment is different everywhere and everywhere it involves great inconveniences. Every year the English *conscription* [Pushkin uses here the old English word *press*] is subject to bitter attacks from the opposition, yet it still exists in full measure. The Prussian *Landwehr*, a powerful system, skillfully adjusted to the state, though not justified yet by experience, already provokes complaints among the patient Prussians. The Napoleonic conscription was accompanied by the loud sobs and curses of all France" (XI, 260).

The narrator appeals to a *raison d'Etat:* "But can the state dispense with a permanent army? Half-measures will not lead to anything good" (XI, 260). He substitutes for Radishchev's discourse of human emotion his discourse of political economy and tries to find rational arguments to justify the system. From an individual concrete situation Pushkin shifts the narrative to a much more abstract level of discourse about institutions. Rather than speaking about concrete individual fates, the narrator appeals to the "general" and "natural" order. Significantly, the traveler's voice dominates; unlike Radishchev, he gives no voice to concrete individuals and avoids any direct speech. The first sentence contains at the outset the thesis: conscription is a universal but necessary evil. To emphasize the universal character of the institution of conscription he uses the word *vezde* several times in a short passage. Even such human emotions as mercy and compassion are subordinated here to *raison d'Etat* and pragmatic causes; to express these ideas the narrator uses impersonal constructions: "It is foolish to sacrifice a useful peasant, a hard working and good father of the family, but to spare a thief and an impoverished drunkard — merely out of respect for a certain rule that we offhandedly adopted" (XI, 261). What is disturbing here is that human beings are defined in terms of "useful" or "not useful," and the law established on the basis of first service (*ochered'*) is dismissed as a "certain rule" (*kakoe-to pravilo*) introduced by "certain philanthropic landowners." If the implication of Radishchev's dramatic and sentimental description is an appeal for radical social changes in order to improve the fate of individuals, the message of the traveler's essay is a philosophical acceptance of the status quo founded on the interest of the state and necessity: "Among the people's services, conscription is the most necessary and the most burdensome duty"; "But can the state dispense with a permanent army?" (XI, 260). The intellectualization of this otherwise political issue necessitates the impersonal mode of narration based on such rhetorical formulations as "there is no need to"; "it is enough to"; "it is better to"; "it is foolish to" (*litsemerit' nechego, dovol'no upomianut' o, luchshe upotrebit' sii prava, bezrassudno zhertvovat'*), etc. Pushkin's use of a different mode of emplotment leads the text to different ideological implications and different concepts of the same phenomenon.

Representation and Responsibility

That Pushkin through his narrator is consciously manipulating the facts, playing with different meanings and different discourses, becomes clear when in the chapter "On the Censorship" (O tsenzure) we read about the role of the written word as such. Pushkin emphasizes the idea, which has been articulated in Western thought as early as Plato, that writers create different discourses by which they manipulate society: "It is clear that the most powerful, the most dangerous aristocracy is that of men who for whole generations, whole centuries, impose their way of thinking, their passions, their prejudices on others. What significance has the aristocracy of birth and wealth in comparison with the aristocracy

of talented writers?" (XI, 264) Pushkin's narrator seems to realize fully that there is no adequate reflection of reality, but only a
"way of thinking." "One's passions, one's prejudices" are always
involved. The author's perspective ultimately defines his representation of historical data. In his argument with Radishchev, Pushkin's narrator tries to show that Radishchev's representation of
events works to promote his program of radical social transformation. Hence his appeal for human emotions. Likewise, Pushkin's
narrator advocates a different representation of reality on the basis
of the same facts in the interest of his own ideology—that of an
aristocrat believing in progressive changes. Pushkin demonstrates
that the traveler's perspective is just as subjective as is that of
Radishchev. And this is why Pushkin needs a fictitious narrator.

But if both perspectives are relative, and if every written word
and literature in general are necessarily ideological, what could be
our reasons for preferring one point of view? Pushkin does not
answer this question directly, but his narrator suggests a classical
formulation as a possible answer: "An idea! What a powerful word!
What else constitutes man's greatness, if not ideas? Let thought be
as free as man should be: *within the limits of law, in full observance
of conditions laid down by society*" (XI, 264). It is "law" and "convention" that should limit the infinite multiplicity of voices, the
unlimited pluralism and relativism.[4] Infinite multivoicedness for
Pushkin's narrator is anarchy. If the knowledge of absolute truth
(even if it exists) is inaccessible to human beings, this truth becomes ultimately a question of faith. But faith is in the domain of
religion. In secular terms the freedom of perspectives is limited by
convention. Certain perspectives, according to the traveler, are not
wrong in themselves, but irresponsible: "But a thought becomes
a citizen, is already responsible for itself, as soon as it has been
born and expressed" (XI, 264). It is no accident that Pushkin uses
here the locution *otvetstvuet za sebia*. Even though all truths are
ideological, not everything is permissible. Ultimately, the choice
of perspective or of point of view should be governed by a moral

law and a sense of propriety.[5] In his drafts Pushkin expresses this idea rather explicitly. Defending the institution of censorship, he writes: "Setting myself to the examination of this article, I consider it my duty to point out that I am convinced of the necessity of censorship in a morally educated and Christian society, whatever laws or form of government it might be subjected to" (XI, 235). In their decisions the censors should be directed by "common sense and the *sense of propriety*" (*zdravyi um i chuvstvo prilichiia*) (XI, 238). Or, in other words, Pushkin's narrator advocates the idea of a "censor-gentleman" or a "editor-gentleman" (to borrow William Todd's terminology).[6]

It would be difficult to comprehend Pushkin's "defense" of censorship in the context of his own painful experience with censors, without considering the close relationship between his notion of censorship and his own aristocratic values of "convention" and "propriety." And indeed, the chapter "On the Censorship" is followed by the one entitled "Etiquette." Advocating the principle of etiquette and hierarchy the traveler writes: "To assume humiliation in the rituals established by etiquette is simply foolishness. The English lord, while introducing himself to his king, kneels and kisses his hand. That does not prevent him from being in the opposition, if he wishes. We daily sign our letters as "your obedient servants," yet no one, it seems, has concluded that we are asking to be promoted to valets" (XI, 265). Etiquette implies a certain set of rules that stress the conventional, non-literal meaning of acts and words. In other words, etiquette conveys the idea that there is no direct connection between a signifier and a referent and, therefore, etiquette not only limits one's freedom but protects it against any totalitarian claim on one and only one literal meaning. Significantly, the narrator points out that the tsars as well as other autocrats experience no need of etiquette: "Of course, sovereigns do not need rituals, which are often tiresome for them" (XI, 265). In this context etiquette becomes something that protects the interests of aristocracy; convention becomes a guarantee of the aristocrats' freedom from the autocrat's "adamic" dictatorship. This is why for the aristocrats, so the narrator's argument goes, etiquette is indispensable: "But etiquette is the law as well; and it is indispensable at court, for everyone who has the honor to come close to the royal family must know his duty and the limits of his service. Whenever there is no etiquette, the courtiers are in constant fear of doing something indecent" (XI, 265). For human behavior, etiquette is as needed as grammar is for language. Without etiquette or grammar there would be a complete arbitrariness of meanings. While emphasizing a free play of meanings, etiquette encourages a conventional meaning that protects against ideological tyranny. Both *etiket* and *tsenzura*, therefore, affirm the idea of freedom within limits (*v predelakh zakona*). Aristocratic society that is used to conventions is a class that may easily understand the complex relationship between freedom and law. And indeed, it is an aristocratic notion of freedom that Pushkin's traveler puts forth. To a multitude of meanings and perspectives, he opposes the notion of taste and etiquette that should control complete arbitrariness of expression.

Radishchev, according to Pushkin's traveler, violates etiquette and is wrong not so much in essence, but in form. This is why the narrator who insists on an aristocratic "polite perspective" accuses him primarily of violating the law of common sense and propriety. Thus, in his criticism of Radishchev he employs such expressions as *derzost'* that belong to the code of etiquette, rather than criticizing Radishchev for some cognitive problems. Radishchev, according to the narrator, "handled Lomonosov's fame with much more circumspection than he treated the sovereign power, which he attacked with such insane audacity" (XI, 248). Radishchev's fault is not in *what* he is saying, but in the perspective he applies to what he is saying.

Thus, to elaborate Siegfried Kracauer's comparison of photography with history, one could say that a good historian differs from a bad historian as a good photographer from a bad one—not in his

or her selection of a subject and not even in the technical instruments he uses (camera, film, etc.), but in the choice of perspective
that allows him or her to avoid major distortion of reality. To be
sure, certain distortions are unavoidable; some of them are inten-
tional, but others are caused by unskilled and negligent shooting.
A proper representation of reality both in photography and historiography should be based on a sense of balance between the parts
and the whole and include some general background or *context* for
the sake of objectivity. Only etiquette or "polite perspective" based
on convention can allow, according to Pushkin, freedom within
limits, or within law. If this convention is denied, then everyone is
free to interpret any word in his or her own way, which leads to an
arbitrary distortion of reality.

Utilizing Hayden White's paradigms of the forms of historical
explanation, one could say that Radishchev in his method assumes
a Mechanistic mode that "turns upon the search for the causal laws
that determine the outcomes of processes discovered in the historical field" and emplots his narrative in the form of tragedy or
drama (White, 17). While analyzing the plight of Russian peasants
and their slavery Radishchev generalizes about the classes: "And
all those who could support freedom, all those owners of large estates, one should expect freedom not from their advice, but from
the very burden of slavery" (1952, 164). The implication of such
a view of history is a call for radical changes. Significantly, when
Catherine the Great was reading Radishchev's book she under-
lined this passage, adding the following comment: "that is, he
counts on a peasant revolt" (Cit. in Makogonenko, 1982, 266).
Pushkin's narrator, on the other hand, constructs his arguments
as a Contextualist. The Contextualist is interested not in the universal laws of cause and effect postulated by the Mechanist, but in
the revelation of the " 'trends' or general physiognomies of periods and epochs" which are "constructed as actual relationships
that are presumed to have existed at specific times and places,

the first, final, and material causes of which can never be known"
(White, 18). The implication of a contextualist mode of argument
is a desire to improve the situation within an existing structure.
Thus, the main disagreement between Radishchev and Pushkin's
traveler is that Radishchev is a revolutionary calling for drastic
changes, while the traveler is an evolutionary, calling for gradual
reforms and improvements. Pushkin inadvertently demonstrates,
however, that his traveler's perspective is just as subjective as is
that of Radishchev.

A Journey from Moscow to Petersburg is a curious example of
rewriting and rethinking history and of Pushkin's critical and historical method. This work demonstrates how two writers may come
to alternative interpretations of the same set of historical events,
depending on a chosen perspective. The ultimate significance of
Pushkin's *Journey* as a work of art, therefore, is not in what Pushkin's narrator says, but in how he differs from Radishchev's narrator. The reader is constantly reminded of the tension and interplay
between the two texts; he is forced to compare, to consider one
narrative against the other and to follow the constantly switching
perspectives. The meaning of *A Journey from Moscow to Petersburg* emerges as a difference between the two texts. What Pushkin
seems to suggest is that a fact in itself does not have any specific meaning, but takes on some significance only in the context.
And as Pushkin's text itself, this process of contextualizing has no
ending.

four   History in the Service and Disservice of Life: "The Hero"

I am certain of nothing but the holiness of the heart's
affections and the truth of imagination—what the
imagination seizes as beauty must be truth—whether
it existed before or not.
—John Keats

History is not an objective empirical datum; it is a
myth. Myth is no fiction, but a reality; it is, however,
one of a different order from that of the so-called
objective empirical fact.
—Nikolai Berdiaev

As brief as it may be, Pushkin's lyric poem "The Hero"
("Geroi"), written in 1830, constitutes one of his poetical mani-
festos.[1] This short poem encapsulates Pushkin's response to
the cultural and historical polemics of his day. Moreover, it is
both a metapoetical and metahistorical poem, constituting one
of Pushkin's most controversial statements on the relationship
between art and history, the nature of truth, and the status of
historical fact. The poem needs to be quoted in full.

ГЕРОЙ

Что есть истина?

Друг

Да, слава в прихотях вольна.
Как огненный язык, она

По избранным главам летает,
С одной сегодня исчезает
И на другой уже видна.
За новизной бежать смиренно
Народ бессмысленный привык;
Но нам уж то чело священно,
Над коим вспыхнул сей язык.
На троне, на кровавом поле,
Меж граждан на чреде иной
Из сих избранных кто всех боле
Твоею властвует душой?

Поэт

Всё он, всё он — пришлец сей бранный,
Пред кем смирилися цари,
Сей ратник, вольностью венчанный,
Исчезнувший, как тень зари.

Друг

Когда ж твой ум он поражает
Своею чудною звездой?
Тогда ль, как с Альпов он взирает
На дно Италии святой;
Тогда ли, как хватает знамя
Иль жезл диктаторский; тогда ль,
Как водит и кругом и вдаль
Войны стремительное пламя,
И пролетает ряд побед
Над ним одна другой вослед;
Тогда ль, как рать героя плещет
Перед громадой пирамид,
Иль как Москва пустынно блещет,
Его приемля, — и молчит?

Поэт

Нет, не у Счастия на лоне
Его я вижу, не в бою,
Не зятем кесаря на троне;
Не там, где на скалу свою
Сев, мучим казнию покоя,
Осмеян прозвищем героя,
Он угасает недвижим,
Плащом закрывшись боевым.
Не та картина предо мною!
Одров я вижу длинный строй,
Лежит на каждом труп живой,
Клейменный мощною чумою,
Царицею болезней . . . он,
Не бранной смертью окружен,
Нахмурясь, ходит меж одрами
И хладно руку жмет чуме,
И в погибающем уме
Рождает бодрость . . . Небесами
Клянусь: кто жизнию своей
Играл пред сумрачным недугом,
Чтоб ободрить угасший взор,
Клянусь, тот будет небу другом,
Каков бы ни был приговор
Земли слепой . . .

Друг

Мечты поэта —
Историк строгий гонит вас!
Увы! его раздался глас, — *
И где ж очарованье света!

Поэт

Да будет проклят правды свет,
Когда посредственности хладной,

Завистливой, к соблазну жадной,
Он угождает праздно! — Нет!
Тьмы низких истин мне дороже
Нас возвышающий обман . . .
Оставь герою сердце! Что же
Он будет без него? Тиран . . .

Друг

Утешься . . . . . .

29 сентября 1830
Москва

- - - - - - - - - - - -

*Mémoires de Bourrienne (Pushkin III: I, 251–53).

HERO

What is truth?

Friend

Yes, fame is capriciously willful.
Like a tongue of flame, it
Flies over the heads of the Chosen
Disappearing from one today
It can be seen instantly atop the next.
To run docilely after novelty
Is what the mindless masses are used to;
But to us that brow is sacred
Above which that tongue of flame has sparked.
On a throne, on a bloody field,
Among citizens of different vocation
From all these Chosen Ones
Who overpowers your soul the most?

Poet

It is him, it is him — this warlike stranger,
He who had all the kings humbled,

This warrior who was crowned by freedom
And disappeared like the shadow of the dawn.

Friend

When does he strike your mind
With his wondrous star?
Is it when he gazes from the Alps
Upon the depths of sacred Italy;
Is it when he takes up the banner
Or the dictator's rod; is it when
He carries far and wide
The swift flame of war,
And victories fly above him in succession
Each victory following another;
Is it when the host of the hero applauds
Before the colossus of the pyramids,
Or when deserted Moscow glimmers,
Receiving him — and keeps silent?

Poet

No, not on the bosom of happiness
Do I see him, and not in battle,
Not as the caesar's son-in-law on a throne,
Not there where on his cliff
He sat tormented by the punishment of peace,
Ridiculed by the nickname "hero,"
Where, motionless, he gradually withered,
Covered by his martial cloak.
That is not the picture before me!
I see a long row of death-beds,
A living corpse stretched out on each,
Stigmatized by the mighty plague,
The queen of malady . . . He,
Not midst martial death,

Walks among the death-beds, frowning,
And in cool blood he shakes the hand of the plague,
And in a perishing mind
Gives birth to vigor . . . By the heavens
I swear: the one who risked his life amidst somber
      disease
In order to enliven an extinct gaze,
I swear, he will be a friend of heaven,
Whatever is the verdict
Of the blind earth . . .

Friend

        A poet's reveries,   .
The strict historian chases you away!
Alas! his voice resounded, — *
And where is the enchantment of the world!

Poet

Let the light of truth be cursed,
When it pleases vainly
The cold mediocrity,
Envious and greedy for temptation! — No!
To the multitude of low truths
I prefer an illusion that elevates us . . .
Let the hero keep his heart! What
Will he be without it? A tyrant . . .

Friend

Be consoled . . .

                    September 29, 1830
                    Moscow

- - - - - - - - - - -

*Mémoires de Bourrienne

Pushkin's treatment of history in "The Hero" is founded on his belief in the psychological truth and moral worth of legend and tradition. In part, Pushkin is engaged here in polemics with Enlightenment historians who overemphasized reason in their distinction between the true and the false in history. As White observes in his study *Metahistory,* "the Enlighteners believed that the ground of all truth was reason and its capacity to judge the products of sensory experience and to extract from such experience its pure content *against* what the imagination wished that experience to be." "This meant," White continues, "that whole bodies of data from the past—everything contained in legend, myth, fable—were excluded as potential evidence for determining the truth about the past." That is, White concludes, such historians ignored or dismissed "that aspect of the past which such bodies of data directly represented to the historian trying to reconstruct a life in its integrity and not merely in terms of its more *rationalistic* manifestations" (52).

For Pushkin and for many Romanticist poets, by contrast, legends are an indispensable source of historical knowledge; imagination has a heuristic value. Pushkin, however, does not go so far as to deny "scientific" history as well as he does not adhere to a Romanticist synthesis of myth and science.

Goethe's and Pushkin's Readings of *Mémoires sur Napoléon* by Louis-Antoine de Bourrienne

"The Hero" was written in October 1830, during Pushkin's stay at Boldino. It is connected to a number of historical events that are either mentioned or implied in the poem. As the dateline "September 29, 1830. Moscow" reveals, the poem was inspired by the visit of the Emperor Nicholas I to Moscow during a cholera epidemic. Since Pushkin deliberately changed the dateline of the poem's composition (the poem was written in October), it is obvious that the date was important to him and must be considered part of the text. Indeed, this is how Pushkin's contemporaries and later scholars have interpreted it. Pogodin accompanied the second publication of "The Hero" with the following note: "There is no need, of course, to remind anyone that the date placed by Pushkin under the poem, after the significant *Be consoled,* 29 September 1830, is the day of the arrival of the sovereign Emperor in Moscow during the cholera epidemic" (Sovremennik 143). This visit was deemed an act of true heroism by the public and was eulogized in contemporary periodicals. (Whether Nicholas I's behavior deserved to be hailed as "heroism" is an issue that cannot be taken up here.) The dateline, however, and the last line of the poem, "Be consoled" (*utesh'sia*), are the only words in the poem that could be interpreted as an allusion to Nicholas' visit to Moscow.

Another "event" that is reflected in the author's footnote to the poem is the publication in 1829–30 of *Mémoires sur Napoléon,* allegedly written by the emperor's former secretary, Louis-Antoine de Bourrienne. The book provoked major controversy among the reading public as it attempted to discredit many legends about Napoleon. One of these—the legend Pushkin uses in his poem— was the story of Napoleon's visit during his Egyptian campaign in 1799 to soldiers infected with the plague in the hospital in Jaffa. It was widely believed that Napoleon, seeking to raise the spirit of the sick and through personal example to prevent his army from panicking, had shaken the hands of plague-ridden soldiers and even touched their sores. Bourrienne did not deny the story of Napoleon's visit to the hospital, but he significantly undermined it by placing the episode at the end of the Syrian campaign rather than at its beginning. Of greater importance, he denied that the emperor had actually touched any of the infected soldiers. Instead, he suggested that the plague-stricken soldiers had been given a potion to accelerate a painful death. Bourrienne writes:

> Bonaparte made a quick tour of the overturned ramparts of this small town and then went to the hospital: there were amputees, wounded men, many soldiers afflicted with ophthalmia, crying out in a most pitiable manner, and plague victims there. The beds of the plague victims were on the right of the entrance to the first room: I

walked at the general's side. I can affirm that he did not
touch a single one. And why should he have? They were in
the final stages of their illness. None of them said a word.
Bonaparte knew very well that he was not immune to
contagion. [. . .] Bonaparte quickly passed through the
rooms, lightly tapping the yellowed edge of his boot with a
whip which he was carrying in his hand. [. . .] There were
barely sixty plague victims there. Any estimate which
states the number as higher has been exaggerated. Their
absolute silence, their complete exhaustion, and their
general lifelessness announced their imminent demise.
To take them away in such a state would have meant
spreading the plague throughout the rest of the army.
[. . .] When a historian has not witnessed an event,
when there is disagreement, one must lean toward the
most probable of the contradictory assertions and benefit from antecedents. [. . .] It has been said, for example, that the plague victims were boarded onto ships
of war, but such ships did not exist. And where would
they have disembarked? Who would have received them?
What would have been done with them? No one speaks of
this (256–59).

Although the *Mémoires* were subsequently found inaccurate (in
1830 a number of French generals and statesmen published refutations of the *Mémoires* in a two-volume work entitled *Bourrienne
et ses Erreurs*),[2] many people still accepted the *Mémoires* as a, for
the most part, credible eye-witness account of Napoleon's life.
Goethe, for example, was one of them. In a conversation with
Eckermann (6 April 1829), he remarked of Bourrienne's *Mémoires:*
"The power of truth is great. Every halo, every illusion which jour-
nalists, historians, and poets have conjured up about Napoleon,
vanishes before the terrible reality of this book; but the Hero becomes no less than before; on the contrary, he grows in stature as
he increases in truth" (Conversations 387). It is interesting to note
that in his reaction to, and interpretation of, this literary event

Goethe focuses on the same notions that will concern Pushkin in his poem—heroism, truth, and illusion.

Curiously, however, Goethe did not pay the slightest attention to such details as de Bourrienne's categorical denial that Napoleon had touched or spoken to any of the infected soldiers. Goethe was completely satisfied with the mere fact that this visit took place. The following day, according to Eckermann, Goethe again spoke about Bourrienne's book:

> I am now reading Napoleon's campaign in Egypt,— namely, what is related by the hero's everyday companion, Bourrienne, which destroys the romantic cast of many scenes, and displays facts in their naked sublime truth. [. . .] We see, by this book, continued Goethe, how many fables have been invented about the Egyptian campaign. Much, indeed, is corroborated, but much is not, and most that has been said is contradicted. That he had eight hundred Turkish prisoners shot is true; but the act appears as the mature determination of a long council of war, on the conviction, after a consideration of all circumstances, that there were no means of saving them. That he descended into the Pyramids is a fable. [. . .] He really visited those sick of the plague, and, indeed, in order to prove that the man who could vanquish fear could vanquish the plague also (Conversations 392).

Goethe passes over the obvious—that to walk among the sick people without really approaching them and touching them hardly means to "vanquish fear," much less to "vanquish plague." Clearly, in his interpretation of this episode Goethe is thinking more about his own idea of the boundlessness of human power than of love, charity, generosity, and readiness for self-sacrifice—virtues that captivate Pushkin's imagination in his interpretation of the same event. Predictably enough, Goethe starts speaking of himself in the very next phrase:[3] "And he was right! I can instance a fact

from my own life, when I was inevitably exposed to infection from
a putrid fever, and warded off the disease merely by force of will. It
is incredible what power the moral will has in such cases. It penetrates, as it were, the body; and puts it into a state of activity which
repels all hurtful influences. Fear, on the other hand, is a state of
indolent weakness and susceptibility, which makes it easy for every
foe to take possession of us. This Napoleon knew well, and he felt
that he risked nothing in giving his army an imposing example"
(Conversations 392–93). Goethe seems to be preoccupied here not
so much with the value of encouraging and helping the diseased
soldiers but rather with the power of human will, with the ability
of Napoleon and of Goethe himself to ward off the disease. Thus
Goethe acknowledges the formal risk to which Napoleon subjected
himself at the hospital, but pays little attention to the actual risk
of touching the sick.

Pushkin, by contrast, does not accept the "truth" of the *Mémoires* as unhesitatingly as Goethe. At the time he wrote "The
Hero" Pushkin could not have read *Bourrienne et ses Erreurs* and
could not, therefore, have any evidence against Bourrienne, nevertheless Pushkin turns out to be unexpectedly pedantic and makes
the Poet in his poem insist on the actual touching of the pestiferous
soldiers. Both Goethe and Pushkin admired the French Emperor.
Goethe's admiration, however, was the admiration of a great poet
who subconsciously identified himself with this "master of kings"
and looked for nothing more than a form, a great symbol for the
splendor of human achievements. As Hans Blumenberg demonstrates in his study *Work on Myth*, Goethe installed Napoleon in
the realm of "the demonic," —a category neither metaphysical nor
moral, but more nearly aesthetic. For Goethe the image of Napoleon, Blumenberg continues, "remains separate from the effect of
his actions" (480).

Pushkin, by contrast, sought some moral foundation to sus-
tain his reverence of Napoleon, while at the same time viewing
with irony any attempts at identification with him (note, for ex-

ample, the remark in *Eugene Onegin:* "We are all eager to become Napoleons"). Throughout his works, Pushkin sets forth the ideal of a true genius who is always characterized by generosity—be it the genius of art (Mozart) or perfect ruler (Duke from *Andzhelo*), whereas Goethe's concept of genius and heroism is quite different: it is grounded in the intensity of the "productive power" by which great deeds are generated. Goethe admired the Hero. Pushkin admired the Hero with a heart ("Let the hero keep his heart!"), the Hero who runs a risk not for the sake of proving the power of his will but genuinely in order to encourage and aid others. The power of Man that Goethe exalts is opposed to the power of man inspired by God that Pushkin extols (cf. "He will be a friend of heaven"), or in Vladimir Solov'iov's terms, Man-god to God-man (*chelovekobog/bogochelovek*). In these two visions of Napoleon we can see the clash of two ideals: Prometheus and Christ.

Romantic tradition often represents Napoleon either as Satan or as Prometheus (Blake, Shelley, and Byron provide outstanding examples).[4] Pushkin seeks rather to invest his Hero with Christian values, no doubt inspired more by his ideal of a perfect ruler and a model for imitation than by the real historical character.[5]

Significantly, "The Hero" has for its epigraph Pontius Pilate's famous question "What is truth?" (John 18: 28–38), the question that is echoed at the end of the poem: "To the multitudes of low truths / I prefer the illusion which elevates us." This proclamation does not mean, however, that Pushkin—who certainly cannot be completely identified with the Poet of his poem—refuses to know the truth about Napoleon; or that he does not wish to recognize, in Goethe's words, some "terrible reality" about him out of fear of sacrificing the sacred image of the Hero. Pushkin's purpose in the poem is different: two events—Napoleon's visit to the hospital in Jaffa during the epidemic of plague and Nicholas I's visit of Moscow during the epidemic of cholera—and Bourrienne's evidence are all brought together in order to question the validity of the historical "fact" and of the meaning or creation of history in general.

"The Hero" is indeed permeated with a Biblical subtext—one not limited to the poem's epigraph and one that discloses an essentially religious view of history. Significantly, Pushkin himself referred to his poem as an "Apocalyptic song." In his letter to Pogodin he wrote: "I am sending you from my Patmos an Apocalyptic song. Publish it whenever you wish, even in *Vedomosti,* but I implore you and demand in the name of our friendship—do not reveal my name to anyone" (XIV, 121–22). Although Pushkin uses this comparison half-jokingly, the reference to the Book of Revelation implies more than just an analogy between apocalyptic horrors and the picture of Napoleon in the midst of the plague at Jaffa. It is of interest that Pushkin considered the Book of Revelation and the Gospel of John to be the work of the same author. This would seem to suggest that Pushkin viewed his own poem as a kind of revelation and historical prophesy.

A close reading of the whole poem discloses how the Biblical allusions operate within the poem. The paradox contained at the end of the poem has attracted the attention of scholars.[6] As a rule, analysis of the poem had been limited to the discussion of its last lines. It is important, however, to consider how the poem unfolds beginning with the discussion of human greatness and the notion of heroism and culminating with the argument on the opposition between, on the one hand, "strict" history and fiction and, on the other, the relation between historical fact and higher divine truth.

The Generic Hero

"The Hero" is constructed as a dialogue between the Poet and his Friend. As the title and the epigraph of the poem suggest, the two main topics that form the thematic core of the poem are heroism and truth. Heroism is discussed in terms of the relationship of human greatness to the sacred, and the generic hero is depicted as one of the elect (The poem's vocabulary is significant: "tongue of fire" (the Holy Spirit, of course); "anointed heads"; "sacred brow"; "the tongue of flame has sparked"; "from those elected";

"his miraculous star"). The Friend begins the discussion with a meditation on the capriciousness of earthly glory and asks the Poet whom he would choose as the true hero. The Poet offers as an example Napoleon.

The next thirty-eight lines of the poem are devoted to the discussion of what constitutes an act of true heroism, or, in other words, what precisely makes the hero a hero. The Friend offers a number of trite images which in fact were common to Napoleonic iconography of the time. Napoleon appears in them as a warrior and conqueror (cf. Byron's words "conqueror and captive of the earth"). But Pushkin's Poet dismisses all these pictures of earthly glory and triumph, even those of noble suffering that Napoleon might have experienced as a prisoner of St. Helena and which Pushkin himself once celebrated in his poem "To the Sea."[7]

Instead of such bellicose and victorious avatars of a Romanticist Promethian image of the Emperor, the Poet advances the image of Napoleon risking his life amidst the plague at the hospital in Jaffa in order to raise the spirit of the soldiers infected with plague.

In the final lines the discussion shifts from the theme of heroism to the problem of historical truth. The Friend, referring to a newly published book—allegedly written by the emperor's secretary, Bourrienne, *Mémoires sur Napoléon*—dismisses this legend about Napoleon in Jaffa. The Poet, reluctant to accept the evidence set forth in the *Mémoires*, responds with an unexpected paradox:

> Да будет проклят правды свет,
> Когда посредственности хладной,
> Завистливой, к соблазну жадной,
> Он угождает праздно! — Нет!
> Тьмы низких истин мне дороже
> Нас возвышающий обман . . .
> Оставь герою сердце! Что же
> Он будет без него? Тиран . . .

> Let the light of truth be cursed,
> When it pleases vainly

The cold mediocrity,
Envious and greedy for temptation! — No!
To the multitude of low truths
I prefer an illusion that elevates us . . .
Let the hero keep his heart! What
Will he be without it? A tyrant . . .

This assertion does not mean, however, that Pushkin — who, again, should not be identified with the Poet of his poem — refuses to know the truth about Napoleon for fear of sacrificing the sacred image of the Hero. Pushkin's purpose in the poem is to establish the paradigm of heroism and to raise the question of the validity of the historical "fact" and the meaning of history in general. Two events are therefore juxtaposed; the authenticity of Napoleon's visit to the hospital in Jaffa, however, is called into question, whereas Nicholas I's visit to Moscow is given the status of fact by the date that the author affixes to the poem. The reader, therefore, is sent back to the title and to the epigraph of the poem: Who is the hero? and "What is truth?"

Significantly, Napoleon is never specifically named. Both the Friend and the Poet refer to him as "he" and "hero." Nor does Pushkin mention Nicholas I in person: the date alludes to an event, not to the agent of the event. Quite deliberately, Pushkin avoids naming the hero: the poem, after all, is not about *a* hero but about the heroic model in general. Pushkin, to be sure, was far from idealizing either the historical Napoleon or even more so Nicholas. The absence of names underscores the abstract, theoretical level of discourse. He is more concerned with creating a paradigm of a hero than with treating specific historical characters. Through this generalization, Pushkin establishes an archetypal hero who takes on a mythological dimension in addition to the historical one.

What are the characteristics of this generalized image of a hero — one which serves the author as an emblem of greatness? The Poet's choice of the Jaffa episode from Napoleon's life suggests the centrality of moral values to his definition of a hero; more precisely, this choice points to the importance of Christian values and of Christ as a model for imitation and an "antecedent hero" for Napoleon himself.

The classical representation of the Jaffa episode can be found in Antoine-Jean Gros's "Les Pestiférés de Jaffa" (1804)—a painting that was popular in artistic and literary circles at the time of its appearance. In this work Napoleon is depicted as a Christ figure or a saintly healer typical of religious paintings; he touches with his fingers the sores of the sick as if healing them. As the art historian Edgar Munhall points out in his article "Portraits of Napoleon," the representation of Napoleon in this painting "follows the traditional figures of St. Roch, the patron of the plague-stricken, and San Carlo Borromeo, as the 1804 Salon title indicates: *Bonaparte, General-in-Chief of the Army of the Orient, shown at the moment when he touches a pestilential tumor, while visiting the hospital at Jaffa*" (Munhall 7). It is interesting to note that the authors of *Bourrienne et ses Erreurs,* in their refutation of Bourrienne's book, considered Bourrienne's interpretation of the Jaffa episode as one of the main calumnies against Napoleon and, indirectly, against Gros's painting. Insisting on the accuracy of the painting, one of the authors concludes his account of the event in these words: "Ainsi, M. le rédacteur, le tableau de la peste de Jaffa, qui fait tant d'honneur au beau talent de notre illustre peintre Gros, et qui peut-être est son chef-d'oeuvre, n'a pas été fait d'après une scène imaginaire, comme le dit trop légèrement M. de Bourrienne" (Thus, Mr. Editor, the painting of the plague of Jaffa, which did so much honor to the fine talent of our illustrious painter Gros, and which is perhaps his master-piece, was not fashioned after an imaginary scene, as M. de Bourrienne has too lightly claimed. Erreurs 46). Although Pushkin could not have read *Erreurs*, he could well have had in mind this painting while writing the poem. (He may have seen a reproduction of the painting or read about it in the contemporary press.) More significant, however, is that the very choice of the episode and the manner in which it is depicted evokes religious paintings of traditional Christian saints or of *Christ Healing the Lepers*. Significantly, the Poet himself refers to his description of Napoleon as a "picture" or "painting" (*kartina*). And indeed, the role of visual detail is of great importance in his descriptions, emphasized by his repeated use of the verb "to see": "No! not on the bosom of happiness do I see him"; "I see a long row of death-beds." He creates, as it were, a verbal painting. The literary device of verbal painting was commonly used at the beginning of the nineteenth century; the literary genre of historical painting in Russia dates back at least to Karamzin's article "On the Events and Characters in Russian History which May Serve as Subjects of Arts" "O sluchaiakh i kharakterakh v Rossiiskoi istorii, kotorye mogut byt' predmetom khudozhestv" (1802), where Karamzin speaks about the past and historical events in terms of imaginary pictures.

Let us look at the diction and imagery Pushkin uses to depict the Poet's apocalyptic vision or the picture (*kartina*) of the hero. The portrayal is based on a tension between several oppositions: life-death, light-darkness, heaven-earth. The figure of Napoleon who brings death on the battlefield ("not midst martial death") and who conquers life or "kings" as a symbol of earthly power ("he who had all the kings humbled"; "not as the caesar's son-in-law on a throne") is opposed to that of a hero who brings life, who conquers death and revives corpses. Since *odr* means not only "bed," but also "death-bed," the hero who "walks among death beds" (*khodit mezh odrami*) seems to descend into the kingdom of death: he is surrounded by "living corpses" and confronted with the "queen" of death ("queen of diseases")—the plague. He not only encourages the dying men, but enters into a duel with death itself. The shaking of hands of dying people is metonymically transformed into a handshake with the plague, or death: "And in cool blood he shakes the hand of the plague." Death and destruction are then conquered by the hero who actually "gives birth [*rozhdaet*] to vigor." Light is opposed to darkness: "the one who risked his life amidst somber disease in order to enliven an extinct gaze." The Poet's "hero" is ready to sacrifice himself and his life not for the sake of earthly glory (note, that earth is connected with blindness or darkness: "the blind earth"), but for some "heavenly" reasons: "The one who risked his life [. . .] will be a friend of heaven." The "blind earth" as opposed to heaven might reject this "hero" and pass sentence on him: "Whatever is the verdict of the blind earth." It is evident that the poet's hero is associated with the origin of life and light, the idea of sacrifice, and ultimate rejection by the blind world. Behind the image of Napoleon hovers that of Christ the Savior.

It is important to note that in the 1830s, Pushkin had a very keen interest in the figure of Jesus and Christianity. Among his plans for dramas was one that was entitled "Jesus" (this plan goes back to 1826). Lotman has made an attempt to reconstruct its plot. Commenting on the sources of Pushkin's interest in the figure of Jesus, Lotman observes:

> It is no coincidence that the image of Jesus tormented Pushkin's imagination. The end of the Napoleonic era and the beginning of a new bourgeois era after the revolution of 1830 were interpreted by different social currents of thought as the end of a vast historical cycle. Hopes for a new historical age evoked in memory images of early Christianity. In the 1820s Saint-Simon named his teaching a "new Christianity." The Russian readers too perceived the teaching of Saint-Simon in this key. In 1831, under the influence of the July Revolution, in a letter to Pushkin, Chaadaev joined the catastrophe of the old world and the appearance of a new Christ: "Tears come to my eyes when I look at the great collapse of the old society, my old society. [. . .] But a vague presentiment tells me that a man soon will appear who will bring us the truth of the centuries (1988, 156).

It is interesting to note that Chaadaev connects the "truth of the centuries" with the appearance of a new Christ. In Pushkin's poem, truth, Christ, and Napoleon merge into one image of a true hero. In this context the epigraph to the poem "What is truth?" acquires a very concrete meaning: truth are those actions which imitate the works of Christ. In the Gospel of John, Pilate does not wait for Christ's answer to his question. So too the poem ends abruptly without providing a definite answer to the question of the epigraph. Pontius Pilate's question (John 18: 38), however, is not left without an answer in the context of the Gospel. The answer is obvious to any Christian reader of the Bible. In the previous chapter (John 17: 17) Jesus says: "Sanctify them by the truth; Your word is truth." As understood by biblical scholars, "truth" in the context of the Gospel of John most often signifies "divine reality."[8] In the Gospel "truth" is linked to "life," "light," and "freedom." Truth is Christ himself: "I am the way and the truth and the life" (John 14: 6); "Then you will know the truth, and the truth will set you free" (John 8: 32). Precisely this kind of "divine reality" corresponds to the Poet's notion of truth and true heroism.[9]

The poem's oppositions — "earth-heaven," "darkness-light," "low-high" — culminate in two hypostases of truth itself: a higher, heavenly truth and a lower earthly one: "To the multitude of low truths I prefer an illusion that elevates us" (cf. Mikkelson 370). The truth for the Poet is not the literal actuality and authenticity of the event but rather the spiritual, "elevating" meaning of the event, that is, the self-sacrificing works of Napoleon and Nicholas I, or the imitation of Christ. To be sure, in his concept of the imitation of Christ, Pushkin follows the medieval Christian tradition according to which healing was considered a prerogative of kings, and the kings themselves were viewed as the Lord's Anointed ones and imitators of Christ.

Fact versus Legend

Once the archetypal paradigm of a hero as Christ is established, one can see how the image of Christ implicitly functions in the poem and how it modifies the author's attitude toward the problem of fact and legend in history. In "The Hero," Pushkin suggests a profound connection between legend and fact through a succession of archetypal models: the legend about Christ gives birth to Christian deeds, Christian morality helps to shape the legend about Napoleon, the legend about Napoleon serves as an archetypal model for the real event—Nicholas I's visit to Moscow. Indeed, it is likely that the historical Nicholas I, consciously or subconsciously, actually did imitate Napoleon; the Jaffa legend may well have influenced his decision to visit cholera-infected Moscow. In this sense it is not important whether the episode in Jaffa actually took place. What matters is that this legend turned out to be a model which found its embodiment in the event that really did take place and the *reality* of which was not questioned: the visit of the Russian emperor to Moscow.

Significantly enough, the poem ends with a "factual," "historiographical" detail: the date of the tsar's arrival to Moscow. The date is introduced neither by the historian nor by the Poet but by a third party, the author, and is given, therefore, a larger degree of objectivity. Thus the poem undergoes its main metamorphosis: *legend is transformed into fact.* The Jaffa legend becomes a fulfilled prophesy. It is in this sense that one can understand the Poet's claim that he prefers an "elevating illusion," or "deceit" (*vozvyshaiushchii obman*) to "the multitude of low truths." In Pushkin's time and in his vocabulary, *obman* could mean both "deceit," "lie," and "fiction" (*vymysel; fantaziia*); it is not lie or untruth but a "true" legend or "true" fiction that the Poet prefers to the barren fact. The legend—or "the elevating deceit" that is realized in life or has a potential of influencing life—is preferable to the stifling fact, and on the spiritual level it is more true. The legend is real and "true" in the sense that what could have happened must happen sooner or later and be realized in life.[10]

The Poet bases his belief on the inner logic of the character, on what is psychologically convincing and in accord with his notion of heroism.[11] (Later the Poet's intuition was proven true: Napoleon's visit at the hospital of Jaffa and his courageous behavior there was confirmed by many eyewitnesses.) If Napoleon is a true hero, then even if he did not act according to the legend, he *could* have acted this way. Thus, truth is not what has happened but what might have happened and could have happened.

The Poet's attitude toward the authenticity of the legend about Napoleon is pertinent to religious and mythological thinking in general. In the European tradition it was reflected in the allegorical exegesis of Christian Fathers of the Church, such as Origen, who were more concerned with the nonhistorical meaning of certain episodes from the Bible than with authenticity of these episodes.[12] In classical antiquity, the perception of history in its more general, "spiritual" meaning was viewed as *poetical*. Aristotle posits a classical opposition between history proper and fiction. A historian, according to Aristotle, writes about what really has happened and is concerned with the authenticity of particular events. A poet's task, on the other hand, is to speak not about what has happened but about what could have happened. In this sense, Aristotle argues, "poetry is something more philosophic and of graver import than history, since its statements are of the nature rather of universals, whereas those of history are singulars" (McKeon, 636).

It is clear that the dialogue between the Poet and his Friend is in part Pushkin's way of discussing the legacy of the old Aristotelian dichotomy of history and poetry—the dichotomy which has been discussed again and again, especially in modern times. It is no coincidence that one of the dialogue's participants is actually called a Poet, whereas the other, although named a Friend, is obviously identified with the "strict historian." Pushkin's portrayal of the Poet's interpretation of the Jaffa episode fully corresponds to Aristotle's understanding of a poet's goal and his subject. Pushkin's Poet is concerned with the general notion of heroism, with what a hero could have done, and with what would be plausible for the hero to do. (As Aristotle said: "By a universal statement I mean one as to what such or such a kind of man will probably or necessarily say or do—which is the aim of poetry, though it affixes proper names to the characters." "And if he [a poet] should come to take a subject from actual history, he is nonetheless a poet for that; since some historic occurrences may very well be in the probable and possible order of things; and it is in that aspect of them that he is their poet"(McKeon, 636).

In "The Hero," however, Pushkin goes beyond merely establishing an opposition between poetical and historical views of history. A certain "inequality" or asymmetry between the Poet's and the Friend's positions is implied by the very shape of the narrative which is *poetical* in the Aristotelian sense of the word—not only in verbal form but in content as well. The poet, Aristotle says, is "more the poet of his plots than of his meters." The Aristotelian theme of poetry vs. history is elaborated upon by Pushkin: the universal meaning, or spiritual truth, which is found in a legend, is ultimately realized in reality and takes on, therefore, some specific "singular" meaning as well. Myth becomes fact, poetry becomes history. This, probably, is what Pushkin meant when he wrote to Nikolai Gnedich that "the history of a nation belongs to the Poet." The poet's method is not based on the presumption of factual objectivity; he uses myth and legend as he might use facts, in order to reach the higher historical vision, that is, get at the "spiritual truth" of history. In his depiction of what might have happened (and probably did happen) he becomes an active prophet for the nation's future. In this sense the Poet is a creator of the national history.

The Principle of Complementarity

The extent to which Pushkin himself can be identified with the Poet of his poem "The Hero," or with the Poet he speaks about in his letter to Gnedich, is still debatable. Although Pushkin structures his poem so as to underscore the truth of the Poet's opinion, it would be wrong to identify Pushkin completely with the Poet.

The voice of Pushkin who aspired to a sober view of history, who painstakingly collected facts and documents for his historical works, and who demanded a scholarly and scientific approach from historians can easily be discerned in that of the Friend. Pushkin, to be sure, wanted to be both a Poet and a Historian, and he creates a dialogue between poetry and history not only in this poem but in his life and his oeuvre. In "The Hero," as in his many other poetical works, Pushkin plays with poetical and historiographical structures (for instance, footnotes and dates). The same device is used in Pushkin's longer narrative poem *Poltava* where, as Lotman suggests, footnotes introduce a dialogue, not so much between poetry and prose as between history and fiction (Lotman 1902, II. 387). This play does not mean, however, that Pushkin's position lies somewhere in-between that of the Poet and the "strict historian." Pushkin challenges the very idea of the opposition between history and fiction and refuses to resolve or synthesize the two points of view in the poem.[13]

I suggest that the relationship between history and poetry in Pushkin's "The Hero" is analogous to "the principle of uncertainty" or the "principle of complementarity" as discussed earlier in the Introduction. The linguistic representation of the "principle of complementarity" can be found in the poem's homonyms. In homonyms, two different and often self-exclusive meanings coexist in their latent form in one phonological and orthographic form, acquiring its concrete meaning only in context. The frequency of homonyms in the poem suggests that Pushkin was consciously playing with "complementarity" and uncertainty in all the crucial notions of the poem. Indeed, Pushkin makes full use of the homonymous nature of such words as *svet, t'ma* and *obman* (*svet* means "light," "world," and "society"; *t'ma* means "darkness" and "multitude"; *obman* could mean "lie" and "fiction," that is, a literary work). The best illustration of Pushkin's skillful use of "complementary" meanings of homonyms can be found in the Friend's and the Poet's respective comments on Bourrienne's *Mémoires.*

The Friend dismisses the legend about Napoleon and relies only on "facts":

> A poet's reveries,
>> The strict historian chases you away!
>> Alas! his voice resounded, — *
>> And where is the enchantment of the world! (*I gde zh*
>>> *ocharovan'e sveta* [emphasis added])

Svet in this case means "world." In the reply to his Friend, the Poet uses the same word—*svet*—but in a very different meaning: "Let the light [*svet*] of truth be cursed." *Svet* here means "light." The Poet and the Friend speak, as it were, "different languages," have different purposes and, therefore, they discover and reveal different meanings of the same word. The meaning of the word *svet* conforms here to the "principle of complementarity" as it depends on the context and the purpose of the speaker. What is true for the Poet does not have to be necessarily so for the strict historian. The position of the "strict historian" and that of the Poet are mutually exclusive, yet they can and probably must coexist as two possible hypostases revealed contextually and diachronically. In other words, Pushkin appears as either a poet or a historian, depending on his purpose and the angle from which a given event is viewed. The truth itself is shown to have two "complementary" hypostases—a higher, heavenly truth, and a lower earthly one—depending on the chosen perspective.

On the one hand, such a play with abstract notions implies the relativity and uncertainty of these notions; on the other, it points to the importance of the vantage point from which these notions are perceived and judged. What is preferable (*dorozhe*) for the Poet need not be so for the "strict historian" or the reader. The answer to the question "what is truth" is transferred from the sphere of rational judgment to the sphere of faith and personal choice, based on personal moral criteria. This is precisely why the Poet in "The Hero" does not deny the "fact" postulated by the Friend, does not assert crudely the priority of illusion over reality, but speaks in terms of preferences: *mne dorozhe.* He *chooses* this elevating illusion without making a claim for objectivity.

In this respect it is interesting to compare "The Hero" with Pushkin's *Mozart and Salieri.* The poem's enigmatic climax, "Let the Hero keep his heart! What will he be without it? A tyrant... ,'" reminds one of the open ending of *Mozart and Salieri.* Its moralistic maxim, "Genius and villainy are two things incompatible" ("Genii i zlodeistvo—dve veshchi nesovmestnye"), is confronted with the uncertainty and ambiguity of the historical evidence— "That's wrong: what about Buonarrotti? Or is that a fable of the obtuse and thoughtless mob—and was the Vatican's creator no assassin?" (*Nepravda: / A Bonarotti? ili eto skazka / Tupoi, bessmyslennoi tolpy—i ne byl / Ubiitseiu sozdatel' Vatikana?*) (VII, 133-4). The incompatibility of art with evil is paralleled in "The Hero" by the incompatibility of heroism with evil. The problem of art is transferred to the problem of history, but the structure of the argument and the general thrust of thought are very similar. Salieri usurps the knowledge of truth and completely ignores the truth in its Christian sense: "Everyone says there is no truth on earth; but there is no truth on high either." Here he equates truth with justice and denies the existence of any divine truth and divine reality.[14] Similarly, the Friend, or a "strict historian" of the poem claims that he knows the truth and knows the fact. Pushkin shows, however, that usurpation of the truth is as damaging for art as it is for history. Significantly enough, the "truth" of the "strict historian" is linked to the "truth" of "mediocrity." All these characteristics— "mediocrity," "cold," "envious," "greedy for temptation" (*posredstvennost', khladnyi, zavistlivyi, k soblaznu zhadnyi*)—can be clearly applied to Salieri. The ultimate "truth" of both the play and the poem is depicted as dependent on an event the authenticity of which is not confirmed within the framework of the text. Therefore, accepting the "truth" of the moral maxims of both the play and of the poem requires not a rationalistic judgment but a leap of faith on the part of a reader. The reader, however, is given a free choice as whether to accept this truth or reject it. In this sense one can say that both Pushkin texts are imbued with religious logic: each requires an attitude analogous to that of a reader of the Bible who has a choice to believe or not to believe in the truth of the Sacred History.

The Paradox of the Elevating Illusion

The idea of complementarity is indeed central to Pushkin's view of the relationship between history and fiction. History and fiction, as the two possible forms of representation of historical material, coexist in Pushkin's historical consciousness and, in fact, induce him to treat the same themes and the same periods in both fictional and historical works. The choice of one genre over another becomes ultimately a moral choice and provides the author with the possibility to view the same event from different perspectives.

As a final observation, it is interesting to note that the same logic that motivates Pushkin's Poet's choice of the "elevating deceit" over "low truths" underlies Dostoevsky's well-known paradoxical statement in his letter to N. D. Fon-Vizina. In this letter, Dostoevsky claims that even if it were proven to him that Christ were outside the truth, he would still prefer to remain with Christ. Dostoevsky, like Pushkin, chooses his vocabulary with care; he avoids the affirmative mood and speaks in terms of preferences: "Even if somebody proved to me that Christ was outside the truth, and it really were true that the truth was outside Christ, then I would rather prefer [*mne luchshe khotelos' by*] to remain with Christ than with the truth" (XXVIII: I, 176). As Robert Louis Jackson points out, Dostoevsky "structures his notion of two kinds of beauty, two ideals, in the framework of a dualistic view of man's nature (corporeal and spiritual) and in terms of a dialectical interaction between the earthly truth of man's nature and the spiritual truth that is revealed in his strivings" (Jackson 70). The statement of Pushkin's Poet, "To the multitude of low truths I prefer an illusion that elevates us" with its distinction between two truths—an earthly truth and a higher "elevating" one—is a literary anteced-ent for Dostoevsky's paradox. In both cases, the notion of a higher truth is associated with the figure of Christ and the choice of the illusion or "untruth" as opposed to the earthly truth is determined by moral criteria and by the ultimate goals these truths serve. The higher spiritual truth signifies the striving for beauty, the good, and potential, whereas the earthly truth serves the lower instincts, mere fact, and pleases "cold, envious mediocrity which is greedy for temptation." It is no coincidence then that in Dostoevsky's novel *The Raw Youth* (*Podrostok*), the two lines from Pushkin's poem "The Hero"—"To the multitude of low truths / I prefer an illusion that elevates us"—are quoted in a conversation between Arkadii and Vasin. Dostoevsky clearly perceives Pushkin's para-dox as central to Russian cultural and ideological debates. "I do not know; I would not be able to decide whether or not these two verses are true," admits Vasin, "The truth may lie, as always, somewhere in-between: that is, in one case a holy truth, and in another—a lie. I only know for certain one thing: this thought will remain one of the main controversial points among people for a long time to come" (XIII, 152).

In their attitude toward "fact," Dostoevsky and Nietzsche are close to Pushkin. "The falseness of a judgment," Nietzsche says in *Beyond Good and Evil*, "is to us not necessarily an objec-tion to a judgment. [. . .] The question is to what extent it is life-advancing, life-preserving, species-preserving, perhaps even species-breeding" (Nietzsche 1988, 17). As White points out, "Nietzsche located the problem of the worth of history (and, a *fortiori* of memory) in the problem of the value or need which it serves" (White 348). Both Pushkin and Nietzsche (one implicitly, the other quite explicitly) differentiated between "scientific" his-tory and history which becomes a form of art providing a higher historical vision. For "the uncontrolled historical sense," accord-ing to Nietzsche, "uproots the future by destroying illusions and depriving existing things of the only atmosphere in which they can live" (Nietzsche 1990, 119). History that is transformed into a work of art, on the other hand, can "preserve or even awaken instincts." Nietzsche warns that "such historiography would be wholly at odds with the analytical and anti-artistic temper of our time; indeed, it would be regarded as a perversion of it. But history which, unless guided by a constructive instinct, only destroys, eventually makes its instruments jaded and unnatural." To support this view Nietzsche cites Goethe: "For such men destroy illusions, and 'the man who destroys illusions in himself and others is punished by Nature, the strictest of all tyrants'" (Nietzsche 1990, 119–20).

It seems that this is precisely what Pushkin objected to in Bourrienne's *Mémoires sur Napoléon*, namely their destructive character, their attempt to dismember the readers' illusions of Napoleon and consequently to present him as a tyrant ("Let the hero keep his heart! What / Will he be without it? A tyrant."). By emphasizing the connection between rejection of illusions and tyranny, Pushkin prefigures the arguments of Nietzsche. Both Pushkin and Nietzsche reveal an aristocratic disdain for positivist historiography when they repudiate history that "pleases vainly the cold mediocrity" — or, in Nietzsche's terms, history that appeals merely to lower instincts of the masses and "individuals hungry for knowledge." Moreover, both the Russian poet and the German philosopher link the value of historical truth to its utility for the historical present and the future of man and culture. Echoing the attack of Pushkin's Poet on the "scientific" truth of mediocrity, Nietzsche insists that "only insofar as a truthful man possesses the absolute will to be just, is there any greatness in the aspiration for truth that the world so mindlessly glorifies" (Nietzsche 1990, 113). Pushkin and Dostoevsky found this "life-serving" and "life-advancing" power in more or less traditional Christian values, whereas behind Nietzsche's notion of the "life-advancing" function there was a notion of "will to power" ("life as such is will to power") or "fear of the void." (These notions are, of course, too complex to be taken up lightly here.) Note that Pushkin's notion of the "elevating illusion" and Nietzsche's attitude toward the problem of fact and legend, history and art, may also contain an inherent danger: once deprived of any moral foundation, this "elevating illusion" may lead to the destruction of life, not to its advancement, as has been fully demonstrated by the tragic history of the twentieth century.[15]

Russian literature, indeed, shows the awareness of the intrinsic danger and dubiousness of "elevating illusion" as well as of its moral worth. If Pushkin and Dostoevsky lean toward the grand "elevating illusion," Lermontov, Tolstoy, and Chekhov are keen on propagating the more "caustic truths" (*edkie istiny*) as Lermontov puts it in the author's Introduction to *A Hero of Our Time*.[16] Though the debate is still open as to what kind of history is "in the service" or "disservice of life," Pushkin's short poetical dialogue, "The Hero," remains one of the key texts in Russian literature that generated and stimulated the discussion of the relationship between fact and legend, "low truths" and "elevating illusion," between history and fiction.

part III *Petra Scandali:* Pushkin Confronts
Peter the Great

In so far as history aspires to meaning, it is
doomed to select regions, periods, groups of men
and individuals in these groups and to make
them stand out, as discontinuous figures, against
a continuity barely good enough to be used as
a backdrop. A truly total history would cancel
itself out — its product would be nought.

—Claude Lévi-Strauss, *The Savage Mind*

five Forging Russian History:
The Blackamoor of Peter the Great

Pushkin's fascination with the figure of Peter the Great and his epoch coincides with the increase of his interest in the historical fate of Russia and the nature of the historical process per se. According to Vladimir Dal', Pushkin was so preoccupied with the image of Peter the Great that he sought to portray him both in fictional and non-fictional genres and considered this one of the main tasks of his life. Dal' describes his conversation with Pushkin in 1832:

> Pushkin then truly got fired up while speaking about Peter the Great and said that in addition to the history of Peter the Great he was definitely going to create a fictional work in his memory as well: "So far I was unable to comprehend, to grasp the whole of this giant at once: he is too large for us nearsighted people; we are still standing too close to him, — we have to step aside for two centuries, — but I comprehend him intuitively; the more I study him, the more amazement and servility prevent me from thinking and judging freely. One should not rush; one should master the subject and study it persistently; time will improve it. But I will make something out of this gold. Oh, you'll see: I will still do so much! (Dal', 262)

Three major fictions by Pushkin — *Poltava, The Blackamoor of Peter the Great,* and *The Bronze Horseman,* as well as his unfinished historiographical work *The History of Peter I* — emerged from his fascination with Peter. Each in their own way and from various perspectives portray Peter the Great and address the role of Peter's reforms for Russia's historical development.

Pushkin strove to look at what he considered to be the central event of Russian history, Peter, from different distances and in various contexts. Only by moving from one angle to another, by considering multiple complementary versions of the same phenomenon, did he expect to achieve a better understanding of historical events and processes.

Begun in July 1827 in Mikhailovskoe, Pushkin's novel *The Blackamoor of Peter the Great* (*Arap Petra Velikogo*) remained unfinished, but even in the eyes of Belinsky it was "infinitely superior to, and better than, any Russian historical novel, whether taken separately or in their totality" (Belinsky 1955, 576). Pushkin completed only six chapters and the beginning of a seventh one—a fragment to which the author's posthumous publishers conferred a title "Arap Petra Velikogo"; Pushkin's editors also distributed epigraphs that Pushkin himself collected but did not assign to specific chapters, except the epigraph chosen for Chapter 4. Later critics devoted much attention to this novel; in most cases, however, they treated it as Pushkin's experiment with a genre of historical novel and considered *The Blackamoor of Peter the Great* merely a stage in Pushkin's literary development culminating in *The Captain's Daughter.* Scholarly analyses of *The Blackamoor of Peter the Great,* therefore, revolve on the causes leading Pushkin to abandon his first historical novel and the speculations concerning the novel's further development.[1] Trying to explain why the novel was not completed, most scholars detect some fundamental flaws in it—such as inconsistencies in Pushkin's mode of narration and lack of a clearly defined point of view. As a result, relatively little is said about the text itself. Without trying to dispute the scholars' conclusions concerning the novel's fragmentary status, I will focus more closely on Pushkin's historical concept in *The Blackamoor of Peter the Great* and his notion of the historical novel in general.[2]

The plot of *The Blackamoor of Peter the Great* is based on a family legend. The novel focuses on one of Pushkin's ancestors,

his maternal great-grandfather, Abram Gannibal, who lived during the reign of Peter the Great and was closely associated with
the tsar. The novel, however, is not a straightforward biography of
Gannibal.[3] Family legend constitutes a core of the plot only formally: the real "hero" of the novel is not Gannibal, Peter, or any
of the characters depicted, but a concrete historical period—Peter
the Great's epoch.

Although traditionally the novel's intent is considered to be a
"domestic" portrayal of Peter, the emphasis is not on Peter's activity, but rather on the result of his activity manifested in cultural
and social changes, in people's norms of behavior and attitudes.
Peter is depicted as a man of enormous personal capacities—very
similar to his portrayal as a "perpetual worker" (*vechnyi rabotnik*)
in "Stanzas" ("Stansy," 1826)—and as a historical figure who was
able to transform Russia by his will and energy. His extraordinary
personal influence on the course of Russian history, however, is
revealed in the novel not explicitly—as in *Poltava* where Peter defeats his enemy in the battlefield—but rather implicitly: in the way
his personality shaped and changed the consciousness of others.
Pushkin intentionally avoids portraying Peter in the moment of
his "historical" or heroic deeds: "nobody could have suspected
this warm and cordial host of being the hero of Poltava, of being
the powerful and formidable reformer of Russia" (VIII: I, 11).
From this passage it is easy to infer that Pushkin attempted to
create an idealized and "warm" (*laskovyi*) portrayal of Peter; and
indeed, this is the traditional view. Thus, Iakubovich concludes:
"The reformist activity of Peter the Great was pushed here on the
foreground as a positive one and all-justifying" (283). Pushkin,
however, did not portray Peter's "reformist activity," but rather
the impact of his activity on different social classes.

Peter's role in the novel could be compared to that of a "host"
who lets his guests speak for him and whose "activity" is felt only
indirectly and revealed not in his own words but in the words of
others. That is why the real center of the novel is a chapter that

Pushkin published separately under the title "Assambleia pri Petre l-m"; as a true "host" Peter appears in this chapter only in the background.[4] The novel, in other words, is not about the "host" but about the "guests"; the character of the "host" is revealed primarily through the nature and activity of his "guests." The idea that the center of the narrative is not Peter or any other protagonist of the novel but the whole of Russia is encapsulated in the epigraph supposedly intended for the entire novel: "Russia transformed by Peter's iron will" ("Zheleznoi voleiu Petra preobrazhennaia Rossiia"). The epigraph, taken from Nikolai Iazykov's poem "Ala," reveals Pushkin's concept in this novel most clearly: it implies that the center of the narrative is a transformed Russia and the results of Peter's reforms (Cf. Lapkina, 298).

Problems of Writing a Historical Novel

It is interesting to note that in his article "Iurii Miloslavskii, or, the Russians in 1612" ("Iurii Miloslavskii, ili russkie v 1612 godu"), 1830, Pushkin defines a novel as a portrayal of a "historical epoch unfolding in a fictional narrative" (XI, 92). Pushkin, like his contemporaries, believed that the task of a historical novelist is to render the unique atmosphere of the age depicted, to recapture it. Significantly, Pushkin seems not to differentiate between a historical novel and a novel in a more general sense of the word. A contemporary novel, according to Pushkin, must be historical to the extent that it aspires to a truthful representation of a social-historical milieu. It is in this sense that one could speak of the historicity of *Eugene Onegin,* for example. For *Eugene Onegin* depicts a panorama of contemporary life and is, indeed, "a historical epoch unfolding in a fictional narrative."[5] Belinsky was the first critic to link the historicity of the novel to the representation of the historical milieu: "First of all we see in *Eugene Onegin* a poetically rendered picture of society, taken in one of the most interesting moments of its development. From this point of view *Eugene Onegin* is a *historical* poem in the full sense of the word, although there is no single historical figure among its protagonists" (Belinsky 1955, VII: 432). If in *Eugene Onegin* Pushkin creates a panorama of Russian life of the twenties, in *The Blackamoor of Peter the Great* he offers a panoramic view of Russian society during the reign of Peter I with all its multifarious social trends and structures.[6] He focuses on different aspects of cultural life and portrays a historical epoch in the process of becoming historical so that the shaping force of history manifests itself as a change in cultural possibilities. The peculiar characteristic of *The Blackamoor of Peter the Great* is that there is no historical event in it, such as a war, rebellion, conspiracy, a struggle for a throne, etc., but only the representation of a historical epoch and a whole range of conventions during the specific historical period. For a long time, however, wars (conquerors, pretenders, and the like) were the central themes of historical narratives. As Mikhail Bakhtin pointed out in his essay "Forms of Time and of the Chronotope in the Novel," "This strictly speaking historical theme [. . .] intertwines, without merging, with the plots of historical figures' personal life (with a central motif of love). The main objective of a historical novel of modern times consisted in overcoming this duality: one attempted to find a historical aspect for private life, and to show history 'in a domestic manner' (Pushkin)" (Bakhtin, 250–51).

Pushkin praised Walter Scott precisely for his ability to portray history in a "domestic manner" (cf. his essay "About the Novels of Walter Scott," "O romanakh Val'tera Skotta"). In *The Blackamoor of Peter the Great* as well, Pushkin strove to demonstrate that "ce qui est historique est absolument ce que nous voyons" (Pushkin 1962–66: VII, 529). However, the historicity of Pushkin's novel is not limited to the representation of a "historical epoch": real historical characters, such as Peter and Gannibal, are portrayed as protagonists of the novel. The presence of real historical characters created a new problem for Pushkin: how does a historical novel differ from a conventional novel—and from history? Although historical novels employ the formal techniques of standard

fiction, the use of historical personages creates new constraints
for a writer. As Herbert Lindenberger noted in his book *Historical Drama: The Relation of Literature and Reality,* the writer has to
coordinate his portrayal with the reader's historical knowledge. In
other words, in addition to the internal probability that has to govern any consistent narrative, the use of historical personages forces
the author to comply with the reality of the external world, or to
external probability as well.[7] This idea is well taken up by Harry E.
Shaw, a student of Scott: "We can say that while in most novels
probability stems from our general ideas about life and society,
in historical novels the major source of probability is specifically
historical" (21). In most pre-nineteenth century historical novels
these two types of probability were not coordinated. In order to
unite them organically, one had to create an internal probability
that would correspond to the external probability, that is, to make
the actions of historical personages both psychologically convincing and consistent with the reader's factual knowledge about these
personages. But when historical facts enter the fictional universe
and are subordinated to internal probability, they can be modified,
since they enter a flexible realm of *probability* as opposed to a stiff
universe of historical document and fact. As Shaw aptly pointed
out, "the idea of internal probability allows us to see why a work
can become more historical, not less historical, if it rearranges
individual aspects of the historical record for the sake of demonstrating a larger pattern" (Shaw, 21–22). This is why Pushkin does
not adhere strictly to historical evidence. For in fiction, historical
truth is not identified with historical fact.

In order to achieve a balance between historical facts and fiction
and to attain the desirable unity of external and internal probability, that is, to solve the "duality" Bakhtin speaks about (the
duality of a historical theme and of a "central motif of love") Pushkin turned to the same kind of sources Scott employed successfully
in his historical novels—legends and historical anecdotes. Since no
formal history of Peter's times existed when Pushkin started his

work on *The Blackamoor of Peter the Great,* he had to look for facts
in various sources: he borrowed historical materials for his depiction of everyday life during the reign of Peter I from Ivan Golikov's
The Deeds of Peter the Great (Deianiia Petra Velikogo), from essays
collected in the volume entitled *Russkaia starina* by the Decembrist Aleksandr Kornilovich, and from a handwritten biography of
Gannibal that Pushkin had acquired from his great-uncle.

Pushkin fully realized the connection between the shape of the
narrative and the choice of historical sources. Speaking about the
"new school" of French historians developed under the influence
of Scott, Pushkin claims "sources" as a shaping force of historical narratives. It was Scott's use of "new sources"—legend—that
influenced, according to Pushkin, the development of both fiction and historiography: "The influence of W. Scott is felt in all
branches of contemporary letters. The new school of French historians was formed under the influence of the Scottish novelist.
He pointed out to them completely new sources, previously un-
suspected in spite of the existence of historical drama, created
by Shakespeare and Goethe" (XI, 121). These sources, according
to Pushkin, inevitably led to the novelistic genre even in history
proper. And indeed, these were the grounds of Pushkin's criticism
of Polevoi: Pushkin disapproved an excessively novelistic nature
of his *History of the Russian People (Istoriia Russkogo naroda)*:
"Mr. Polevoi strongly sensed the merits of Barante and Thierry
and accepted their line of thought with the boundless enthusiasm
of a young neophyte. Captivated by the *novelistic vividness of the
truth* [emphasis added], brought before us in the artless simplicity
of a chronicle, he practically denied the existence of any other kind
of history" (XI, 121). To be sure, Pushkin does not equate "novelistic" elements with literary style or concrete literary devices. On
the contrary, he blames Polevoi for his poor literary style: "At
least style is the weakest side of *The History of the Russian People.*"
Rather he sees "novelistic" elements in the very structure of the
narrative and in its selection of facts. In other words, Pushkin

is convinced that certain sources and their treatment are suitable for historical novels with their "novelistic vividness of truth," but history proper should not be turned into a novel; despite all the advantages of "novelistic" history one has to seek "another kind of history" (*drugaia istoriia*) as well.

Thus, Pushkin selected historical sources that could best satisfy his goal—the writing of a historical novel about Peter the Great's epoch. Although Paul Debreczeny suggested that "in pursuing these sources, Pushkin probably had a historical essay, rather than fiction, in mind," I believe that such sources as a family legend and historical anecdotes invite a novelistic structure of the narrative with a strong emphasis on the depiction of social conflicts and everyday reality revealed in manners, customs, and peculiarities of behavior.[8] Indeed, the genre of anecdote is traditionally viewed as an antecedent for the European novella whose literary development generated the novel. Anecdote is an ideal choice for a historical novel as it combines history and fiction and offers a popular interpretation of a historical event. For it is precisely a combination of history and fiction (*vymysel*) that "makes" a historical novel, according to Pushkin. In his article "Iurii Miloslavskii" he observes: "The events of the novel fit effortlessly into the very broad framework of historical events" (XI, 92). Thus, in a historical novel, fiction and historical fact merge in an integrated narrative. Historical anecdote is an ideal choice for this kind of fusion, for it satisfies two major features of historical novel: unity of history and fiction, and the characterization of a "historical epoch."

Note that Pushkin had an extremely analytical sensitivity toward anecdotes; in their treatment he was able to discern the historical content of an anecdote and differentiate it from a factual and purely fictional one. Thus, for example, in a letter to his wife of 11 October 1833, he writes: "Do you know what people say of me in neighbouring governments? Here is how they describe my occupations: When Pushkin writes poetry—a whole decanter of *glorious* liqueur stands in front of him—he downs three glasses one after another—and here he already starts writing!—This is glory" (XV, 87). What is important for Pushkin in this Kharms-like anecdote is not the fact and the event described (which is fictional), but the reasons why this anecdote was composed. The historicity of this anecdote lies not in what it says about Pushkin, but in what it says about people's attitude toward Pushkin and in the way it reflects the unique atmosphere of his time. The allusion to the "glorious liqueur" is people's only way to react to a historical fact—Pushkin's fame, or glory (*slava*). Moreover, the anecdote reveals a general attitude toward poets and artists as "idle revellers," to use Salieri's phrase (*guliaka prazdnyi*). Concrete details and names stated could be substituted by analogous facts, but the general meaning of the anecdote remains invariable.

In *The Blackamoor of Peter the Great* Pushkin relies fully on anecdote in order to portray a historical epoch. He approaches the store of anecdotes from the perspective of a historian, trying to detect historical kernels in fictional narrative. Yet he refictionalizes the historical kernel in his own fictional narrative, establishing himself not only as a historian, but as a writer as well. Thus, for example, Pushkin rewrites a historical anecdote, borrowed from Golikov, about Peter the Great arranging the marriage of his attendant Rumiantsev with Count Matveev's daughter. Real protagonists and their names are not historically significant in this episode. Historical meaning lies in the fact that Peter indeed *could have had arranged* this kind of marriage—an act that is fully congruous with the character of Peter's reforms: a creation of a new class distinguished not by the privilege of noble birth, but by personal merit. Pushkin reemplots and refictionalizes this episode in his novel, making Peter propose to the Rzhevskiis on Ibragim's behalf. To be sure, Peter's role in Ibragim's marriage is hardly factual—Peter did not take any part in arranging Gannibal's marriage with the boyar Rzhevskii's daughter, and the historical Gannibal married only after Peter's death, his spouse to be not a Russian boyar's daughter, but a girl of Greek origin, Evdokiia Dioper (the daughter of a sea captain). Yet the anecdote Pushkin uses in *The Blackamoor of Peter the Great* is sufficient proof for him that this marriage could have happened, or at least was thought to be a possibility by Peter's contemporaries. The chance of such a marriage is precisely what characterizes Peter's epoch. Thus, Pushkin preserves the "historical truth" contained in Golikov's anecdote, but consciously disregards "factual truth." Anecdote is indispensable in conveying the spirit of the time and in creating the internal probability corresponding to the external probability. Fiction, as opposed to history, plays with possibilities and is not restricted to historical fact.

The emphasis on anecdote reveals Pushkin's approach to the historical novel.[9] Anecdote helps to "divine" (*ugadyvat'*) not facts but the character, the spirit of a historical epoch and the probability of certain facts. Anecdote is a historical probability *per se.* Thus, Pushkin writes about Zagoskin: "Our good common folk, boyars, Cossacks, monks, riotous vagabonds—*all of them are divined,* all of them act and feel as *they must have acted* and felt during the troubled times of Minin and Avraam Palitsyn [emphasis added]" (XI, 92). Pushkin's contemporaries shared this principle of historical fiction. Viazemsky easily recognized the character of Pushkin's historical method in *The Blackamoor of Peter the Great:* "His meeting with his beloved Ibragim in Krasnoe Selo where, informed about his arrival, he waits for him *since yesterday,* perhaps and even likely is not true historically, but it is true psychologically, which is more important. It did not happen, but it could have happened; it corresponds to Peter's character, to his impatient and fervent nature, to the simplicity of his manners and his character (Viazemsky, II, 376). Pushkin believes in the historicity of the character, of customs, and of behavior. Interestingly, precisely in the moments when Pushkin does not strictly adhere to facts, he discloses his concept of history most clearly and reveals a "higher" historical truth as he perceives it. This is especially evident in his portrayal of his ancestor, Abram Gannibal.

The Blackamoor as an Emblem of Peter the Great's Epoch
One of the problems connected with the balance between the historical and the fictional in the novel is the choice of the main protagonist. Walter Scott had to confront the same problem and found a successful solution by introducing his famous "middle-of-the-road hero." Pushkin's Ibragim, however, is different from Scott's protagonists in that he is not an ordinary person. On the contrary, as a Blackamoor he is exotic by definition. Significantly, many critics considered Pushkin's portrayal of Ibragim a failure and the choice of this character not very successful. Thus, Nina Petrunina, a Russian scholar of Pushkin, observes: "Ibragim may feel the impact of the contradictory Russian social structure of the last years of Peter's reign, but he himself developed outside this structure and does not bear in himself—in his views and psychology, in his feelings and life's principles—the consequences of this structure. This is why the inner world of the hero does not help to understand the essence of historical processes and secrets of the 'domestic' life of Petrine Russia" (62). I believe, however, that Petrunina misunderstood Pushkin's purpose and the very genre of the work. *The Blackamoor of Peter the Great* is not a psychological novel, which focuses on the "inner world" of the hero. Like Scott, who is not interested in the inner life of Waverley, Pushkin is not concerned with Ibragim's psychology and his inner world. His goal is to portray the mannerisms and styles of behavior of a specific epoch, rather than the emotional and behavioral characteristics of individual personages. The epoch is reflected not through the psychology of a personage, but rather through his career. Ibragim affords the reader an insight into the domestic life of Peter's age by the very fact of his existence.

Indeed, in order to depict the domestic life of Peter the Great's epoch, the Blackamoor was an ideal choice. As Lotman points out in his article "The Poetics of Everyday Behavior in Russian Eighteenth-Century Culture," "the documents which record the norms of everyday, ordinary behavior for a particular social group as a rule originate with foreigners or are written for them. Such documents take for granted an observer who is located outside the given social group" (Lotman, 231). Pushkin's ancestor was exactly this kind of an outsider. Pushkin introduces Russia through the eyes of a Moor—an intimate of Peter who received his education in France, who lived in Europe for a long time and had only a vague awareness of his African roots, who definitely would have been accepted as a "double" foreigner anywhere in the half-barbarian Russia that he had chosen as his new "homeland." This approach allowed Pushkin a necessary distance needed to observe the ordinary, everyday reality. Yet although Ibragim is an outsider, he eventually becomes an insider; therefore, he is not as alien to the Russian reader as any other foreigner and is not perceived as a stranger by the reader who knows about Ibragim's personal bond both with Peter and with Pushkin. Previously, in *Boris Godunov*, Pushkin had used the same device of introducing his own relative in a fictional narrative. In both cases this device served to stress the continuity of a historical process and to add a personal touch to the narratives. The role of Ibragim, however, is different from that of Gavrila Pushkin in *Boris Godunov*. While the function of Gavrila Pushkin is relatively marginal and limited to his interior position in relation to the society described, Pushkin conferred a central role upon Ibragim and made him both a judge and an interpreter of Russian history, and an emblem of the historical epoch portrayed.

Ibragim's role as both an outsider and insider is further emphasized by his ambivalent position in the narrative: he is both a participant in the historical process and a historian of the same historical process; he is both inside the past and outside the same past. Occasionally, Ibragim seems to know what his narrator knows. Thus, while describing Ibragim's first impressions of Petersburg, the narrator states: "Ibragim looked with curiosity at the newborn capital that had risen from the swamp at the bidding of autocracy. [. . .] There was nothing splendid in the whole city except for the Neva, not yet adorned by a granite frame but already covered with warships and merchant ships" (VIII: I, 10). Such perception could not be that of Ibragim as a participant of the events described—from the point of view of an insider the knowledge about the Neva's "granite frame" is the knowledge of the future. Thus, assuming the role of an outsider, or a historian, Ibragim is able to view Russia in the period of Peter's reforms from the point of view of the narrator's present and to perceive as the past that which he, being inside of the same historical process, would have supposed to perceive as future. This allows Pushkin to unite the perspective of a historian-outsider with the perspective of a participant-insider both on the level of the narrative strategy and subject matter.

Incorporating both perspectives, being both foreign and Russian, Ibragim emerges as the very image of the epoch—as an emblem of the syncretism of Russian culture during the reign of Peter the Great. Ibragim is emblematic of the intersecting of boundaries of race, social status, citizenship, conventions, traditions—all social institutions Peter was trying to reshape. Thus, the very choice of the character—whose personal merits, education, and devotion are opposed to tradition, race, and social origins—is already a historically accurate characterization of the epoch. The character here represents a historical milieu and becomes translucent to allow the historical process to penetrate through him. The reader, therefore, cannot probe the inner world of Ibragim, who speaks infrequently in the novel. Unlike Grinev from *The Captain's Daughter,* who undergoes certain development in the course of the novel, Ibragim does not change in any significant way and enters the novel as an already mature character. Rather than portraying an inwardly complex and growing human being, Pushkin introduces a protagonist whose very career is a commentary on historical process.[10] Ibragim serves not only a plot-constructing function, facilitating the depiction of the historical epoch and the characters, but he embodies important historical processes that were taking shape during this period. Thus, for example, Pushkin makes Ibragim marry a boyar's daughter, Nataliia Rzhevskaia. In this episode Pushkin reveals his historical concept most clearly, for this marriage prefigures changes in the class hierarchy of Russian society and a compromise that was to be achieved between the old Russian nobility and a new class of Peter's supporters.

Pushkin perceived the reign of Peter and his historical mission as a mediation between Russia and Europe, between the old and the new. In a sense, Gannibal with his African origin and European education could be viewed as a symbol of Petrine Russia with its "dark" and unknown past and forced europeanization. In the novel, Ibragim's mission, as viewed by Peter himself, is precisely to attain this union between Russia and the West, between old Russian boyars and a new generation of europeanized reformers. The idea of mediation between Russia and the West was very dear to Pushkin. Moreover, mediation in general is a central concern of Pushkin's philosophy and of his works. Pushkin rarely uses merely binary oppositions in his fictions; his vision is not dualistic, but trinitarian. In his own life too, Pushkin wanted to mediate between his friends, the Decembrists, and the regime. Pushkin's ideal characters, therefore, are always able to mediate between the two opposite realms of reality and to establish a new order. Such is Tatiana in *Eugene Onegin* who succeeds in mediating between country and city, or Nature and Culture, and creates a universe of her own.[11] Likewise, in *The Captain's Daughter,* Grinev mediates between the rebellious Pugachev and the official Russia.

In contrast, Pushkin's more negative characters fail to mediate between opposite forces (cf. Eugene from *The Bronze Horseman;* Hermann from *The Queen of Spades;* Aleko from *The Gypsies*). Aleko's problem is that, unlike Tatiana, he is unable to reconcile Nature with Culture. Rather than mediating between the two spheres of life and introducing a degree of civilization in nature (or vice versa), Aleko believes he could become a man of nature. As a result, he violates the conventions of both realms of reality.

This is why there is a personal touch in Pushkin's choice of the main protagonist of *The Blackamoor of Peter the Great:* in a sense Ibragim is Pushkin's spiritual relative. The reader was surely expected to know that the true child of this cultural mediation was Pushkin himself.

The composition of the entire novel is founded on this central idea of mediation embodied in the character of Ibragim. To make this idea more prominent, Pushkin intensifies the contrasts upon which the novel is built. The poetics of contrast help him to establish the main spheres of social and political life that had to be mediated in order to achieve a new social order in Russia.[12]

The Poetics of Contrasts: French and Russian Chronotopes

The novel opens with an account of Ibragim's sojourn in Paris where he had been sent by Peter with a group of young men "for the acquisition of knowledge essential to a country in the process of reorganization" (VIII: I, 3). Ibragim does not hasten to return to the half-civilized country of his godfather; he enjoys the whirl of the French social life and, most of all, an affair he is having with the Countess D., who becomes pregnant and gives birth to a black child.

Pushkin needs this exposition to set the initial contrast between Russia and France and to provide backbone to the plot, which, according to his project in 1827, had to be strictly symmetrical: Ibragim's future Russian wife, Nataliia Rzhevskaia, was to bear him a white child and to be sent for that to a monastery. The two stories were clearly reversed to produce an effect of irony and humor. In Paris, Ibragim had a successful liaison with a married woman, but his marriage with any member of the gentry probably would not have been approved of by society. In France, Ibragim merely aroused the curiosity of the ladies who "wanted to see *le Nègre du czar* at their houses" and treated him as an exotic man good for relieving the monotony of life: "As a rule, people looked at the young black man as a wonder, they showered him with salutations and questions; and their curiosity, though disguised as courtesy, offended his pride. [. . .] He felt that in their eyes he was a kind of rare animal, a peculiar and alien creature who had been accidentally transported into a world that had nothing in common with him" (VIII: I, 4–5).

But in Russia, Ibragim managed to charm the most conservative part of Russian nobility, even though he was doomed to fail as a lover: "During your illness the Moor succeeded in casting a spell over everybody. The master is out of his mind about him, the Prince raves about no one else, and Tatiana Afanas'evna says: 'It's a pity he is a Moor, but it would be a sin to wish for a better suitor' " (VIII: I, 32). To enhance the contrast between Ibragim's Parisian lifestyle and his Petersburg career Pushkin even changes his narrative style when he switches from the portrayal of France to Russia. From "French" prose with its light and ironic tone, focusing on romantic relationships, Pushkin turns to "Russian" prose and Russian history and looks for a new "formula" to depict it. From the realm of love he carries the reader to the realm of *history*.

The description of France helps to put the situation in Russia into historical perspective and to establish Russian national identity. The search for national identity is a common discourse in European Romanticism. However, the peculiar characteristic of Russian endeavor at discovering its national self-consciousness is that Russian identity is always contrasted to, and defined against, a European one. Russia is able to recognize itself only vis-à-vis Europe with various degrees of attraction or alienation.

Indeed, in *The Blackamoor of Peter the Great* Pushkin contrasts France to Russia on different levels of generalization: luxury / modesty; leisure / work; lightmindedness / seriousness; decline / rise; old / new; dissipation / moderation; pleasure / duty; consumerism / economy; disappearance / appearance (emergence); laughter / seriousness; falling apart / forming; homogeneity / diversity; glamour / simplicity; superficiality / sincerity, etc. Pushkin gives an incisive account of the state of French society:

According to the evidence of all historical records, nothing could compare with the frivolity, folly, and luxury of
the French at that time. [. . .] The orgies at the Palais
Royal were no secret to Paris, and the example was con-
tagious. [. . .] greed for money was united to a thirst
for enjoyment and dissipation; estates vanished; morals
degenerated; the French laughed and calculated, and the
state was falling to pieces to the playful tunes of satirical
vaudevilles. [. . .] Superficial courtesy took the place of
profound respect. [. . .] But the thought of exchanging
this dissipation, these splendid amusements for the aus-
tere simplicity of the Petersburg Court was not the only
thing that terrified Ibragim (VIII: 1, 10).

One of the most revealing contrasts between Russia and France
consists in a different treatment of space, different concepts of
space associated with Russia and France. The social space of
France is depicted as homogeneous, yet a kind of a negative homogeneity—in Paris, cultural and social diversities are leveled by
fashion: "Education and the longing for amusement drew together
all the different estates. Wealth, courtesy, fame, talent, even ec-
centricity—everything that provided food for curiosity or gave
promise of enjoyment was received with equal indulgence. Literature, scholarship and philosophy abandoned their quiet study
rooms and appeared in the circles of the haut monde, to please
fashion while at the same time governing its opinions" (VIII: I,
3–4). This society has a clearly defined center—"the circle of the
haut monde" (*krug bol'shogo sveta*). Space shrinks; spatial diversities are nullified—even scholars "abandoned the quiet of their
studies"—to reduce social space to its center—the salon. With his
unique economy of description, Pushkin provides a set of spatial and temporal characteristics of French society which I call a
chronotope of the salon. In France, all events, meetings, and conversations occur in salons (*videt' u sebia; veselye vechera; uzhiny; baly;*

prazdniki). Pushkin sensed that the *salon* embodied the "formula" of French history of this time, as it was fully revealed in the works of Balzac and Stendhal. Hence, Pushkin claims the *historicity* of his account, referring to "the evidence of all historical records."

Russian space is not homogeneous and lacks any clearly definable center. The events and conversations that take part in Russia occur in various places and settings: in the inn, in the palace, at the boyars' residence, on the embankment of the Neva, in the bedroom of Natasha, etc. Russian space is not yet defined and stabilized. A new way of life in Russia and its new history is represented in the process of taking on shape. A new "space" of Russian history is only being created. Still in the process of being built, Petersburg, therefore, embodies the state of Russian history of this time: "Ibragim looked with curiosity at the newly-born capital that was rising out of the marshes at the bidding of autocracy. Open dikes, canals without embankments, wooden bridges testified everywhere to the recent victory of human will over the resistance of the elements. The houses seemed to have been built in a hurry. There was nothing splendid in the whole city except for the Neva, not yet adorned by a granite frame but already covered with war- and merchant-ships" (VIII: I, 10). This description reproduces a picture of chaos that is only beginning to be ordered. A new Russia is still unshaped and is being born from nowhere. If in *The Bronze Horseman* Petersburg emerges as a center of the world with the monument to Peter the Great as its axis, in *The Blackamoor of Peter the Great* the center is absent: even on the new territory of Petersburg the boyars' residences and Peter's palace are still competing for predominance. Petersburg represents an amorphous space with no clear sense of boundaries. Thus, all potential borderlines are defined in negative terms: *obnazhennye plotiny; kanaly bez naberezhnoi; Nevy, ne ukrashennoi eshche granitnoiu ramoiu* (Cf. the emphasis on boundaries in *The Bronze Horseman: V granit odelasia Neva; Tvoikh ograd uzor chugunnyi*). Evidently, the negative presupposes the positive.[13] Thus, one could say, that in

The Blackamoor of Peter the Great, Pushkin describes Petersburg not only in terms of what it was, but in terms of what it is going to become. This is a glance into the past from the point of view of the future. The description of Petersburg in terms of its future potential has an obvious implication: Petersburg is a space of the future; Russian space and history are open to the future.

By contrast, the narrator depicts France not in terms of its future potential, but in terms of its forfeited past: "The last years of Louis XIV's reign, which had been characterized by the strict piety of the court, by pomposity and propriety, left no trace" (VIII: I, 3). Hence, the predominance of the terms implying destruction in Pushkin's portrayal of France: *ischezat', gibla, rasseiannost', raspadalas'.* While France is falling apart, Russia is being built. Pushkin introduces numerous details that place in relief the idea of construction: Peter works in the *turnery*—even when occupied "with affairs of the state" (VIII: I, 11); in the dockyard; on the "mast of a new ship." Ibragim too "considered it his duty to work hard at his own machine-tool." Moreover, the entire Russia appears to Ibragim as a "huge workshop": "Russia appeared to Ibragim as one huge workshop, where only machines moved and where each workman, subject to an established order, was occupied with his own job" (VIII: I, 13). Thus to the French *chronotope of the salon,* emblematic of France's decline and stagnation, Pushkin juxtaposes a Russian *chronotope of the workshop*—the place where Russian history is being forged.

It is not surprising, then, that it is in France—in the amorous space of salon—that Ibragim has a successful affair with a woman. In Russia not only his actions but even his thoughts are much more stern: " 'To marry!' thought the African. 'Why not? [. . .] The Tsar is right: I must secure my future. Marriage with the young Rzhevskaia will unite me to the proud Russian nobility, and I shall no longer be a stranger in my new fatherland. I will not demand love from my wife, but will be content with her fidelity' " (VIII: I, 27). A political union, facilitating Ibragim's participation in Rus-

sian history, takes on the place of the romance, and gives way to
Pushkin's writing of the historical novel.

Historicity of Speech, Manners, and Customs

The poetics of contrasts in *The Blackamoor of Peter the Great* are
subtle and not limited to the opposition of Russia and the West.
Pushkin creates a whole set of contrasts: the contrast between
Ibragim and Russian nobility, between Korsakov and Ibragim,
between Korsakov and the boyars, between Ibragim and French
society, etc. By using multiple contrasts, Pushkin demonstrates
the complex social situation of the time, the epoch when different
attitudes and different modes of behavior confronted one another,
clashed and produced various levels of mediation. The poetics of
contrasts allowed Pushkin to concentrate on everyday behavior, on
specific details of Russian *byt*, norms, and rituals of Russian life
manifested in the likes of speech, mannerisms, costumes, and traditions.

The central opposition between the foreign and the native helps
to analyze speech peculiarities characteristic of this historical period. Pushkin demonstrates the ways in which historical process
is mediated through language. According to Lotman, the descriptions of everyday speech "are nearly always oriented towards an
outside observer. [. . .] Both everyday behavior and one's own
language are semiotic systems which are perceived by their immediate bearers as 'natural,' as belonging to Nature rather than
to Culture. Their semiotic and conventional character is apparent
only to an outside observer" (1984, 231–32). In order to represent the linguistic changes occurring during the reign of Peter the
Great and which were accelerated by his reforms, Pushkin had to
introduce two poles of linguistic orientation, that is, conservative
Russian nobility who were able to observe (and to criticize) the foreign lexis in Russian speech, and Russian "foreigners" — a group
of Westernized young men educated abroad — who perceived the
boyars' conversation and their way of speaking merely as a "gibber-

ish" (*bredni*). The confrontation between the foreign and the native exposes the existence of diverse styles of behavior and speech.

Indeed, Pushkin is a master of employing different layers of lexis of language and colorfully depicts various styles of speech. The boyars' speech is clearly contrasted to that of Korsakov, and also to Ibragim and Peter. Korsakov, Ibragim's Parisian friend, speaks either French or inserts French words in his talk. His conversational style is chatty and "westernized." This is how the narrator introduces Korsakov in the novel: "He [Ibragim] was sitting in his study one morning, surrounded by business papers, when he suddenly heard a loud greeting in French" (VIII: I, 14). Throughout the novel Korsakov keeps speaking French: " '*Entre nous*', he said to Ibragim, 'the Emperor is a very strange man' " (VIII: I, 14); " '*Que diable est-ce que tout celà?*' — Korsakov asked Ibragim under his breath" (VIII: I, 16); "If I were you, *j'aurais planté là* the old prattler and all his kin" (VIII: I, 30).

To be sure, Korsakov's "foreign" talk is exactly what excites the indignation of Russian noblemen: "He is not the first, nor will he be the last, to come back a clown from those German lands to holy Russia. What do our children learn there? To shuffle their feet, to talk in God knows what tongue, to disrespect their elders, and to dangle after other men's wives" (VIII: I, 22). In order to ridicule a new, or "foreign," way of speaking, therefore, a boyar's fool, Ekimovna, uses all foreign words when she parodies Korsakov: "Ekimovna the fool seized the lid of a dish, put it under her arm as if holding a hat, and began making grimaces, shuffling and bowing to all sides, while saying again and again: '*monsieur . . . mamselle . . . assemblée . . . pardon.*' " (VIII: I, 22). In Ekimovna's buffoonery, encouraged by Prince Lykov, the clash of the two antagonistic styles of speech is fully disclosed:

—Здравствуй, Екимовна, —сказал князь Лыков, — как*ово* поживаешь?
—Подобру-поздорову, кум: по*ючи* да пляш*учи*, женишков поджида*ючи*.

—Где ты была, дура? —спросил хозяин.

—Наряжалась, кум, для дорогих гостей, для Божия праздника, *по царскому наказу, боярскому приказу, на смех всему миру,* по немецкому *маниру* [emphasis added] (VIII: I, 20).

"Good day, Ekimovna," said Prince Lykov. "How are you doing?"

"Quite well, my good friend: singing and dancing, awaiting bridegrooms."

"Where have you been, fool?" asked the host.

"I was dressing up, my good friend, for your dear guests, for the holy day, by the Tsar's command, by the boyars' demand, to make the whole world laugh, in a German manner."

Ekimovna achieves a comical effect by combining an old way of speaking—which Pushkin reproduces by employing a language belonging to common parlance (cf. colloquial forms of gerunds ending with *-ючи* and the form *каково* instead of *как*)—with a consciously ridiculous neologism formed from a foreign word, *манир*. She starts with a traditional folk formula—*по царскому наказу, по боярскому приказу*—but ends the traditional formula with an allusion to new, "foreign" manners and norms of behavior introduced by Peter.[14]

Tatiana Afanas'evna too, while attacking modern fashions and customs, consciously avoids using foreign words: "Just look at today's beauties—you have to laugh and weep at once: their hair is all fluffed up like tow, greased and covered with French flour" (VIII: I, 20–21). Thus, she uses the Russian term *nasaleny* instead of a more foreign *napomazheny; mukoiu* instead of *pudroiu*. All the boyars employ many terms and locutions that could already sound archaic to the nineteenth-century reader: *kolymaga; zhal' sarafana, devich'ei lenty i povoinika; ispodnitsy; kutaf'ia; baldykhan.* To create a linguistic distance between Russian nobility of the eighteenth-century and nineteenth-century aristocrats, Pushkin makes the boyars speak a more colloquial language full of folklore elements (*Skazal by slovechko, da volk nedalechko; Kak nam znat', batiushka-bratets; Ali predlozhil byt' v posol'stve?*) (VIII: I, 21, 24).

The two polar styles of speech—old Russian and a modern "westernized" one—struggle with one another and are defined in relation to each other through their mutual estrangement. Against this linguistic background it is significant that Peter's language sounds very modern and almost identical with that of Pushkin's contemporaries. Peter addresses Ibragim and the boyars in a very informal way: " 'Hey! Ibragim?' he shouted, getting up from the bench. 'Welcome, godson.' " (VIII: I, 10); " 'I notice, brother, that you are in low spirits. Tell me frankly, is there anything you want?' " (VIII: I, 27) Peter's somewhat colorless language induced some critics to perceive Peter's speech as Pushkin's artistic failure. Thus, Victor Vinogradov in his analysis of the linguistic peculiarities of *The Blackamoor of Peter the Great* concludes: "The principle of individualization and social characterization of the speech of some personages is widely used in *The Blackamoor of Peter the Great*. This principle, however, has little relevance to Peter's speech and no application at all to the speech of Ibragim. Peter's speech does not correspond to his documented historical style" (Vinogradov, 588). Vinogradov seems to be unaware that by employing different linguistic characterization of his personages, Pushkin's purpose is not to "correlate" their speech with "documented historical style," but rather to use diverse literary styles in order to reproduce a historical epoch as he understood it. I suggest that, even though Peter's speech does not exactly correspond to his style as it was documented in historical sources, it does reveal Pushkin's historical concept of Peter the Great as a reformer modernizing the patriarchal Russia. This is why Peter's is a simplified modernized Russian language; Pushkin consciously wanted to reduce a gap between Peter and the contemporary reader in order to show that Peter is a progenitor of a new order and a new tradition.

Peter's language is abrupt, colloquial and simple in vocabulary: "You are becoming prettier day by day" or "Well, I have disturbed you. You were eating your dinner; please sit down again, and so as for me, Gavrila Afanas'evich, would you offer me some aniseed vodka'" (VIII: I, 23). (The simplicity of speech is a historical trait of Peter). His conversation consists almost exclusively of verbs—a peculiar characteristic that conveys the idea of action and of moving forward. Thus, it is through his speech that Pushkin portrays Peter as a man of action, as an emblem of a modern man who started a new era in Russian history and even in Russian literary language. Although Peter has a good command of foreign languages (Pushkin does not miss the opportunity to demonstrate that Peter spoke German: "The emperor spoke in German with a captive Swede about the campaign of 1701") (VIII: I, 23), when he speaks Russian he does not introduce foreign words into his speech as Korsakov does. Neither is Peter a master of the rich language of the boyars—one saturated with folklore elements. He avoids both Russian archaisms and foreign terms and even seems to ridicule Korsakov for his excessive use of the French language: "'Aha! said Peter, seeing Korsakov, 'You've been caught, brother! Now drink, if you please, *monsieur* [*mos'e*], and do not make faces" (VIII: I, 17). Clearly, Peter employs the word *mos'e* here as a derogatory term. In his attacks on Korsakov's francophilia he echoes Ekimovna—a detail implying that Pushkin wanted to portray Peter as a moderate westernizer. This idea is further stressed by Peter's predilection for some Russian customs (cf. "After dinner the Emperor, in keeping with Russian custom, retired to rest") (VIII: I, 11).

If Peter's language is different from that of both Korsakov and the boyars, Ibragim manages to mediate between the two styles of speech. Although Ibragim is fluent in French, he—like Peter—does not use any single French word in his speech. Significantly, Ibragim speaks a correct and simple Russian language, occasionally even flavored with Russian proverbs: "Do you know the proverb: it's not your duty to rock other people's babies" (*Znaesh' poslovitsu: ne tvoia pechal' chuzhikh detei kachat'*) (VIII: I, 30). Some critics criticized Pushkin for making Ibragim, who grew up abroad, use Russian proverbs. For Pushkin, however, it was important to demonstrate Ibragim's integration into Russian society and to portray him as a real mediator between the West and old Russia. It is by employing proverbs that Ibragim symbolically enters the alliance with the nobleman Rzhevskii.

In addition to speech peculiarities, the contrast between Russia and the West helps Pushkin to characterize the *modes of behavior* typical of the age. As Lotman observes, in the time of Peter the Great a "way of speech, deportment and clothes unfailingly indicated what place any person occupied in the stylistic polyphony of everyday life" (1984, 236). In *The Blackamoor of Peter the Great* history penetrates all levels of human existence. Old Russian customs are portrayed through the eyes of a "Russian foreigner" Korsakov, whereas Western attitudes and fashions are depicted primarily from the point of view of Russian nobility.

Pushkin contrasts the boyars' tenor of life to the Western style of Korsakov in the scene of a dinner party at Rzhevskii's. The narrator characterizes Rzhevskii as an "hereditary Russian nobleman" (*korennoi russkii barin*), who "could not endure the German spirit and strove to preserve in his household the customs of olden times that were dear to him" (VIII: I, 19). Pushkin depicts a family holiday governed by old Russian rituals and strict hierarchy: "They sat—men on the one side, women on the other—according to the rank of their family, thereby evoking the happy old days of *mestnichestvo*" (VIII: I, 20). The main target of the boyars' attacks on Peter's reforms are, of course, new Western trends transplanted to Russia by Peter.[15] Korsakov embodies all that looked strange to Russian noblemen and that was associated with the West: speech, clothes, manners, disregard for old Russian rituals and their sense of hierarchy, frivolous attitude towards women. Therefore, Rzhevskii nicknamed Korsakov a "French monkey": "but the dodginess and dandyish appearance of this young fop did not please the proud boyar, who gave him as a result the witty nickname of French monkey" (VIII: I, 19). Rzhevskii dislikes not only Korsakov's clothes, but his "dexterity" that manifests itself in his manners.

Curiously, in Pushkin's account of Peter the Great's epoch and his characterization of the old Russian and new European manners, even movements and a way of walking become historical traits. Thus, an epigraph for the chapter depicting the dinner at Rzhevskii's—four lines from Pushkin's own poem *Ruslan and Liudmila*—is quite revealing:

> Не скоро ели предки наши,
> Не скоро двигались кругом
> Ковши, серебряные чаши
> С кипящим пивом и вином (VIII: I, 19).

> Our forefathers did not eat fast.
> Jars and silver chalices
> With foaming ale and wine
> Did not go round fast.

Ne skoro is a pace of old Russia and of the boyars. Westernized Russians, by contrast, move in a very different tempo. This is why Korsakov's speed and his way of walking are criticized by the boyars: "The next day I suddenly see somebody driving straight into my courtyard. Who on earth could this be, I thought. Isn't it perhaps Prince Aleksandr Danilovich? Nothing of the sort: it was Ivan Evgrafovich! Could not he have stopped at the gate and troubled himself to come up to the porch on foot? No way! He just flew in! He bowed and scraped, spitting out the words!" (VIII: I, 22) Indeed, Korsakov never walks slowly, but always runs or dashes, so that a rapid pace becomes one of his main characteristics and, by extension, one of the main attributes of the West-oriented supporters of Peter. The narrator consistently contrasts Korsakov's speedy pace with the "lofty immobility" (*velichavaia nepodvizhnost'*) of

Rzhevskii's steward and with the dignified manners of the boyars: " 'I've only just arrived,' said Korsakov, 'and ran directly to see you"; "he spun around on one heel [*povernulsia na odnoi nozhke*] and ran out of the room"; "he began dressing hastily"; "the Emperor [. . .] did not notice Korsakov, as much as he hovered [*vertelsia*] around them"; "Korsakov rushed up [*razletelsia*] to her and asked her to do him the honor of dancing with him"; "Korsakov [. . .] ran out into the entrance hall, giving his host no chance to see him off" (VIII: I, 14, 15, 17, 31).

Korsakov's bustling is emblematic of the extremes and hastiness of some of Peter's reforms. Korsakov functions as a representative of a new type of man generated by Peter's westernizing politics. The reader, however, is not expected to sympathize with him, as Pushkin describes him rather negatively not only through the eyes of the boyars, but also through the condescending remarks of Peter (" 'Listen, Korsakov,' Peter said to him, 'the pants you're wearing are made of velvet, of a kind even I don't wear, though I am much richer than you. This is extravagance; watch out that I don't quarrel with you' ") or the narrator (for example, the narrator repeatedly uses the deprecating diminutives in his portrayal: "They quickly powdered his wig in the anteroom and then brought it in. Korsakov thrust his close-cropped small head [*golovku*] into it"; "he spun around on one heel [*na odnoi nozhke*]") (VIII: I, 17–18, 15, 15). Korsakov is a real parody of "westernizers" who too quickly adopted a new identity. Paradoxically, Peter's reforms encouraged both a xenophilia and a xenophobia. Significantly, one of the epigraphs Pushkin selected for the novel is from the mock poem of Ivan Dmitriev's "The Diary of a Traveler" ("Zhurnal puteshestvennika"). In this poem, Dmitriev ridicules the gallomania of Vasilii Pushkin: "I am in Paris; I have begun to live, not just breathe." [16] A relatively prominent role of Korsakov in these chapters is to comment on the activity of Peter the Great himself: Peter may be a fascinating figure having some higher goals and striving for the well-being of Russia, yet his reforms unleashed forces in society which Pushkin expects the reader to deplore—the appearance of Westernized lightweights, of new aristocrats that broke completely with all tradition, denied Russian past, and, therefore, were "foreigners" in their own native land.

If Korsakov seems "foreign" to the boyars and his behavior violates their conventions (Rzhevskii's daughter, for example, does not know how to behave in his presence: "The young beauty looked at him with embarrassment, not knowing, it seemed, what to say to him"), so does Peter's Russia seem strange and "barbarian" ("this barbarian Petersburg") to Korsakov (VIII: I, 17). Predictably, he does not know how to behave in Russian society: "But I am a total stranger in Petersburg: during my six-year absence I have completely forgotten the local customs. Please be my mentor, come to pick me up and introduce me" (VIII: I, 15). His expectations of social life are immediately frustrated. Korsakov's impressions of his first encounter with the Tsar are particularly revealing, since Korsakov mentions those details of Russian life that could have been noticed only by an outsider and which represent, therefore, the most characteristic traits of the epoch (cf. the formalists' principle of alienation): " '*Entre nous,*' he said to Ibragim, 'the Emperor is a very strange man: just imagine, I found him wearing some sort of sack-cloth shirt on the mast of a new ship, where I had to clamber with my dispatches. Standing on a rope ladder, I did not have enough room to make a proper curtsey and became all confused, which had never happened to me before' " (VIII: I, 14–5). Korsakov, who is used to a "French space," has to confront a very different reality and finds himself literally out of place (*ne imel dovol'no mesta*): instead of a salon he has to enter a new Russian space—"the mast of a new ship" and "a rope ladder." Russian history enters the novel through a new type of Russian space, emblematized by a "workshop," "dockyard" or a "rope ladder"—an adventurous, but shaky promise for the future.

For Korsakov, who looks at Russia from outside and from the distance, everything is strange in this country: time, space, clothing, modes of behavior. Violating traditional conventions, however, was, in fact, a trait characteristic of Peter's age that was marked by the Emperor's disregard of social positions and his attempt to reshape social institutions across the board. Korsakov, therefore, is able to notice the most characteristic details of Peter's time, because they are different from the norm he is familiar with. In Russia he finds himself not only out of space, but also out of time. Used to a different daily routine, he is almost late for Peter's Assembly and is surprised that it has started so early: "Korsakov was sitting in his dressing gown, reading a French book. 'So early?' he said seeing Ibragim. 'For goodness' sake!' the latter responded; 'it's already half past five. We'll be late; get dressed quickly and let's go' " (VIII: 1, 15).

Korsakov is so accustomed to French norms of behavior and the French chronotope, that he fails to read Russian rituals and anticipate correct reactions. His failure to integrate into Russian society reaches its peak in the scene depicting Peter's Assembly where Korsakov is forced to drink a "Goblet of the Great Eagle" as a punishment for violating the rules established by Peter. (Assemblies at Winter Palace represented a new institution introduced by Peter who required strict attendance of these scheduled gatherings from his retinue.) Significantly, the chapter that describes Peter's Assembly was published separately in *Literaturnaia gazeta* in 1830, #3, with a title "Assambleia pri Petre I-om." For the Assembly represents the whole of Peter's epoch in miniature.

To stress the fact that Petrine Russia is a unique phenomenon different from both Europe and traditional Russia, Pushkin introduces narratorial remarks that express Korsakov's astonishment: "Korsakov was dumbfounded"; "Korsakov could not come back to his senses"; "he was struck by an unexpected sight"; "Korsakov stared at this intriguing sport with his eyes widely opened and bit his lips" (VIII: I, 16–17). Indeed, everything appears unexpected to Korsakov, for everything looks like Europe, yet is very different. Pushkin paints a tableau of Russian life consisting of a

set of incongruities. The palace hall is full of "the clouds of to-
bacco smoke"; Eastern rituals and "the most melancholy music"
take place in the ballroom and are combined here with Western
dances; instead of the court or chamber music one hears "the
uninterrupted sound of the music of wind instruments"; the luxury of new European fashions (the young ladies "glittered with
all the splendor of fashion. Their dresses were brilliant with silver and gold; from luxuriant farthingales their slim waists rose
like flower-stems; diamonds sparkled in their ears, in their long
curls and around their necks") mingles with "dimity skirts and
red jackets" of "the wives and daughters of the Dutch skippers"
who are "knitting their stockings." The guests form an eminently
eclectic society: "magnates with blue ribbons across their shoul-
ders, ambassadors, foreign merchants, officers of the Guards in
their green uniforms, shipmasters in jackets and striped trousers."
The eclecticism of the age of Peter the Great is encapsulated in
the dressing style of old ladies: "The elderly ladies strove to slyly
coalesce the new mode of dress and the old styles frowned upon:
their head-dresses were very like the Tsaritsa Natalia Kirilovna's
sable hat, and their gowns and mantles resembled somehow sara-
fans and wadded jackets" (VIII: I, 16).

Indeed, Pushkin shows the eclecticism to be the main trait of
the Petrine Russia that emerges as an amazing admixture of different social classes, nationalities, old traditions and new fashions. To
the style of French society Pushkin juxtaposes an anti-style of Russian life and an unshaped nature of Russian history. Eclecticism
appears a fundamental principle of not only the reign of Peter the
Great, but of Russian history in general. To be sure, eclecticism is
not merely a Petersburg phenomenon. In his *Journey from Moscow
to Petersburg*, Pushkin describes Moscow in similar terms:

> The most innocent quirks of the Muscovites were signs of
> their independence. They lived as they would, entertained
> themselves as they would, and cared little for the opinions

of neighbors. It would happen that a rich oddball would, on one of the main thoroughfares, build himself a Chinese house with green dragons and wooden mandarins beneath golden umbrellas. Another would drive out to Maria's Grove in a carriage of the best hammered silver. A third would put on the running board of his four-person sleigh five Arabs, valets and footmen and in tandem was dragged along the pavement on a summery day. The fashionable belles, borrowing Petersburg fashions, would put their indelible mark on the clothes as well (XI, 246).

In fact, an attempt to "slyly coalesce" (*khitro sochetat'*) Eastern and Western customs or a new way of life with the "banished style of the past" (be it in fashions or in architectural fancies) was not Peter's innovation, but rather the continuation of an old Russia tradition and the very spirit of Russian character.[17] Russian history is bound to be eclectic: first, an oriental eclecticism of Moscow; then a European eclecticism of Petersburg. In Russia an anti-style of eclecticism becomes Russia's natural style and a "formula" of Russian history. Western customs on Russian soil are different, and, in fact, coexist with ancient practices. This is why a Parisian Korsakov perceives Peter's Assembly merely as a styleless and disordered crowd and is unable "to take part in the general gaiety," whereas a Blackamoor Ibragim fits very well into this heterogeneous and variegated society.

Indeed, if the boyars and Korsakov represent two social poles of the Petrine Russia, Ibragim embodies its very idea; in other words he "slyly coalesces" Russia and the West. Ibragim is identified neither with a caricature of "westernizer" Korsakov, nor with humorously portrayed "slavophiles"—Russian noblemen. Just as he manages to mediate between the two styles of speech, he succeeds in mediating between the two antagonistic modes of behavior: he is clothed in European dresses, but does not wear a wig; he is not particularly slow in his movements, but is not as fast as Korsakov either—rather he is "sedate" (*stepennyi*); European by education, he is African by blood; he participates in Peter's reforms and his new customs, yet he does not outrage the boyars' sense of propriety. Ibragim successfully communicates both with the reformers and the conservatives, and even earns the favor of Russian nobility: "'Of all the young people educated abroad (God forgive me), the Tsar's Blackamoor is the one that most resembles a man.'— Yes, indeed,' remarked Gavrila Afanas'evich, 'he is a solid and respectable man; you can't compare him with that weathercock.'" (VIII: I, 22). Significantly, the "weathercock" (*vetrogon*) Korsakov seems more alien to Russian noblemen than a Blackamoor Ibragim. The understanding of the social code wins over the prejudices of race. Now we can understand how important it was for Pushkin to make Ibragim a main hero. For Ibragim's fate discloses the main trend of the epoch: the priority of behavioral code over social position or blood ties.

As a mediator between old Russia and Europe Ibragim embodies the ideal to which Pushkin's Peter the Great strove. In this sense, Ibragim represents Peter's idea more than does Peter himself. Pushkin depicts a peculiar situation in which the monarch is alien to practically everyone around him. Both the Russian nobility and Korsakov look upon him with reservation, since he violates both norms of behavior. In a polyphony of various behavioral styles, Peter remains highly unconventional and beyond all codes. For Peter is not a mediator, but the one who orchestrates mediation. This is why Peter chooses Ibragim as his friend. And this is why Pushkin puts the idea of the union between the conservatives and the reformers into the mouth of Peter himself: "Listen, Ibragim, you are on your own in this world, without birth or kindred, a stranger to all except myself. If I were to die today, what would happen to you tomorrow, my poor Blackamoor? You must get settled while there is still time; find support in new ties, enter a union with the Russian nobility" (VIII: I, 27). Peter seems to be wise enough not to regard favorably the extreme form of Europeanization represented by Korsakov, but he does not approve the conservatism of Russian nobility either. At the same time Peter is not totally hostile to them; after all, this is Peter who understands the boyars' ambitions and persuades Ibragim to compromise, to flatter their vanity, and to conform to their conventions: "I've arranged a match for you. Tomorrow go to see your father-in-law; but look—honor his boyar pride: leave your sleigh at the gates, cross through his courtyard on foot; speak to him about his merits, about the nobility of his birth, and he will be crazy about you" (VIII: I, 28). Peter's match-making is symbolic. For Ibragim, in fact, implements the marriage of Russia and Europe, tradition and innovation, noble parentage and personal merit.

Through his elaborated poetics of contrast and an oscillating narratorial point of view, Pushkin creates an illusion of a moving camera that depicts various aspects of everyday life during the reign of Peter the Great.[18] The historicism of *The Blackamoor of Peter the Great* consists precisely in Pushkin's understanding of the specifics of the epoch as a moment of transformation where different styles coexist. In his study of the semiotics of the culture of eighteenth-century Russia, Lotman—without analyzing Pushkin's novel *The Blackamoor of Peter the Great*—arrives at similar conclusions: "during the Petrine period there was a confusion of the most varied forms of behavioral semiotics: official church ritual, parodies of church ritual in the blasphemous rites of Peter and his friends, the practice of foreign modes of conduct in everyday life, intimate unofficial behavior which was consciously opposed to ritual" (Lotman 1984, 235). In *The Blackamoor of Peter the Great*, Pushkin demonstrates that in Petrine Russia, different styles of behavior struggle with each other and conventions are not clearly defined; Russia undergoes a transformation of consciousness, of identity, of clothing, and of behavior. The unifying theme of the novel, therefore, is the idea of transformation and coalescence. Hence, Pushkin's image of Petrine Russia as a "huge workshop" (*ogromnaia masterovaia*) where Peter the Great is trying to forge Russian history by his "iron will," his talents, and his *dubinka*. In *The Blackamoor of Peter the Great* there is no traditional historical action, event, or conflict, as in *Boris Godunov, Poltava,* or *The Captain's Daughter.* Here Pushkin depicts a stream of history in the process of being shaped. He portrays this unshaped and eclectic quality of Russian life—like the "caps" of elderly ladies at Peter's Assembly—that would puzzle generations of Russian thinkers and would give them only a faint hope that "things will shape themselves" (*vsio obrazuetsia*). In *The Blackamoor of Peter the Great* Pushkin attempted to shape a discourse on Russian history in prose, as later he would do in poetry and historiography. Pushkin's novel, however, like Russian history remained a "workshop."

Like most of his historical fictions, *Poltava* (1828), Pushkin's longest dramatic poem, not only represents Pushkin's interpretation of the specific historical event but also is a statement on the nature of historical process. Written in a few days, this majestic tour de force of three cantos stands between the two other major Petrine narratives—*The Blackamoor of Peter the Great* and *The Bronze Horseman*—as a glaring and assertive hymn to Russian nationalism. Indeed, some critics interpret the poem as an unambiguous and almost blatant defense of Russian imperial power and as a categorical condemnation of any revolt that could threaten it. In scholarly literature, *Poltava* is often viewed as Pushkin's attempt to reconcile himself to the historical reality of Russia after the defeat of the Decembrist revolt. Other critics suggest a counterargument to this narrow interpretation. They call attention to the multiplicity of the narrative voices in the poem and to Pushkin's "dynamic polyphonic mode of characterization," which allow the critics to "rehabilitate" Pushkin from the charge of creating a panegyric to Russian imperialism.[1] The multiplicity of voices points to some conflicting characterizations in Pushkin's text; it does not explain, however, the nature and roots of these conflicts. The question remains: is there anything in the poem that would allow us to reintegrate the multitude of voices into an integral historical concept, and to what extent can this concept be attributed to Pushkin?

Pushkin's Selection of Facts

Pushkin's philosophy of history and his view of Peter the Great can be ascertained not only from the different narrative voices present in the poem (including the author's Introduction and Notes) but also from the way he *selects* and *modifies* historical facts connected with the battle of Poltava and historical characters depicted in the poem. Pushkin claims to represent a true history in *Poltava*. "In my poem, Mazeppa acts exactly as in history," he declares in "Refutations of the Critics," "and his speeches explain his historical character" (XI, 158). However, in his representation of Mazeppa and Matrena Kochubei, whose historical name Pushkin changed to that of Mariia in his poem, he draws from documents and also from legends (for example, the episode in which Peter I tweaks Mazeppa's mustache), from Russian poetic tradition, and from his own creative imagination which conveys, according to the author, the psychological truth about the characters: "Someone in a Romantic tale portrayed Mazeppa as an old coward. [. . .] It would be better to develop and explain the real character of the rebel Hetman, without arbitrarily distorting a historical figure" (Pushkin 1962–66: IV, 519). Blaming others for historical distortions, Pushkin seems to be unaware of his own deviations from historical fact. Needless to say, Pushkin did not include all the data he knew about this specific historical event and the characters it involved. A constant and consistent omission of some of the information available about Mazeppa (all his charismatic and positive characteristics, such as the breadth and refinement of his European education and his personal courage) should be considered, therefore, as Pushkin's inadvertent historical statement.

As has been noted in the scholarly literature about *Poltava*, the love story in the poem differs significantly from what it was in reality.[2] After Mazeppa, then aged sixty-five or more, was denied the hand of Matrena Kochubei, a young eighteen-year-old Ukrainian beauty and the daughter of Mazeppa's friend and Judge General, Vasilii Kochubei, the young girl, passionately and mutually in love with the Hetman, decided to flee from her parents' house to Mazeppa. The evidence suggests, however, that for the sake of her reputation Mazeppa sent the fugitive back almost immediately. The relationship and a secret correspondence between

Mazeppa and Matrena continued for a while, though it is hard to say for how long. Eventually, however, Matrena got married. In Pushkin's poetical rendering this episode takes quite a different turn: Mazeppa allegedly participates in Matrena-Mariia's elopement and accepts Mariia as his mistress; his defection and the callous execution of his former friend and Mariia's father, Kochubei, coincides with his longlasting romance with Mariia; as a result of Mazeppa's perfidiousness Mariia goes mad. Why does Pushkin transfer the timing of the event, which took place in 1704 to 1708, and why does he make a really tragic love affair out of the relatively brief episode of young Matrena Kochubei's elopement with Mazeppa? Clearly, Pushkin's historical concept is revealed not only through his authorial voice or voices within the poem, but also, and primarily, through the general thrust and construction of the plot and those aspects of the narrative in which he actually deviates from history. It is evident that Pushkin highly exaggerates Mazeppa's cruelty and darkens his image. By incorporating the tragic romantic plot into the historical epic Pushkin dramatizes Mazeppa's wickedness. Yet the poem generates further questions: does Pushkin distort some historical facts merely in order to evoke more condemnation of the Hetman and to defend the "Russian cause" by undermining the image of its political antagonist? Might alterations have had some deeper interpretative value? If so, how does the depiction of Mazeppa's total wickedness contribute to Pushkin's historical concept? Why does Pushkin cast a slur upon Mazeppa and prove the innocence of Kochubei to the point of introducing certain logical inconsistencies in the authorial evaluation of these two characters in the poem? I suggest that the myth Pushkin creates in *Poltava* helps to account for these inconsistencies and the poem's internal contradictions.

History as Holy War

As the title of the poem indicates, Pushkin puts a special emphasis not on any individual character but rather on the significance of a historical event.[3] Byron calls his poem *Mazeppa;* Ryleev's poem dealing with the same period in Russian and Ukrainian history is called *Voinarovskii;* Hugo's is entitled *Mazeppa.* In this context the emphasis on event rather than on character is polemical and constitutes a historical statement in itself. Indeed, although a love story plays a role here, Pushkin's *Poltava* is not a Romantic poem focusing on the adventures and the inner world of its protagonist similar to Byron's *Mazeppa,* but a combination of the Romantic poem with the epic. Some contemporary critics, however, who did not grasp Pushkin's historical idea in the poem claimed that the title must have been a mistake and expected it also to be *Mazeppa.* In response to this Pushkin writes: "In *The Messenger of Europe* it was noted that the title of the poem was erroneous, and that I probably didn't call it Mazeppa so as not to recall Byron. Correct. But there was another reason for this too—the epigraph. Thus, in the manuscript, 'The Fountain of Bakhchisarai' was called *The Harem,* but the melancholy epigraph (which is, of course, better than the whole poem) seduced me" (XI, 165). However, Pushkin does not explain why he had chosen precisely these lines from Byron's *Mazeppa* as an epigraph for his poem: "The power and glory of the war, / Faithless as their vain votaries, men, / Had pass'd to the triumphant Czar." The epigraph, however, points to the three main aspects of Pushkin's "myth" of Poltava which correspond respectively to each of the three lines of the epigraph: the notion of war; the origin of political evil conceived as betrayal and disloyalty; and the Tsar's triumph. Indeed, the poem follows the general "theme" of the epigraph: victory in a war. Pushkin is interested not so much in the personality of the "romantic hero"—even though he focuses his attention primarily on the "treason" of the Ukrainian challenger Mazeppa—but rather in a historical conflict seen as a battle and confrontation of two historical forces. History is not a background for the unfolding of the romantic plot and the fate of characters, but the very center of the narrative. The fate of the state and of a nation, which lies at the core of any war, is seen as depending not merely on the individual historical figures but rather on the nature of the conflict itself. This is why the character of Mazeppa is so one-sided and lacking any psychological dimension — a fact that Pushkin admitted himself: "That I depicted Mazeppa as evil I confess: I do not find him good [. . .] not a single kind, benevolent emotion! Not a single consolatory feature! Seduction, enmity, treason, slyness, cowardice, ferocity . . ." (XI, 158–60).

The central historical opponents — Peter the Great and Karl XII — are represented in the poem not as real full-blooded characters but rather as something like historical forces. Both monarchs appear in person only briefly in the third canto and are practically mute: Peter pronounces a few words: "To work, with God!" (*Za delo, s Bogom!*) (V, 56); Karl utters a single sentence to rouse Mazeppa from sleep: "Ho! It is time to get up! Mazeppa, rise! The dawn is coming." (*Ogo! pora! Vstavai, Mazeppa. Rassvetaet.*) (V, 63); Karl even makes the command to launch his troops into battle by gesture, not by word: "Suddenly, with a languid sign of hand, / He launched his troops against the Russians" (*Vdrug slabym maniem ruki / Na russkikh dvinul on polki*) (V, 57). But although Peter I and Karl XII are barely sketched and lack any psychological characterization, they stand as emblems of power, and their presence in the poem provides the two main points of orientation against which other characters are tested. These two poles can be defined as Tsar and Adversary. The other characters (no matter how much more important in terms of the narrative space) — Kochubei, Mazeppa, Mariia, a young Cossack, etc. — are portrayed and judged in relation to these forces.

The polarity between the Tsar and his Adversary is portrayed in terms of cosmogonical struggle between the forces of Order and Chaos (or on the level of ethics, between Good and Evil). Pushkin introduces the historical theme of Peter's wars with the image of a discord (*smuta*) or primordial battle that coexists with the act of creation, in this case the creation of the new Russia:

Была та смутная пора,
Когда Россия молодая,

В бореньях силы напрягая,
Мужала с гением Петра (V, 23).

That was an age of discord
When young Russia,
Exerting all her strength in struggles,
Came of age with Peter's genius.

At the same time the image of confusion and political instability
caused by the struggle of young Russia with its enemies appears as
a resurgence of the ancient chaos:

Украйна глухо волновалась.
Давно в ней искра разгоралась.
Друзья кровавой старины
Народной чаяли войны,
Роптали, требуя кичливо,
Чтоб гетман узы их расторг (V, 23).

The Ukraine was mutely seething.
A spark had smoldered there for a long time.
The friends of ancient, bloody time
Sought for a civil war;
Grumbling, demanding arrogantly,
That the Hetman annul their bonds.

Peter and Petrine Russia are associated with youth, vigor, light,
the color white ("with the enemies of the white Tsar" [*s vragami
belogo tsaria*]) (V, 31), and order: "But a line of gleaming, orderly
regiments / Obedient, swift and calm, / And an array of firm
bayonets" (*A nit' polkov blestiashchikh, stroinykh, / Poslushnykh,
bystrykh i spokoinykh, / I riad nezyblemykh shtykov*) (V, 53). Peter's
enemies, by contrast, are united through the images of old age
(Mazeppa's age is repeatedly emphasized in the poem), ailments
(both Mazeppa and Karl XII suffer: one from illness, another from
wounds), darkness, the color black ("those black thoughts her love
would not chase away" [*chernykh pomyshlenii / Ego liubov' ne uda-*

lit]) (V, 34), theft ("Like thieves in the darkness of night / They carry on their negotiations" [*Vo t'me nochnoi oni, kak vory, / Vedut svoi peregovory*]) (V, 29), blood, confusion, and instability. Mazeppa is continuously associated with night and darkness: "In him the spirit of darkness had no peace" (*V niom mrachnyi dukh ne znal pokoia*). Moreover, Mazeppa is also compared to a serpent: "Where did he flee from the pangs of his snake-like conscience"; "You do not know what a serpent you caress on your bosom" (*Kuda bezhal ot ugryzenii / Zmeinoi sovesti svoei; Ne znaesh' ty, kakogo zmiia / Laskaesh' na grudi svoei*) (V, 42, 32). The scene of the execution of Kochubei contains the same imagery: "The road is full of people and moves like a serpent's tail" (*Doroga, kak zmeinyi khvost, / Polna narodu, shevelitsia*) (V, 47). A notion of abyss (note that the Greek χαοσ means "abyss") also appears several times in relation to Peter's enemies: "Bold Charles was sliding above an abyss"; "Partly he [Mazeppa] revealed [to Kochubei] the abyss of his rebellious and insatiable soul" (*Otvazhnyi Karl skol'zil nad bezdnoi; Dushi miatezhnoi, nenasytnoi / Otchasti bezdnu otkryval*) (V, 23, 26). The imagery of the abyss plays a special role in the characterization of Mazeppa:

> Кто снидет в глубину морскую,
> Покрытую недвижным льдом?
> Кто испытующим умом
> Проникнет бездну роковую
> Души коварной? . . . (V, 24–25).

> Who would descend into the sea chasm,
> Covered with unmoving ice?
> Who, with a searching mind,
> Can penetrate the deadly abyss
> Of the vicious soul?

It is evident that on the mythopoetic plane Peter and his Enemy represent the main antagonists of any cosmogonical mythology, in which the forces of Cosmos triumph over the forces of Chaos.

Chaos is often associated with the elements (especially the watery element — cf. "the sea chasm" of Mazeppa's soul). In the system of Indo-European mythology this struggle appears as a battle between the storm god (in Slavic mythology — Perun) and a serpent. Significantly, while Mazeppa is compared to a serpent, Peter is described as a deity and is directly linked to the storm god: "He is a true embodiment of God's storm" (*On ves', kak bozhiia groza*) (V, 56). Peter's army too is compared to a storm: "And the tsar launched his troops thither. / They rushed like a storm" (*I tsar' tuda zh pomchal druzhiny. / Oni kak buria pritekli*) (V, 53). Likewise, the word "storm" is employed when a possibility of Peter's retribution for Mazeppa's deeds is suggested: "Listen! All is not yet done. A storm will burst out; who knows what awaits me?"; "Meanwhile, unaware of the [approaching] storm, perturbed by nothing, Mazeppa keeps plotting his designs" (*Postoi. / Ne vsio svershilos'. Buria grianet; / Kto mozhet znat', chto zhdet menia?; Grozy ne chuia mezhdu tem, / Ne uzhasaemyi nichem, / Mazeppa kozni prodolzhaet*) (V, 37, 29).

An interpretation of the battle of Poltava in terms of cosmogonical struggle explains Pushkin's attitude toward Peter the Great's reforms. The battle was viewed by Pushkin as an emblem of Peter's political achievements and the initiation of a new era and new order in Russian history. It is a pivotal moment: "Russia entered Europe like a newly launched ship — to the sound of hammers and the thunder of guns. But the wars undertaken by Peter the Great were beneficent and fruitful. The success of the national reforms [*preobrazovaniia*] was the result of the battle of Poltava, and European Enlightenment moored to the shores of the conquered Neva" (XI, 269). In his introduction to the first edition of *Poltava*, Pushkin writes: "The battle of Poltava is one of the most important and fortunate events of Peter the Great's reign. It freed him of a most dangerous foe; it strengthened Russian dominion in the south; it secured the new conquests in the north and proved to the state the success and necessity of the reform [*preobrazovaniia*] which was being accomplished by the Tsar" (Pushkin 1962–66: IV, 518).

In both quotations Pushkin stresses the idea of reform, or transformation. The idea that cosmos is a reorganization of chaos is typical of all mythologies: "Cosmos is always secondary in relation to chaos, both in terms of time and in terms of the elements that constitute it. Cosmos emerges in time, and in many cases it emerges out of chaos (often this happens by means of 'elucidation' of the characteristics of chaos: darkness is transformed into light, void into fullness, amorphousness into order, continuity into discreteness, formlessness into form, etc.) or out of the elements intermediate between chaos and cosmos" (Mify narodov mira 1982, 9–10). The view of Peter's epoch as a new Order resulting from the reorganization of the old Chaos explains the narrator's somewhat ambiguous treatment of the past in the poem. On the one hand, he blames the rebels for forgetting the past:

> Так, своеволием пылая,
> Роптала юность удалая,
> Опасных алча перемен.
> Забыв отчизны давний плен,
> Богдана счастливые споры,
> Святые брани, договоры
> И славу дедовских времен (V, 24).

> Thus, burning with self-willed desire,
> Grumbled brave youth,
> Greedy for dangerous changes;
> Forgetting their fatherland's ancient captivity,
> Bogdan's fortunate quarrels
> Sacred truces, treaties,
> And the glory of their grandfathers' times.

On the other hand, he insists on the dismissal of the past by calling the rebels "friends of the bloody olden times" (*druz'ia krovavoi stariny*). Thus the narrator creates an opposition between "the bloody olden times" and sacred glorious old times — "the glory of their grandfathers' times." One past has to be forgotten, another always has to be remembered. "The bloody olden times" represent the chaos from which the cosmos of the Russian empire was born. And this is this cosmogonical victory that has to be remembered. Therefore the memory which Pushkin's narrator advocates is not *historical* but *mythological*. The notion of "the holy wars" (*sviatye brani*) is essential for the establishment of Pushkin's mythology of Russian history. The battle of Poltava appears as the re-enactment of the myth of creation and the battle itself also gains the status of a holy war.

The Wicked Enemy and the Sacralization of the Tsar

The notion of a holy war inevitably raises the question of political evil, its nature and origin. In his book *The Symbolism of Evil*, Paul Ricoeur distinguishes four types of myths concerning the origin and the end of evil. The first type he calls "the drama of creation." According to this type "the origin of evil is coextensive with the origin of things; it is the *'chaos' with which the creative act of the god struggles.*" The fundamental traits of this type of myth constitute, according to Ricoeur, "the identity of evil and 'chaos,' and the identity of salvation with 'creation'" (Ricoeur 1969, 172).[4]

It is evident that Pushkin's representation of the battle of Poltava in terms of the cosmic combat between the Tsar and his Enemy coincides with this type of myth concerning the origin of evil. As Ricoeur points out, "Any coherent theology of the holy war is founded on the first mythological 'type' of Evil. According to that theology, the Enemy is a Wicked One, war is his punishment, and there are wicked ones because first there is evil and then order. In the final analysis, evil is not an accident that upsets the previous order. [. . .] Indeed, it is doubly original: first, in the role of the Enemy, whom the forces of chaos have never ceased to incarnate [. . .]; second, in the figure of the King, sent to 'destroy the wicked and the evil' by the same ambiguous power of devastation and of prudence that once upon a time established order" (Ricoeur 1969, 198). Indeed, *Poltava* is a story in which good and evil have their most striking "representatives." The characters are clearly divided into two groups: one includes Peter the Great and his followers, another "the enemies of Russia and of Peter." The first group is identified with a "common wealth" (*obshchee dobro*), the second one takes on the collective epithet "the enemy" (*vrag* standing for both the Swedes and the Ukrainian rebels: *i vrag bezhit*) and is repeatedly referred to as "evil" (V, 59). Significantly, the word "evil" is one of the most recurrent words in the poem, and together with its derivatives (*zlodei, zlobnyi, zloba, zlobit'sia*) it is employed twenty-six times in the poem, of which none apply to Peter, only a few relate to Kochubei, and the rest refer to "Russia's enemies," mainly to Mazeppa. Mazeppa is consistently called an "evildoer," or malefactor (the English word "villain" does not adequately render the meaning of the Russian word, *zlodei*); he appears as the very incarnation and embodiment of Evil. Thus the battle of Poltava is seen in terms of the cosmogonical battle between Good and Evil. The figure of the King (Tsar) plays the crucial role in this "theology of the Holy War" (Ricoeur, 196).

Within the structure of the myth that represents "the drama of creation," it becomes clear why it is essential for Pushkin to make Mazeppa completely evil in order to preserve his concept of Peter the Great as the founder of the new Order. The idea of the new European Russia was crucial for the formation of Russian national identity. Once this idea was identified with the figure of Peter the Great, the order established by him had to be preserved and defended, and any enemy had to be considered not only evil, but impious and sacrilegious. Indeed, Mazeppa encroaches on everything sacred:

> Не многим, может быть, известно,
> [. . . . .]
> Что он не ведает святыни,
> Что он не помнит благостыни,
> Что он не любит ничего,
> Что кровь готов он лить, как воду,

Что презирает он свободу,
Что нет отчизны для него (V, 25).

Not many, perhaps, know

. . . .

That he recognizes no holiness
That he remembers no benefaction
That he loves nothing
That he is ready to spill blood like water,
That he scorns freedom,
That fatherland does not exist for him.

He not only simulates illness (Kochubei also does) but takes the sacraments, as if expecting to die any moment, thus committing a sacrilegious act. He violates the religious law in relation to Mariia, not just by being her lover but by doing so as her godfather (which in Orthodoxy is equated with incest). Therefore Mariia's mother calls Mazeppa an "impious elder" (*starets nechestivyi*) and the possible marriage to him a "sin." He emerges as a "destroyer of holy innocence" (*sviatoi nevinnosti gubitel'*) as he brings ruin to the house "where a peaceful angel dwelled" (*gde mirnyi angel obital*).

The satanic nature of Mazeppa is also revealed in the motif of his demonic spell. Here are a few examples that demonstrate Mazeppa's association with the devil: "You do not know what a serpent / You caress on your bosom. / What enigmatic power / Has so attracted you / To his ferocious and lecherous soul?"; "His cunning conversation"; "The couch spread by seduction"; "The elder has bewitched you"; "Oh, stop! Don't confuse my heart! / You are a tempter" (V, 32, 38). Use of such words as "serpent," "inexplicable power," "cunning," "seduction," "bewitch," and "tempter" clearly points to the demonic nature of Mariia's seducer.

Mazeppa profanes the Church's sacraments, mysteries, prohibitions, and, finally, he betrays the Tsar—the Lord's Anointed One, and even encroaches upon his throne: "They bargain over the head of the Tsar"; "With him a Jesuit, who shares his power, / Stirs up a

popular uprising / And promises him a shaky throne"; "And soon
in turmoil and martial strife / I may raise myself a throne" (V, 29–
36). Significantly enough, Mazeppa is called "Judas" several times:
"The Tsar himself consoled Judas" (V, 30); "Where did Judas flee
in fear?" (V, 60). Mazeppa says about himself: "I am sent to Peter
as punishment; / I am a thorn in the leaves of his crown" (V, 60).
Thus, Peter seems to be implicitly identified with Christ wearing
a "crown of thorns" as a result of Judas' betrayal. It is interesting
that, according to Zhivov and Uspenskii, Russian scholars of the
semiotics of culture, Peter would appear before the people wearing
a crown of thorns while coming out of the monastery of Our Lord
the Savior (Spasskii monastyr') (Zhivov and Uspenskii, 107).

The identification of Mazeppa with Judas and of Peter with
Christ is more than just a rhetorical device. Pushkin was fully
aware that Old Believers identified Peter the Great with the anti-
Christ. (See his *History of Peter the Great*). Yet, there was another
tradition in which the figure of the tsar was deified and actually
referred to as "christ" (*khristos*). At first this term was used as a
simple borrowing from Greek in a sense of "anointed." Zhivov and
Uspenskii, in their illuminating work dedicated to the problem of
the sacralization of the figure of the tsar in Russia, quote many
sources in which Peter the Great is named Christ. They write:
"This association of the tsar with Christ, which goes beyond the
framework of etymology, is most clearly revealed in the texts dedicated to the victory of Poltava. Inasmuch as Peter is named Christ,
Mazeppa is called Judas, and Peter's partisans—the apostles" (Zhivov and Uspenskii 1987, 77–78). In his "Sermon on the victory
of Poltava over the king of the Swedes in 1709" ("Slovo o pobede
nad korolem Shvedskim pod Poltavoiu 1709 goda"), Stefan Iavor-
skii exclaims: "Christ the Victor from the tribe of Judas had won
through our Christ the Tsar" (Zhivov and Uspenskii, 80). This
mythological perception implies that to be the tsar's enemy is to
be Christ's enemy. This is why Mazeppa was excommunicated and
anathematized.

While Mazéppa and the Enemy in general are presented in the poem as the incarnation of evil, the figure of the Tsar is sacralized. As I have mentioned, none of the many words related to the notion of evil are applied to Peter. Even when Peter has every reason to be angry (*zlit'sia*) he displays not anger but wrath. The difference between anger (*zlost'*) and wrath (*gnev*) is a crucial one in the Russian language: God can experience wrath (*gnevat'sia*) but cannot be angry (*zlit'sia*). The Tsar, as God, can be *wrathful* but cannot be *angry*. As opposed to Peter, Karl XII, although a king, is angry (*I, zlobias', vidit Karl moguchii*) (V, 53). In accordance with the actual Russian tradition of sacralization of the figure of the tsar, Peter is depicted as the only *true tsar*, the Lord's only Anointed One. In this connection Zhivov's and Uspenskii's observations concerning the difference between a "true tsar" and a "false tsar" are especially valid:

> The concept of the special charisma of the tsar radically changes traditional beliefs: the juxtaposition of a righteous tsar and an unrighteous one turns into the juxtaposition of the true tsar and the false one. In this context "the righteous one" may signify not "just," but "right"; the "rightness," in turn, is determined by the choice of God. In this way, a true tsar is defined not according to his behavior but according to predestination. In addition to that, the problem emerges of how to distinguish a true tsar from a false one, a problem that cannot be solved rationally: if true tsars receive their power from God, false ones get it from the devil. Even the church rite of sacred coronation and unction does not impart grace to the false tsar, for those acts preserve nothing but appearance; in reality these are demons who crown and anoint him under the order of the devil (59).

Karl XII, although a lawful monarch, is not chosen by God and therefore does not have this unique royal charisma. Significantly, the idea that Karl actually does not possess the truly royal charisma is implied in such verses as: "And you, the lover of martial glory, who preferred the helmet to your crown" (*I ty, liubovnik brannoi slavy, / Dlia shlema kinuvshii venets*) (V, 53). Karl seems to prefer the status of warrior to the tsar's charisma, and his place in the mythological hierarchy is strictly defined as that of a *hero* (*Vozhdi geroia shli za nim; Shchadiat mechty pokoi geroia; S nikh otrazhal geroi bezumnyi*) (V, 57, 61, 63). Thus he is "crowned with a vain glory" (*venchannyi slavoi bespoleznoi*). Therefore, his deeds and those of his accomplices are also deprived of God's grace: "The design is both daring and weak, and there will be no grace in it" (*Rasschet i derzkii i plokhoi, / I v niom ne budet blagodati*) (V, 53).

By contrast, Peter and his supporters are under the protection of God's grace (Pagan and Christian symbolism is mixed in the poem; I will discuss this mixture later): "And each of our steps is marked by the grace of the god of war" (V, 56). Peter bears the sign of glory (cf. Karl's "vain glory"): "His eyes glow with glory" (*I slavy polon vzor ego*) (V, 59). (Note that in liturgical texts Christ is called "the King of Glory.") Peter is clearly depicted as the one chosen by God and "inspired from above." Moreover, the figure of the tsar merges with that of a god. Peter himself is described as a deity descending from above to his people:

> Тогда-то свыше вдохновенный
> Раздался звучный глас Петра:
> "За дело, с Богом!" Из шатра,
> Толпой любимцев окруженный,
> Выходит Петр. Его глаза
> Сияют. Лик его ужасен.
> Движенья быстры. Он прекрасен,
> Он весь, как Божия гроза.
> Идет. Ему коня подводят.
> Ретив и смирен верный конь.
> Почуя роковой огонь,

Дрожит. Глазами косо водит
И мчится в прахе боевом,
Гордясь могущим седоком (V, 56).

Then, heavenly inspired,
Peter's sonorous voice resounded:
"To work, God bless!" From the tent,
Surrounded by a crowd of his favorites,
Steps forth Peter. His eyes
Shine. His visage is terrible.
His movements are quick. He is splendid,
He is like a God's storm itself.
He goes forth. A steed is led to him.
Spirited and docile is the trusted steed.
Sensing the fatal fire,
He trembles. His eyes roll wildly,
And he races in the dust of battle
Proud of his mighty rider.

Peter also appears as a very incarnation of the god of battle, Mars: "He galloped in front of the troops, mighty and joyful as a very battle" (*I on promchalsia pred polkami, / Mogushch i radosten, kak boi*) (V, 57).

As already noted, Pushkin uses both Christian and pagan symbolism here. Peter is identified alternatively with the storm god, Mars, and Christ. However, the mythological pattern of the poem —the cosmic struggle of the King and his Enemy—remains intact. In coalescing Christian and pagan imagery, Pushkin actually follows the eighteenth-century Russian literary tradition. Sacralization of the figure of the tsar and of Peter the Great in particular was typical of Russian eighteenth-century culture. Examples of Peter's deification and of his likening to both Christ and pagan gods (often in the same poem) are too many to be quoted.[5] The important thing, however, is that Pushkin chose to follow this tradition.

Kochubei: How the Traitor Becomes a Martyr of Faith

Only within the mythological structure of cosmological combat, which is marked by the Tsar-Enemy relation, can one understand how Kochubei, who commits an immoral deed by writing a denunciation, remains somehow a positive character and even an "innocent" victim. It is difficult to comprehend how the malicious and vindictive Kochubei ("But furious in his bitter spite"; "but his inventive spite / He hid deeply in his heart"; "[. . .] the impatient wife / Is hurrying her spiteful husband") (V, 27) suddenly turns out to be "a victim of bold righteousness" (*zhertva smeloi pravoty*) in his wife's words (V, 46). Moreover, he becomes almost a saintly martyr: "In it [in a cart], at peace with both the world and heaven, / Fortified by mighty faith, / The innocent Kochubei was riding" (V, 47-8). At first sight this seems to be an almost absurd incongruity. Kochubei is driven by thirst for revenge. His actions hardly can be called courageous—he writes a denunciation but does not attack Mazeppa openly, although it is clear that he has all the means and opportunities to do so:

Богат и знатен Кочубей.
Довольно у него друзей.
Свою омыть он может славу.
Он может возмутить Полтаву;
Внезапно средь его дворца
Он может мщением отца
Постигнуть гордого злодея;
Он может верною рукой
Вонзить . . . но замысел иной
Волнует сердце Кочубея (V, 22-3).

Kochubei is famous and wealthy.
He has plenty of friends.
He can cleanse his honor.
He can raise up Poltava;
Suddenly, amid his court,

He can, with a father's vengeance,
Overtake the arrogant villain;
He can, with a sure hand,
Thrust . . . but a different plan
Stirs the heart of Kochubei.

He shows no more courage in prison:

Давно сознался я во всем,
Что вы хотели. Показанья
Мои все ложны. Я лукав,
Я строю козни. Гетман прав (V, 41).

Long ago I have confessed all
That you desired. My depositions
Are deceitful. I am cunning,
I plot vile schemes. The Hetman is correct.

This obviously contradicts the image of the "innocent" and "reconciled with heaven" Kochubei who suffers for the lofty cause. Kochubei's righteousness is also doubtful. First, he seeks the cruelest kind of punishment for his former friend (the rack, tortures, etc.). Second, he chooses the meanest kind of revenge—betrayal of the secret entrusted to him by his friend:

Так! было время: с Кочубеем
Был друг Мазепа; в оны дни,
Как солью, хлебом и елеем,
Делились чувствами они.
Их кони по полям победы
Скакали рядом сквозь огни;
Нередко долгие беседы
Наедине вели они—
Пред Кочубеем гетман скрытный
Души мятежной, ненасытной
Отчасти бездну открывал

И о грядущих измененьях,
Переговорах, возмущеньях
В речах неясных намекал.
Так, было сердце Кочубея
В то время предано ему (V, 26).

And yet, time was when with Kochubei
Mazeppa was a friend; in those days,
Like salt, bread, and oil
They shared their feelings with each other.
Their horses, on the fields of victory,
Would gallop side by side through fires;
Often they would have long discussions
When they were alone.
Before Kochubei the secretive hetman
Would open up the abyss
Of his mutinous, insatiable soul.
And of approaching changes,
Negotiations and disturbances
He would hint at obliquely in his talks.
Yes, Kochubei's heart
Was loyal to him at that time.

It is clear that Kochubei had to share the rebellious projects of his friend in order to be his confidant. He is anything but a sincere Russian patriot. Significantly, the patriotic aspect of Kochubei's and Iskra's enterprise is not elaborated on in the poem. Quite the opposite: Mazeppa's enemies are shown to have personal reasons for their confrontation with him (cf. the Cossack). In general, Kochubei's actions are no better than Mazeppa's: they are vindictive, mendacious, and devious. In a way, Mazeppa's cruelty in respect to Kochubei is even more understandable, as he is motivated by the instinct of self-preservation and perhaps the higher cause of the Ukrainian uprising, whereas Kochubei, who dreams of tortures on the rack for his friend at the hands of Moscow's executioners, is driven by the desire for sheer revenge. Nevertheless, one is labeled an "evildoer," while the other emerges as a "victim." Quite unexpectedly Kochubei's denunciation is transformed from personal revenge to the "common good" (*obshchee dobro*):

Удар обдуман. С Кочубеем
Бесстрашный Искра заодно. [...]
Но кто ж, усердьем пламенея,
Ревнуя к общему добру,
Донос на мощного злодея
Предубежденному Петру
К ногам положит, не робея? (V, 27–28).

The strike is planned. With Kochubei
Fearless Iskra will go along. [...]
But who, burning with zeal,
Striving for common weal,
The denunciation of the powerful villain,
At the feet of biased Peter,
Will lay without trembling?

Pushkin hardly could view writing denunciations and giving evidence against one's friends as honorable acts. Unfortunately, the Decembrists' behavior during the investigation was a vivid reminder of the moral flaws of those who, "flushed with zeal and contributing to the common good," wrote detailed reports to the tsar, confirming their own and their friends and fellow conspirators' guilt. Indeed, in *Poltava*, Kochubei himself fully realizes that he has lost his honor: "To lose life—and honor alongside, / To drag one's friends to the execution, / To hear their curses above one's grave."; "My foremost treasure was my honor, / The torture took this treasure from me" (V, 39, 41). How is it possible, then, that Kochubei is ultimately justified in the poem? Such is the law of mythologization of the cosmic Order and sacralization of the Tsar. Kochubei is granted "innocence" only because he happens to be a supporter of the *true tsar*. Mazeppa, on the contrary, commits the ultimate crime: he enters the war against the Tsar and wants to usurp his throne. Sacralization of the Tsar implies that his defense is a *holy* duty, whereas a fight against him appears as devilish intrigue. When the attitude toward the tsar is in essence religious, loyalty to the tsar has to be equated with faith in God. This is why Kochubei is "reconciled to heaven" and "strengthened with mighty faith." Loyalty to the Tsar is a religious act; suffering for the Tsar makes Kochubei a martyr of faith.

> Несчастный думает: вот он!
> Вот на пути моем кроавом
> Мой вождь под знаменем креста,
> Грехов могущий разрешитель,
> Духовной скорби врач, служитель
> За нас распятого Христа,
> Его святую кровь и тело
> Принесший мне, да укреплюсь,
> Да приступлю ко смерти смело
> И жизни вечной приобщусь! (V, 40)

> The poor man thinks: Here he is!
> Here on my bloody path
> My leader under the banner of the Cross,
> The great remitter of sins,
> Physician of the soul's grief, and a servant
> Of Christ who was crucified for us.
> He who brought to me
> His sacred blood and body, so that I fortify myself,
> Approach death bravely,
> And join eternal life!

While mounting the executioner's block, Kochubei and Iskra pray for their enemies as real Christian martyrs:

> Безмолвно молится народ,
> Страдальцы за врагов. И вот

Идут они, взошли. На плаху,
Крестясь, ложится Кочубей (V, 48).

Silently, the people pray,
The sufferers pray for their foes. And now,
They step forth, they mount. Onto the
    executioner's block,
Crossing himself, Kochubei lays his head.

This is how his personal revenge gains vicariously the status of "holy," or "sacred" revenge: "But I preserved my final treasure, / My third treasure: sacred revenge. / That I shall take with me to the Lord" (V, 41). (Cf. Zhivov and Uspenskii: "Later on the epithet *holy* may be applied to all that is related to tsar. [. . .] In 1880s the archbishop Avgustin Vinogradskii, who was in charge of the Moscow eparchy, mentions the 'holy will' and 'holy prayers' of the tsar") (Zhivov and Uspenskii, 74).

Similar logic underlies the description of the Cossack fatally enamored of Mariia. Motivated by personal hate for Mazeppa he makes an attempt to kill him during the battle, but gets mortally wounded himself:

[. . .] Но казак
Уж умирал. Потухший зрак
Еще грозил врагу России;
Был мрачен помертвелый лик,
И имя нежное Марии
Чуть лепетал еще язык (V, 59).

[. . .] But the Cossack
Was already dying. His extinguished gaze
Still threatened the foes of Russia;
His visage was somber in death,
And the gentle name of Mary
Still softly issued from his lips.

Significantly, in this scene Mazeppa is first referred to as "Russia's enemy" and only after that as the seducer of Mariia. Mazeppa is the Cossack's personal enemy, but he is called here "Russia's enemy." Thus the personal revenge of the Cossack undergoes the same transformation as that of Kochubei: he appears to avenge Mazeppa for being a traitor to Russia, but in fact he simply seeks revenge against his rival. On the level of plot, both Kochubei and the Cossack seek revenge against Mazeppa for Mariia; on the mythopoetical level, however, the image of Mariia merges with that of Russia, and both Kochubei and the Cossack appear as martyrs for Russia and the tsar.

Mariia's Tragedy: An Inverted Fairy Tale

The fate of Mariia is also depicted in relation to the main structural opposition of the poem—"Tsar / Enemy." The description of Mariia's love for Mazeppa follows a folktale pattern not only in terms of rhetorical devices, but also in the very structure of the intrigue. It represents an inverted version of the common folk motif of a girl who has to marry a monster who is later transfigured into a beautiful prince. Although others perceived Mazeppa as a real monster and a "serpent," the "enchanted" Mariia sees him as a prince and a true tsar: "Oh, my dear, / You are to be the tsar of our native land! / A crown would so suit / Your silver hair!"; "You are so mighty! Oh, I know: / A throne will be yours" (V, 36–7). But Mariia mistakes a usurper for the real tsar. The traditional folktale device of recognition and liberation from a demonic spell is reversed here: in her "prince" Mariia discovers a monster:

Я принимала за другого
Тебя, старик. Оставь меня.
Твой взор насмешлив и ужасен.
Ты безобразен. Он прекрасен (V, 62).

I took you for another,
Old man. Leave me alone.

> Your gaze is mocking and terrifying.
> You are loathsome. He is splendid.

Significantly, this description follows the rhythmical and semantic scheme of the description of Peter the Great (with a caesura after the second feet and the same rhymes):

> Толпой любимцев окруженный,
> Выходит Петр. Его глаза
> Сияют. Лик его ужасен.
> Движенья быстры. Он прекрасен (IV, 56).

> By his favorites surrounded,
> Peter appears. His eyes
> Shine. His visage is terrifying.
> His movements are fast. He is splendid.

Peter and Mazeppa appear as doubles whom Mariia confuses. Their deceitful resemblance (*Lik ego uzhasen* and *Tvoi vzor nasmeshliv i uzhasen*) stresses only more dramatically their polarity and the image of Mazeppa as a Pretender: "You are loathsome"—"He is splendid" (the last sentence, "He is splendid," is the same in both descriptions). Since the expression "He is splendid" (*On prekrasen*) first was applied to Peter, the same sentence in Mariia's description of Mazeppa may imply "Peter is splendid." Significantly, the epithet *prekrasnyi* seems to be an attribute of Peter's image:

> Пирует Петр. И горд и ясен,
> И славы полн взор его.
> И царский пир его прекрасен (V, 59).

> Peter revels. Proud and bright,
> And full of glory is his gaze.
> And his royal feast is splendid.

The whole description of Peter's triumph is built on alliterations of "*p-r*", which confirm the semantic connection *Piotr—pir—pre-*

krasen. (In 1835, Pushkin will write a poem entitled "The Feast of Peter the Great" ["Pir Petra Pervogo"] in which he creates a truly holy image of this "giant-miracleworker.") The real tsar is "beautiful," or splendid (*prekrasen*); a usurper is "loathsome," "ugly" (*bezobrazen*). Mariia's tragedy is that she succumbs to temptation and takes an anti-tsar for the tsar, a prince of darkness for a holy prince. For this she is punished with madness.

Pushkin claims to be very close to history in his representation of historical facts and events. Yet in contradiction to his own statement that nothing is known about Mariia's fate, he indulges in poetic imagination and makes Mariia go mad. Why does he do this? What is this fatal mistake that leads Mariia to madness? It is obviously not her liaison with Mazeppa in itself. One can argue that to be the lover of one's father's murderer is enough to drive one mad. But it would be more accurate to say that it is not the situation itself but the causes which led to this situation that drive Mariia crazy. Her fate is decided when she says to Mazeppa: "Oh, don't be angry! All, anything I am ready / To sacrifice to you, believe me" (V, 38). Indeed, even before Mariia's vow the narrator puts blame on Mariia for preferring Mazeppa to everything and everyone:

Его кудрявые седины,
Его глубокие морщины
[.   .   .   .   .   .]
Тебе всего, всего дороже:
Ты мать забыть для них могла,
Соблазном постланное ложе
Ты отчей сени предпочла (V, 32).

His gray curls,
His deep wrinkles
[.   .   .   .   .]
Are the most precious to you:
You could have forgotten your mother for them,

> The couch spread by temptation
> You have preferred to your father's house.

Indeed, Mariia confesses to herself that she actually forgot everything for Mazeppa: "Listen, Hetman: for your sake / I forgot everything in the world" (V, 34). Although she speaks about sacrificing herself for Mazeppa, it is obvious that in fact she sacrifices everything for *her passion* for Mazeppa, for her *personal* happiness. As opposed to fairytale maidens who as a rule sacrifice themselves for their parents, relatives, or homeland by marrying a monster and who are rewarded for this with a transfiguration of reality — with the happy revelation of actually being wedded to a prince, Mariia sacrifices everything for her *personal* interest and is, therefore, punished with disfigured reality — madness.

The Problem of Political Good and Evil

This inverted fairy tale constitutes an integral part of the myth of the cosmic Russian empire Pushkin creates in his poem. All characters are tested by their attitude toward the Tsar. Those who happen to be on the side of Peter's Enemy are shown to have only personal interests. Whereas Peter's supporters, even though they might have as many personal interests as their enemies, are transformed into sufferers for "the common good." It is important to note that evil is always linked in Pushkin with the triumph of the personal and egotistical in human beings. Most of "Russia's enemies" are possessed in Pushkin with personal anger; such are Radishchev, Mickiewicz, the Polish rebels, and Eugene from *The Bronze Horseman*. The pursuit of personal interest often has, according to Pushkin, a diabolical source. Significantly, Hermann in the *Queen of Spades*, this typical representative of the Faustian man, is compared to Mephistopheles. Hermann claims that he searches for independence, but independence for him is not true freedom, but a personal interest. It seems that Mazeppa's notion of independence is quite similar. He claims that he aspires for freedom:

Без милой вольности и славы
Склоняли долго мы главы
Под покровительством Варшавы,
Под самовластием Москвы.
Но независимой державой
Украйне быть уже пора:
И знамя вольности кровавой
Я поднимаю на Петра (V, 36).

Without sweet liberty or fame
We bent our heads for a long time
Under the patronage of Warsaw,
Under the autocracy of Moscow.
But it is time for the Ukraine
To be an independent state:
And the banner of bloody liberty
I raise against Peter.

Yet, this claim clearly contradicts that of the narrator, who says about Mazeppa the following:

Что он не любит ничего,
Что кровь готов он лить, как воду,
Что презирает он свободу,
Что нет отчизны для него (V, 25).

That he loves nothing
That he is ready to spill blood like water,
That he scorns freedom,
That fatherland does not exist for him.

Thus Mazeppa's notion of freedom is significantly different from that of the narrator. The narrator's concept of freedom seems to coincide with that of Pushkin's traveler as expressed in his *Journey from Moscow to Petersburg:* "What else constitutes man's greatness, if not ideas? Let thought be as free as man should be: *within the limits of law, in full observance of conditions laid down by society* (XI, 264). This is a freedom within Order, within Cosmos. Mazeppa's freedom, by contrast, is lawless, and therefore chaotic and bloody. *Svoboda* is juxtaposed to *vol'nost' krovavaia* which is identified with the chaos of "the rebellious greedy soul" (Cf. Aleko from *The Gypsies*). The element of patriotism is significantly undermined in Mazeppa by Pushkin's suggestion of personal revenge as the source of his political activity:

> Давно решилась непреложно
> Моя судьба. Давно горю
> Стесненной злобой. Под Азовом
> Однажды я с царем суровым
> Во стане ночью пировал:
> Полны вином кипели чаши,
> Кипели с ними речи наши.
> Я слово смелое сказал.
> Смутились гости молодые . . .
> Царь, вспыхнув, чашу уронил
> И за усы мои седые
> Меня с угрозой ухватил.
> Тогда, смирясь в бессильном гневе,
> Отмстить себе я клятву дал;
> Носил ее — как мать во чреве
> Младенца носит. Срок настал (V, 54–55).

> Long ago my fate was decided
> Irreversibly. I burn with long-restrained
> Anger. Near the Azov,
> I feasted one night in the general's quarters
> With the severe tsar:
> The goblets boiled, full of wine,
> And with them boiled our conversations.
> I said a bold word.
> The young guests felt embarrassed . . .

The tsar flushed, dropped his goblet
And grabbed me by my silver
Mustaches with a threat.
Then, humbled in my powerless rage,
I gave an oath to revenge myself;
I carried the oath — like a mother in her womb
Carries her child. And now time has come.

The reading of *Poltava* in terms of the Tsar/Enemy opposition helps to reconcile different points of view in relation to the characters presented in the poem. The establishment of such conflict is instrumental for the poet's evaluation of the protagonists and for his definition of political good and evil. The universe that is dominated by the Tsar/Enemy opposition strictly determines the historical fate of each individual. Historical or political good and evil do not necessarily coincide with personal moral worth: one can be morally wrong, Pushkin seems to suggest, and still be historically right (or morally right and historically wrong, as is Eugene from *The Bronze Horseman*). The fact that Kochubei acted out of low personal interest is a *low truth* (*nizkaia istina*), which is refuted by the *elevating deceit* (*vozvyshaiushchii obman*) of his suffering and belonging to the "right" side. It is interesting that Kochubei's belonging to the "right" side is presented in the poem as a haphazard event, unconditioned by his convictions. Peter himself, although his image is highly sacralized, as has been shown in this analysis, is far from being impeccable in his everyday behavior. Although indirectly, he is depicted in the poem as a person with limited insight into human nature (he cannot distinguish between his friends and his enemies), a person who makes hasty decisions (he sent Palei as well as Kochubei's relatives to Siberia), and has an impetuous and cruel temperament (he insulted Mazeppa by pulling his mustache). However, it is not Peter's behavior or even his errors that define him as a true Tsar, but his historical predestination. Compare Zhivov's and Uspenskii's observation: "It is not behavior but predestination that determines who is a true tsar" (59). In essence this is a religious historical concept: *ex cathedra* Peter is marked by God's grace, and in decisive moments he acts as a *true* Tsar. Peter creates history and fulfills Russia's historical predestination:

> В гражданстве северной державы,
> В ее воинственной судьбе,
> Лишь ты воздвиг, герой Полтавы,
> Огромный памятник себе (V, 63).

> In the citizenship of the Northern Empire,
> In its martial fate,
> It is you alone, Poltava's hero, who raised
> An enormous monument to yourself.

The concept of Peter the Great as a *true* Tsar, as a progenitor of Russian history, is confirmed by the collective memory of the nation. Memory functions in the poem as a litmus test for distinguishing between the true and false, the good and evil of history. Memory preserves only what represents higher truth. This is why in the epilogue, Pushkin makes popular memory the ultimate judge of events. The epilogue reproduces "the degrees of memory" that correspond to degrees of significance and truthfulness. Peter is on the top of this hierarchy—he holds a unique place in Russian historical memory and, therefore, he has erected "a colossal monument to himself." Mazeppa as Peter's antagonist and as an embodiment of political evil in the poem is lost in oblivion, having no grave and no monument (which are the material signs of memory), and also is condemned to the anti-memory of anathema:

> И тщетно там пришлец унылый
> Искал бы гетманской могилы:
> Забыт Мазепа с давних пор!
> Лишь в торжествующей святыне
> Раз в год анафемой доныне,
> Грозя, гремит о нем собор (V, 64).

And vainly a sad traveler
Would have searched there for the grave of the hetman:
Mazeppa is forgotten from ancient times!
Only the triumphant church,
Once a year, resounds threateningly
With the anathema to his name.

Extremely scant is the memory of Peter's main historical opponent — Karl XII:

Три углубленные в земле
И мхом поросшие ступени
Гласят о шведском короле (V, 63).

Three stairs half-buried in the earth
And overgrown with moss
Bear witness to the Swedish king.

Although the memory of him is not the anti-memory of Mazeppa, his "monument" — "three stairs half-buried in the earth and overgrown with moss" — is a kind of a *negative monument,* since it actually goes not up but *down* into the earth and is overgrown with moss, the symbol of oblivion.

Mariia, who happened to be on the "wrong" side, has no grave and no monument; she is completely eliminated from the national memory:

Но дочь преступница . . . преданья
Об ней молчат. Ее страданья,
Ее судьба, ее конец
Непроницаемою тьмою
От нас закрыты. [. . .] (V, 64).

But the guilty daughter . . . the legends
Are silent about her. Her sufferings,
Her fate, her end
Are hidden from us
By an impenetrable darkness.

However, out of compassion and sympathy the poet feels for this "sinful maiden," he grants her a bit of poetical memory: "A blind Ukrainian singer / . . . / Speaks briefly to the young Cossack girls / About the sinful maiden" (V, 64).

By contrast, Kochubei and Iskra are the only characters in the poem who are said to have graves. Memory of them is preserved in lore and their graves are honored:

> Но сохранилася могила,
> Где двух страдальцев прах почил:
> Меж древних праведных могил
> Их мирно церковь приютила (V, 64).

> But the grave was preserved,
> Where the dust of two martyrs rests;
> Among ancient graves of the righteous
> The church has peacefully given them repose.

Even more significantly, in his "Notes" to the poem, Pushkin introduces the text of the epitaph on Kochubei's and Iskra's tombstone—a documentary piece of memory about them. This epitaph fully reflects Pushkin's own mythological interpretation of these characters and is a curious example of the reconstruction of historical personages' biography in accordance with the norms of myth. It represents them as "sufferers for truth and loyalty to the Monarch," as real holy martyrs: "[. . .] And for our truth and loyalty to the Monarch / We drained the chalice of suffering and death" (V, 67). Thus the polarity between political good and evil is paralleled by a descending hierarchy of degrees of memory attributed to the respective characters. This can be represented in the following scheme:

The Tsar	Peter	Colossal monument
The Tsar's men	Kochubei and Iskra	Honorable grave and epitaph
Historical lawful enemy	Karl XII	Negative monument
Involuntary "enemy"	Mariia	Poetic memory only
Lawless enemy (rebel)	Mazeppa	Anathema: anti-memory

In *Poltava* Pushkin creates not so much a panegyric to Peter the Great or even to the figure of the Tsar, but rather a myth of the "origin" of the present political system that allows him to overcome "the terror of history" (Eliade) and the anxiety arising from the instability of this system, shaken by the Decembrists' revolt. *Poltava* is not a metaphor for the Decembrists' revolt, yet it raises the same questions that tormented Pushkin after 1825—the relationship between personal morals and political good, the discrepancy between personal and political good and evil. This anxiety induces the poet to explain the origin of the present order of things and of political evil by the "primordial evil" in Russian history.

The mythologizing of the figure of the Tsar results in a specific sort of history and specific modes of interpreting it. Placed in the perspective of the creation myth or the cosmic struggle between the Tsar and his Enemy, traditional values change, depending on their relation to the "cosmic" opponents. Moreover, the characters' belonging to the right or wrong party is often random, yet they must bear full responsibility for their actions. Pushkin knew this very well from his personal experience: he shared many of the political aspirations of his Decembrist friends, yet he happened to be on the "right" side, whereas his friends were "guilty without guilt" and had to endure execution. Moreover, many of them participated in the uprising or, on the contrary, did not join it, by sheer accident. The Decembrists indeed represented a complex moral and psychological problem for Pushkin. On the one hand, Pushkin did not endorse their political method of violence and revolution, and he could not admire the moral behavior of most of them (denunciations, acceptance of guilt, etc.) during the investigation; on the other hand, Pushkin was bound to many Decembrists by bonds of personal friendship and he shared their striving for emancipation and freedom. He could neither condemn nor fully justify the Decembrists. For Pushkin, who considered himself to have been saved from participation in the Decembrist revolt only by chance, the myth of the holy war represented a *scape-myth*, helping to face the cruelty of history and to reconcile himself to his moral conflict. The reality which cannot be justified often becomes mythologized. Pushkin's myth of the holy war condemned historical errors (Mazeppa), but excused some personal weaknesses (Kochubei). Such was in general Pushkin's attitude toward the Decembrists—"mercy for the fallen" as he put it in his poem "Ia pamiatnik vozdvig sebe nerukotvornyi." Such was his portrayal of Pugachev in *The Captain's Daughter* and, to a certain extent, of Grishka Otrep'ev in *Boris Godunov,* and Radishchev in the eponymous article "Alexander Radishchev"—a mixture of political disapproval and personal sympathy.

The same search for paradigmatic myth and archetypal hero that helps in tolerating reality and gives some philosophic currency to it is found in "Stanzas" (1826). Pushkin wanted to see in Nicholas I the second Peter the Great. He thus followed the tradition of the Russian ode, according to which "every new monarch revives Peter the Great" (Zhivov and Uspenskii, 129). Pushkin dispenses with the baroque and classicist rhetoric but develops the mythological aspect of the Russian ode. Indeed, events of Peter the Great's epoch were favorable for the creation of a national mythology and sacralization of the figure of the monarch. As founder of the new European Russia, Peter was identified as the progenitor of a new dynasty and became an archetypal ancestor. Once Peter is understood as a primordial ancestor, the events of his time become paradigmatic for interpreting all consequent events in Russian history: all wars are viewed as the re-enactment of the original battle in which Order was won, and all true Tsars have to resemble their archetypal ancestor in order to preserve the established Order. Thus, in "Stanzas," Pushkin reveals a deeply mythological consciousness by attempting to explain the present by the past and even to use the past as a prophecy for the future:

> В надежде славы и добра
> Гляжу вперед я без боязни:
> Начало славных дней Петра
> Мрачили мятежи и казни (III: I, 40).

In hopes of fame and good to come
I look ahead without fear:
The beginning of the glorious days of Peter
Were darkened by revolts and executions.

Only knowledge of the origins ("of the beginning of the glorious days of Peter") helps him to overcome the anxiety of the present and "to look ahead without fear." The past (and past glory) seems to be a guarantee for future glory and well-being. Thus he conjures the monarch not to deviate from the archetypal pattern but rather to re-enact the same myth that involves the cosmic struggle of the Tsar with his enemy, his victory over him and his clemency:

Семейным сходством будь же горд;
Во всем будь пращуру подобен:
Как он, неутомим и тверд,
И памятью, как он, незлобен (III: I, 40).

Be proud, then, of your family resemblance;
In all things be like your forefather:
Like him, tireless and firm,
And, like him, not holding a grudge.

The motif of forgiveness makes a "humanized," "Christianized" version of the old paradigmatic myth of the combat between the forces of Cosmos and Chaos. Pushkin urges the monarch to conform to this myth and to its "elevating deceit" (*vozvyshaiushchii obman*).

The tension between personal and historical perceptions of reality in *Poltava* is, of course, represented by the very structure of the plot. We will see the same interweaving of the stories—a personal story and a mythologized historical event—in *The Bronze Horseman*, Pushkin's last fictional narrative dealing with Peter the Great. Significantly, the description of the flood in *The Bronze Horseman*, introduced by the line "A fearful time there was" (*byla uzhasnaia pora*), echoes the opening words in Pushkin's portrayal of the time of turmoil in *Poltava:* "A troubled time there was" (*Byla ta smutnaia pora*). Like the political conflict in *Poltava*, the flood in *The Bronze Horseman* is depicted in terms of a battle. Once again Pushkin portrays Peter as founder of a new order, or cosmos. The rebellious forces, by contrast, in both poems are associated with primordial Chaos. If in *Poltava*, Pushkin raises the problem of political good and evil and of personal *involvement* in historical events, in *The Bronze Horseman*, Pushkin addresses the issue of personal, individual *attitude* toward history and an already established order. The final verdict, however, remains similar in both poems. The rebellious participants in Poltava's events and an individual revolting against the legacy of his land's historical past are equally devoured by history and perish, leaving no trace.

The function of Eugene's story in *The Bronze Horseman* is also similar to that of Mariia in *Poltava*. In both cases personal fate unfolds against the background of a historical event. The historical event turns out to be a test for personal integrity. Both Mariia and Eugene commit a crime against Order (Eugene rebels against Russian history embodied by Peter the Great; Mariia rebels against social and religious laws) and happen to be on the side of Peter's antagonists: rebellious elements represented by the Neva in *The Bronze Horseman* and the Ukrainian uprising, represented by Mazeppa, in *Poltava*. Although Mariia and Eugene do not participate directly in the cosmic struggle, both of them are swept away by historical turmoil. Both of them are concerned with personal happiness, and in both cases personal interests are defeated and the heroes go mad and perish. Close analysis of *The Bronze Horseman* and of the plight of Eugene is, however, the subject of the next chapter.

The subtitle of Pushkin's poem *The Bronze Horseman: A Petersburg Tale* (*Mednyi vsadnik: Peterburgskaia povest'*, 1833) is explicitly ambiguous: a tale, a genre that is primarily prosaic,
turns out to be a poem. The tension between poetry and prose
is further increased because the poem itself is enclosed in the
prosaic frame of the Introduction and the Notes. The Introduction and the Notes are intended to create the illusion of trust-
worthiness and documentary precision—a common device of
the Romantic historical fiction used for the most part in prose
genres. The ambiguity of the subtitle, however, is not limited to
blurring the boundary between poetry and prose. It is not clear
whether the definition "a tale" refers to the history of Petersburg or to the story of Eugene in Petersburg. The very duality
of the subtitle indicates that one has to deal with two different
types of tale, which form the plot (*siuzhet*) of the "Petersburg
tale," that is, of the whole poem. These two tales differ struc-
turally from one another. One of them describes the history
of the creation of Petersburg, or, more precisely, it reiterates
the Petersburg myth. It would be appropriate to point out that
numerous sources, citations, and subtexts discovered by Pushkin scholars in the text of the Introduction play in this case a
functional role.[1] The old theme of the Petersburg ode and the
traditional theme of Peter I-demiurge,[2] which Pushkin replays
in his poem, acquire a specifically mythological dimension partially because of the device of literary citation and variation. In
The Bronze Horseman, myth embraces not only the history of
the foundation of Petersburg but also the picture of the flood
and the description of the monument of the Bronze Horseman itself. This potentially could have been repeated and even

Count Khvostov might sing about it in his verses. Another trait that distinguishes this type of tale is its *reality*. The story of the creation of Petersburg, the Bronze Horseman, and the flood are real in the sense that they form part of history, that they either still exist or have really existed, a fact that is verified even in documents. Significantly, Pushkin mentions this detail in his Introduction. In mythic consciousness, all these traits are identified as a "true story." Thus Pushkin insists: "The event described in this tale is based on truth." Mircea Eliade, an expert in the patterns of mythic archaic consciousness, defines the aborigines' concept of true and false as follows: "The Pawnee differentiate 'true stories' from 'false stories' and include among the 'true' stories in the first place all those which deal with the beginnings of the world; in these the actors are divine beings, supernatural, heavenly, or astral. [. . .] Thus in the 'true' stories we have to deal with the holy and the supernatural, while the 'false' ones on the other hand are of profane content. [. . .] The Herero consider the stories that relate the beginnings of the different groups of the tribe 'true' because they report facts that really took place" (Eliade 1975, 8–9).

The other tale, connected with Eugene's plot-line, does not reiterate but depicts a singular event, or an excess. Obviously, the story of Eugene cannot be repeated, for it is *not real;* that is, it is not testified historically or supported by documents. Needless to say, the "curious ones" after consulting the "report compiled by Berkh," would find there neither the story of Eugene's adventure with the Bronze Horseman, nor any mention of Eugene himself. The "unreality" of the story of Eugene is not limited, however, to the fact that it has no documentary foundation. Everything that is related to the hero of this "tale" is unclear, imprecise, and may be characterized by the indefinite adverbs "somewhere" and a dubious "perhaps." Eugene serves "somewhere" (*gde-to sluzhit*), hopes to settle down "somehow" (*Uzh koe-kak sebe ustroiu / Priiut smirennyi i prostoi*—Eugene's thoughts), and feels no regret that

his presently neglected family name "may have shined" in the past
(*Ono, byt' mozhet, i blistalo*).³

The interweaving of those two "histories," or stories, in one tale
is accomplished in full accord with the semiotic theory of a plot.
The plot emerges, according to Lotman, as a result of the tension
between the mythological aspect of the text and its *fabula*.⁴ The
peculiarity of *The Bronze Horseman* consists in the fact that it is
the hero's attitude toward myth that turns out to be the basis of
fabula itself. The interrelationship between these two lines of the
text requires further exploration.

The Myth of Petersburg

The tale about Petersburg forms a mythological text that includes
three parts: the creation of Petersburg, the Bronze Horseman, and
the flood. As has been pointed out more than once in Pushkin
scholarship, the Introduction reproduces a cosmogonic myth, the
myth of creation, in which Peter I performs the role of the creator-
demiurge.⁵ The first noun in the poem—"the shore" (*na beregu*)
points to the notion of a borderline and introduces the initial
opposition *earth—water,* which later is recodified into the opposition *empty—full.* The myth of Petersburg's creation includes
three main components: the subject, the source, and the object.
As a result of the transforming activity of the subject, in place
of the forest a *city* arises, *palaces* appear instead of *huts,* instead
of a *poor canoe* (*bednyi cheln*)—the *ships;* in place of *swamps* now
gardens grow, etc. In order to enumerate all the transformations
one would have to rewrite the whole Introduction. These transformations illustrate central oppositions: cultured—uncultured;
dry—humid; firm—soft (granite and swamp); light—darkness;
definite—indefinite (*nevedomye vody* as opposed to the Neva); cen-
tripetal movement—centrifugal movement. Compare "The river
was rushing past; alone, a poor canoe was drifting over" (*Reka nes-
lasia; bednyi cheln / Po nei stremilsia odinoko*) and "the flock of

ships from all the ends of the earth rush toward the rich piers"
([. . .] *korabli / Tolpoi so vsekh kontsov zemli / K bogatym pristaniam
stremiatsia*). These oppositions in turn are easily reduced to the
main opposition of any mythology: cosmos — chaos. Petersburg is
born as a result of the transformation of unorganized chaos into
organized cosmos. In this connection, the opposition Moscow —
Petersburg takes on a special meaning:

> И перед младшею столицей
> Померкла старая Москва,
> Как перед новою царицей
> Порфироносная вдова (V, 136).

> And the old Moscow faded
> Before the younger metropolis,
> As a porphyry-wearing widow
> Before the new Empress.

"Chaotic" Moscow gives way to "cosmic" Petersburg, which marks
the beginning of the new order and new history, history "according to Peter the Great."

Pushkin depicts Petersburg not only as the center of Russia
and its capital, but as a sacral center of the world. Petersburg is
radically separated from the rest of the world. It is no coincidence
that all kinds of borderlines — embankments, bridges, railings —
play such an important role in depicting the city: "The Neva was
clothed in granite"; "The granite of her embankment"; "The cast-
iron pattern of your railings"; "The bridges were hung above the
water" (*V granit odelasia Neva; Beregovoi ee granit; Tvoikh ograd
uzor chugunnyi; Mosty povisli nad vodami*). Everything located beyond these borders is perceived as periphery, the "ends of the
Earth," or chaotic elements that during the time of crisis flood the
city. Cf. "And Petropol surfaced like Triton, / Immersed in water
to his waist" (*I vsplyl Petropol', kak Triton, / Po poias v vodu pogru-
zhen*). Petersburg is marked vertically as well: it *arose* from "the

quagmire of swamps" (*iz topi blat*). In the description of the city's architecture, images that emphasize its striving upwards predominate: "Enormous stately palaces and towers cluster together"; "And bright are the enormous sleepy masses of deserted streets, and light is the Admiralty's needle" (*Gromady stroinye tesniatsia / Dvortsov i bashen; I iasny spiashchie gromady / Pustynnykh ulits, i svetla / Admiralteiskaia igla*).

In Petersburg there is a monument located on the junction of three worlds: heaven, earth, and the underground world. It is erected on earth, but "above the abyss itself," "above the outraged Neva," raising "its bronze head in darkness." This may allow us to speak about the Bronze Horseman as an equivalent of the "world pillar," or the "world tree," which is located in the sacred center of the world and occupies a vertical position.[6] Indeed, the monument has a definite vertical trichotomous structure: the lower part — "the pedestal of the idol" and the serpent (an underworld chthonic animal) that the horse crushes with its hoof; the middle part — the horse (in mythology the hoofed animals, horses in particular, often correspond to the middle part of the world tree, its trunk); the upper part — Peter himself with his "outstretched arm" (the arm stretching upward could be easily identified as a branch of the world tree).[7] The vertical cosmic model of the monument also discloses the juxtaposition *the past — the present — the future*. The Bronze Horseman emerges as a temporal symbol of the fate of Russia, of its past (the fateful foundation of the city), its present, and its future ("Where are you galloping, proud steed, / And where will you put down your hooves?"). The merging of all time into one image of the Bronze Horseman is stressed grammatically. A relatively short passage, dedicated to the depiction of the Bronze Horseman, includes all three grammatical tenses: the past tense ("Who was rising motionlessly"; "Beneath the sea the city was founded"; "[You] raised Russia to stand straight up"), the present tense ("Terrifying he is in the surrounding gloom! / What thought upon his brow! / What strength concealed in him! / And what fire there is in this steed! / Where are you galloping, proud steed"), and the future tense ("And where will you put down your hooves?").

The horizontal structure of the Bronze Horseman as a world tree is characterized by its central location vis-à-vis "all the world's ends" and its position within the square or a circle. (Cf. "The poor madman made a circle / Around the idol's pedestal.")

In addition to these details that imply sacralization, the Bronze Horseman clearly reveals the traits of the storm-god.[8] As often happens in mythology, the anthropomorphous deity merges with a world tree. Like the monument to Peter the Great, the idol of Perun, the Slavs' storm-god, was located in the capital, Kiev, and erected on the top of the hill, from where it was thrown down into the Dnieper. According to the myth, "Perun, initially under the image of the rider on the horse or the chariot (cf. the later iconography of Ilia the Prophet), strikes the serpent-like enemy with his weapon" (Mify narodov mira: II, 307).[9] The connection between the Bronze Horseman and Perun (or his later folklore transformation, Ilia the Prophet) is not limited, however, to outward resemblance. Locutions that evoke in one way or another the image of a storm appear repeatedly in the text of the poem: "Bridges overthrown by the storm" (*Grozoi snesennye mosty*); "in that stormy [terrible] year" (*v tot groznyi god*), and finally the face of the "fearsome tsar" (*groznogo tsaria*). In the main draft of the poem there are even more expressions linked either etymologically or semantically to the idea of a storm: "the idol on the bronze horse" appears "threatening with his immobile arm" (*grozia nedvizhnoiu rukoiu*) (in a variant Pushkin adds: "in the stormy silence" [*v groznoi tishine*]; after the flood, finally "[the storm] subsided" (cf. also: "the morning's ray [. . .] found no trace of yesterday's storm"). In different variants of the scene of Eugene's rebellion, the monument is described as follows: "What a [immobile] fearsome coldness"; How fearsome "?" is his "?" visage "?" in darkness]"; "fearsome gaze" (*Kakoi [nedvizhnyi] groznyi khlad; Kak grozen ⟨?⟩*

lik ⟨*?*⟩ *ego* ⟨*?*⟩ *vo mgle; groz*⟨*nyi*⟩ *? vzgliad"*) (V, 478). (Cf. also in *Poltava:* "He is splendid, / He is like a storm of God").[10] It is not surprising then that the appearance of the "stormy tsar" is accompanied by thunder (*grom*).[11] Frightened by the Bronze Horseman, Eugene "runs and hears after him— / Something like the rumbling of thunder." (In other variants: *Zvucha v okrestnoi tishine / Gremia nesetsia Vsadnik Mednyi; Prostershi ruku v vyshine / So gromom Vsadnik Mednyi*). In this context the very movement of the Bronze Horseman becomes not only natural but predictable, for it may be interpreted as a relapse of the myth of Ilia the Prophet riding his chariot across the sky.

The theme of Perun is clearly also present in the description of the flood. Pushkin's depiction of the flood is characterized by six main elements:

1. The flood is described in terms of war or struggle (cf. "Siege! Assault! ferocious waves"; "in this way the villain, / Bursting into a village, breaks, slaughters, / Smashes and plunders; / [There are] screams, gnashing, / Violence, swearing, alarm, and howls! . . .").

2. The space is divided into two zones: the center (the sacral center, St. Petersburg, and its monument, which rises to "unshakable height") and the periphery (the chaos of water, or the Neva, that surrounds the city and the monument from all sides). The water element represents the other world (cf. "the coffins from a washed-out graveyard").

3. The Bronze Horseman and Nature's elements represent the central antagonists in this war and are associated with the oppositions *top—bottom* and *center—periphery*.

4. The antagonist of the Bronze Horseman is described as a *robber* and a *beast* ("Ferocious waves, like thieves, sneak in windows"; the Neva "smashes and plunders" and "frenzied, like a beast, she rushed on the city").

5. A woman (Parasha) is among the goods amassed by the robbery of the Bronze Horseman's antagonist.

6. The victory over the elements is accompanied by their "per-

secution," chasing, and the redemption of the stolen riches ("The Neva retreated, / Admiring her perturbation / And abandoning her booty / With carelessness"; "And, weighed down with pillage, / Tired, in fear of pursuit, / The robbers hurry home, / Dropping their loot on their way back").

This scheme generally coincides with one of the main subjects of Slavic and Indo-European mythology: the duel between the storm-god and the serpent (in the earliest variant of the myth it is a cattle god, Veles, who corresponds to the serpent; in the variant of Ilia the Prophet he is referred to as a "ferocious beast").[12] Perun is located on the summit of the hill, while Veles is associated with the dale. Veles kidnaps people and cattle; in some variants the myth mentions the abduction of a woman, Mokosh (Mokosh is a female deity of the Old Russian pantheon), the act that causes the struggle. Perun chases his enemy, strikes the serpent and sets free everything the serpent has stolen. Pushkin slightly deviates from the mythic paradigm in his poem: although the robbers retreat, "dropping their loot on their way," Parasha is not taken away from the usurper: she disappears, leaving no trace. It is interesting to notice, however, a curious coincidence connected with the name of the poem's heroine. The Christian name "Paraskeva" (Parasha) is an equivalent of the pagan name "Mokosh": "After the acceptance of the Orthodoxy, Paraskeva-Piatnitsa became a direct continuation of the image of Mokosh" (Mify narodov mira II: 169). It seems that since the name "Mokosh" is etymologically connected with the root *mokr-* (*mokryi, moknut'*), St. Paraskeva acquired a number of characteristics associated with contact with water: hence the customs according to which "one should not bathe children on Fridays; and those who do not fast on a Holy Friday may drown" (Mify narodov mira II: 357). It is no coincidence either that the Neva is compared to a beast. As Boris Gasparov aptly points out, the flood and the "frenzy" of the beast in *The Bronze Horseman* enter the paradigm of images that correspond to the revolt of elemental, other-worldly forces (Gasparov 1984, 146, 344). Perun's struggle with the serpent is perceived in this case on the plane of the suppression of the elements, or of the chaos of water. Significantly, according to Evgenii Meletinskii, in most mythologies the serpent "is connected with water, often as its thief, so that he threatens with either flood, or drought, that is, with violation of the norm, the water balance" (Meletinskii 1976, 208).

Thus one could say that the portrayal of the flood, if associated with the myth of Perun, may be interpreted as a cosmogonic struggle signifying the victory of the forces of cosmos (Petersburg with the monument to Peter the Great in its center) over the forces of chaos (the Neva). In this way the flood reproduces the cosmogonic theme of the Introduction. The reemergence of chaos and its defeat represent one more cycle of the spiral in the system of the cosmic cycle. The cosmogonic myth, or "true story," ends with a picture of the revived city and the re-establishment of the old order ("the crimson [radiance of the morning's rays] / Covered up the harm. / Everything returned to the old order").

Such is the trinomial cosmic model of the "Petersburg tale." A historical event, which lies at the basis of the poem (the flood), serves as convenient material for creation of the real "tribal myth": the history of Petersburg and of its creator, that is, of the beginning of the new europeanized Russia. As we have seen in our discussion of *Poltava* in the previous chapter, even later, in 1834, while speaking about the positive role of Peter the Great's wars in Russian history, Pushkin employs the same image of the defeated, conquered Neva: "The success of the national reforms was the result of the battle of Poltava, and European enlightenment moored to the shores of the conquered Neva" (XI, 269).

The Individual Facing History

Despite differences of interpretation and approach, the mythological essence of Pushkin's description of Petersburg in general provokes no controversy. As I have demonstrated, the portrayal of Petersburg and the flood reproduces a "tribal myth" of sorts.

The image of Eugene, however, generates disagreements among scholars. What led Eugene to his perdition? What is the author's attitude toward his hero?

In the scholarly literature dedicated to *The Bronze Horseman*, it became a tradition to consider Eugene as a victim, be it a victim of the state (Mirsky), a victim of imperialism (Lednicki), or a victim of the statue (Jakobson). Such an approach is based on the clear reduction of the poem to the opposition *Eugene—the Bronze Horseman*. Roman Jakobson formulated this idea most explicitly in his famous article "The Statue in Pushkin's Poetic Mythology." Jakobson labels the Bronze Horseman "the citizen's persecutor," and calls Eugene "the victim of the state" (Jakobson, 262–3). For several reasons I cannot agree with this view. Jakobson's concept of the "destructive statue" is based on the comparative analysis of three of Pushkin's narratives: *The Stone Guest* (*Kamennyi Gost'*); *The Bronze Horseman,* and *The Tale of the Golden Cockerel* (*Skazka o Zolotom Petushke*). Jakobson discerns the common thematic kernel of these works:

> 1. *A man is weary, he settles down, he longs for rest, and this motif is intertwined with desire for a woman.* [. . .]
> 2. *The statue, more precisely the being which is inseparably connected with the statue, has a supernatural, unfathomable power over this desired woman.* [. . .]
> 3. *After a vain resistance the man perishes through the intervention of the statue, which has miraculously set itself into motion, and the woman vanishes* (Jakobson 1979, 240–41).

When applied to *The Bronze Horseman*, however, the invariant motifs discovered by Jakobson do not correspond to at least two of the named above points. Thus, the woman, or "heroine" in *The Bronze Horseman,* as opposed to the rather real Dona Anna and Shamakhanian Empress, seems to be a purely fictitious character (I will develop this point later). It does not follow from the text of the poem that the Bronze Horseman has any power over Parasha, or that she vanishes as a result of the statue's malicious intervention. Neither is there reason to give credence to the revelations of Eugene who, according to Jakobson, "in his sudden madness [. . .] clairvoyantly perceives that the real culprit is the guardian of the city, the renowned Bronze Horseman, Tsar Peter" (243). In this regard, I fully support the observation of Richard Gregg: "What reason is there to believe that Pushkin wished us to share his hero's sudden 'illumination'?" (1977, 173).

In addition to these objections, there is one more argument against Jakobson's scheme: if Don Juan and Tsar Dodon really perish as a result of the intervention of statues that miraculously set themselves into motion, nothing of the sort occurs in *The Bronze Horseman*. Eugene's revolt in front of the monument of Peter the Great changes nothing in his fate. Eugene goes mad *before* he has a confrontation with the Bronze Horseman, and he remains in this state *after* his escapade as well. In *The Stone Guest* and *The Tale of the Golden Cockerel*, by contrast, the protagonists' deaths occur *instantaneously* as a result of the intervention of the supernatural power.

Attempts have often been made to interpret the character of Eugene on the basis of Pushkin's own biography. Thus, for example, both Lednicki and Jakobson succumb to the temptation of drawing the parallel between the relationships of Eugene to Peter I and Pushkin to Nicholas I. Jakobson therefore reasons: "What circumstances accompanied the origin of this *second version of Puškin's myth of the destructive statue?* Remembrance of the lonely fiancé's tempestuous autumn in involuntary exile at Boldino, [. . .] mounting fear of the tsar, who was enslaving the poet and courting his wife, and indignation both at the whole imperial environment, which was wanton and seditious, and at the capital [*nevolja nevskix beregov*]" (260). Likewise, Jakobson connects Eugene's matrimonial yearnings with Pushkin's own decision to get married—a detail in which both the author and his hero seem little different from other mortals: "Originally Puškin's own deliberation about matrimony had passed over into *The Bronze Horseman* from the eighth chapter of *Eugene Onegin*" (1979, 262).

In his otherwise remarkable book dedicated to *The Bronze Horseman*, Waclaw Lednicki observes a certain affinity between the hero of the poem and its author, namely the similarity of their social status, that is, of their belonging to the impoverished Russian nobility: "Such a stylization of the figure of the 'humble' hero of the poem, of the 'poor' Eugene, who in the first drafts of the poem was endowed with another characteristic trait — an inclination for poetry — reveals Pushkin's feeling of offense at the existing state of affairs in Russia, a feeling which is skillfully and deeply concealed in the poem" (Lednicki, 69). It is highly doubtful that a simple "inclination for poetry" and the poor clerk's desire to get married are sufficient to claim the resemblance with Pushkin. At least in *Eugene Onegin*, Pushkin attempted to defend himself against such analogies:

Как будто нам уж невозможно
Писать поэмы о другом,
Как только о себе самом (VI, 29).

As if it were impossible for us
To write poems about others
And not only about ourselves.

Neither Lednicki nor Jakobson observes that Pushkin speaks about his hero's inclination for poetry with unconcealed irony just as he mocks Onegin's or Belkin's unsuccessful attempts to become poets. Regarding Eugene's emphatically prosaic yearnings Pushkin remarks: "And like a poet he got lost in dreams" (*I razmechtalsia, kak poet*). Significantly, Pushkin employs the same device of ironic juxtaposition of poetry and prose some lines below: Count Khvostov, a "poet loved by the heavens," appears with his "immortal verses" on the most prosaic background (which is emphasized in the poem on the level of rhythm as well). It has to

be noted that irony toward Eugene is not accidental; it is implied
in the very name of the hero. As Lotman points out, "Beginning
with the second satire of Kantemir, Evgenii (Greek "well-born")
is a name that designates a negative, satirically portrayed personage, a young gentleman using the privileges of his ancestors without having their merits" (Lotman 1983, 113). Lotman continues:
"Significantly, in granting the hero of *The Bronze Horseman* the
same name, Pushkin preserves the semantics of a loss. However, if
in the moralistic literature of the 18th century "Evgenii" signifies
a nobleman [*blagorodnyi*] who lost his spiritual noblesse [*blago-
rodstvo*], the hero of *The Bronze Horseman* is an impoverished de-
scendant of high-born ancestors" (Lotman 1983, 113). One could
add that a "well-born" Eugene not only became impoverished but
lost the memory of his high-born ancestors, for whom he "does not
grieve." About his family name the author simply remarks: "His
further naming is not required" (*Prozvan'ia nam ego ne nuzhno*).
In this way the name "Eugene" turns into a semantic oxymoron
and becomes redolent with clearly ironical overtones.

A similar irony pervades the description of Eugene's thoughts
and dreams. Thus, for example, the parallelism of the lines "And
he thought" (*I dumal on*) (about Peter) and "What did he think
about?" (*O chiom zhe dumal on?*) (about Eugene) emphasizes the
author's rather ironical attitude toward his protagonist. In point of
fact, an analogous parallelism occurs later on in the poem as well.
Pushkin writes about Peter the Great: "Full of great thoughts he
stood" (*Stoial* **on,** *dum velikikh poln*). The author's choice of words
in his description of Eugene is strikingly and ironically similar:
"He roamed silently, full of terrifying thoughts" (*Uzhasnykh dum /
Bezmolvno poln, on skitalsia*). It is important to stress here the juxtaposition of Eugene's and Peter's "broodings" (*dumy*), and that of
the stasis of Peter and everything connected with him (cf. "Stand
in all your splendor, city of Peter, and stand steadfast, like Russia" [*Krasuisia, grad Petrov, i stoi / Nekolebimo, kak Rossiia*]) with
Eugene's chaotic movement ("he roamed"). Still more ironical and

even parodical is the picture of Eugene riding the marble lion, for it clearly contrasts with a real rider — the bronze Peter on his horse.

These considerations do not allow me to share the traditional view of Eugene as a tragic hero. Jakobson referring to Mirsky articulates this standard opinion: "Evgenij, as a critic rightly points out, is indeed wretched but not even slightly farcical: in spite of his external shabbiness he grows into a tragic hero, and his death arouses not disdainful pity but terror and compassion" (Jakobson, 264).

The plot-line connected with the story of Eugene could be summed up as follows:

1. The hero appears; his appearance more or less coincides with the beginning of the flood.

2. The hero recalls his beloved and dreams about marriage.

3. The flood turns out to be the main obstacle to the hero's reunion with his fiancée.

4. In search of his fiancée the hero crosses the river, but does not find his beloved and goes mad.

5. He remains in a state of madness and roams around without coming back to his house. During his wanderings, he experiences a strange incident of a half-real and half-hallucinatory nature. This event, however, has no decisive influence on his fate.

6. The rambling and madness of the hero end with his death on the threshold of a destroyed house.

From the formal point of view one can say that at the base of this plot lies a failed attempt of the hero to change his social status, or in other words, to perform a transition that is called "initiation" in traditional anthropology. A ritual by means of which adolescents enter adulthood, that is, become marriageable, represents the main form of initiation. According to numerous studies of myth and religion, this transition includes the following necessary components:

1. The transition must occur beyond the boundary of "this

world." Compare Eugene's crossing of the river, which is clearly
perceived as a transition to the world beyond the grave:

Евгений смотрит: видит лодку;
Он к ней бежит как на находку;
Он перевозчика зовет —
И перевозчик беззаботный
Его за гривенник охотно
Чрез волны страшные везет (V, 144).

Evgenii looks: he sees a boat;
He runs toward it, as toward a find;
He calls the ferryman —
And the carefree ferryman
Gladly takes him across the terrible
Waves for a ten-kopeck piece.

In the "carefree ferryman" one can unmistakably recognize Charon, the ferryman who transported the dead over the waters of the
Styx and received a payment for his services — a coin of one obolus.
In this context it is no surprise that Eugene recognizes nothing on
the other side of the river and sees only that "corpses lie scattered
all around, as if on a battlefield (*[. . .] krugom, / Kak budto v pole
boevom, / Tela valiaiutsia*).

2. A symbolic temporary death, which in mythological interpretation is often equated with exit outside the exclusive territory.
In the text of the poem, the fact that Eugene leaves his house and
goes mad corresponds to mythological symbolic death. As a result
of his madness he becomes "neither beast nor man; neither this
nor that; neither resident of this world nor dead ghost" ([. . .] *ni
zver' ni chelovek, / Ni to ni sio, ni zhitel' sveta / Ni prizrak mertvyi . . .*).

3. The required knowledge of tribal myths, which may be staged
in front of the initiated. It is the history of Petersburg and of
its "marvel-working builder," Peter I–The Bronze Horseman, that
serves as such a tribal myth for the resident of Petersburg. In this

connection, Eugene's encounter with the Bronze Horseman—an episode that formally has no influence on the hero's fate—turns out to be exceptionally important, for it demonstrates the hero's attitude toward this myth.

The initiation ends with a "new birth" and with the return of the novice to society, having assumed a new status. Unfortunately, this does not happen to Eugene. Instead of the "resurrection," a second death, this time a real and final one, follows the symbolic death of the hero. There is one more detail that points to the initiatory nature of Eugene's story: nowhere does the author say that Eugene *loves* his fiancée. She represents for him merely a symbol of married life and the matrimonial home. This is why, in his dreams and his fears, Eugene thinks first of all of the house and only afterwards about his fiancée:

> Уж кое-как себе устрою
> Приют смиренный и простой
> И в нем Парашу успокою (Pushkin 1962–66: IV,
> 385).[13]

> Somehow I will make
> A humble and simple refuge for myself,
> And I will settle down Parasha there.

> [. . .] Боже, Боже! там—
> Увы! близехонько к волнам,
> Почти у самого залива—
> Забор некрашеный, да ива
> И ветхий домик: там оне,
> Вдова и дочь, его Параша [. . .] (V, 142).

> [. . .] Oh God, oh God! there—
> Alas! so close to the waves,
> Almost at the very gulf—
> Is an unpainted fence, a willow

And an old flimsy cottage: there they are,
Widow and daughter, his Parasha [. . .]

Looking for Parasha, Eugene does not ask himself where she is, but "where the house is." It is in search of the house, which has become for him a matrimonial symbol (Cf. the role of the house, or a hut, in the initiatory rituals), that Eugene wanders until he finds death on the threshold of an "old flimsy cottage" (*domishki vetkhogo*). It is natural then that Parasha does not appear in the poem at all. Nothing is known either about her looks, her age, or even her social status, which we can only guess. She can claim neither the role of heroine nor that of *dramatis persona* in the poem; she turns out to be in essence a purely "fictitious fiancée," or a theatrical "extra." For Eugene she is not the goal but a means of entering adulthood. (Significantly, the Russian name Paraskeva goes back to the Greek *paraskeue*, which means "preparation," "means," "method").[14]

In more general terms, any initiation may be considered as a transformation of "psychophysic chaos" into "social cosmos," that is, as a socialization of the individual.[15] Such a transformation begins with the moment of birth and of acquiring a name—the event which is perceived as the first link that connects man to his family, his tribe, or to the "social cosmos." This is why it is no coincidence that the reader's acquaintance with the hero of *The Bronze Horseman* begins with the author's choice of the name for the protagonist of the story and with the description of the hero's attitude toward his kinsfolk. Interestingly enough, while in the process of working on the poem, Pushkin vacillated between two versions of his hero's social origin: in one variant he is an aristocrat, in another he is a "clerk of modest means" (*chinovnik nebogatyi*).[16] Such a vacillation may indicate that it was not the hero's birth in itself that was important for Pushkin, but his attitude toward his origins.[17] Pushkin conveys a similar idea in "The Genealogy of My Hero" ("Rodoslovnaia moego geroia"), a poem that includes verses initially intended for *The Bronze Horseman*. In this poem

the poet expresses not so much his dissatisfaction with the current
state of affairs but a protest against the oblivion of the past:

> Мне жаль, что сих родов боярских
> Бледнеет блеск и никнет дух.
> Мне жаль, что нет князей Пожарских,
> Что о других пропал и слух,
> Что их поносит шут Фиглярин,
> Что русский ветреный боярин
> Теряет грамоты царей,
> Как старый сбор календарей. [. . .]
> [.   .   .   .]
> Что геральдического льва
> Демократическим копытом
> У нас лягает и осел:
> Дух века вот куда зашел! (III: I, 427–28).

> I feel sorry that the glamour and the spirit
> Of those boyar families pales away and fades.
> I feel sorry that there are no more princes Pozharskii,
> That others are not even recalled,
> That the buffoon Figliarin defames them,
> That a lightminded Russian boyar
> Loses the charters of the tsars,
> As if they were a pile of old calendars. [. . .]
> [.   .   .   .]
> That in our country, even an ass
> Kicks the heraldic lion
> With his democratic hoof:
> Here is what the spirit of the century has come to! [18]

Any genealogy is typologically close to cosmogonic myths, and
a genealogical tree—to a world tree. This is why a history of ancient families and dynasties often starts with a story of the birth of
the cosmos from the egg (Eliade, 1975, 21–22). (Cf. "The Geneal-

ogy of My Hero" which begins *ab ovo* — a locution that had already become a cliché). The hero's indifference toward his "heraldic lion" is equated in this case with his ignorance of the cosmogonic myth itself and his lack of genealogical knowledge, and thus with ignorance of history in general. The meditations of Vladimir, a protagonist of Pushkin's *Novel in Letters* (*Roman v pis'makh*), are very similar: "The past does not exist for us. A pathetic people! An aristocracy based on rank cannot take the place of a hereditary aristocracy. The gentry's family chronicles should be the nation's historical heritage" (VIII: I, 53). In this context, the image of Eugene "chained" to the lion seems especially parodical, for Eugene, riding the lion (a "heraldic lion"?), is clearly juxtaposed to the Bronze Horseman who, in turn, is associated with the world tree. Eugene's disregard for his "heraldic lion" (for the history of his family) corresponds to his rejection of the Bronze Horseman, a rejection which signifies renunciation of history as a whole in the context of Petersburg mythology.[19] Since the Bronze Horseman, as I have tried to demonstrate, combines the traits of Perun and those of the world-tree, Eugene's rebellion against the Bronze Horseman symbolizes his final defection from cosmos; it is described as sacrilege. In this connection, it is interesting to note that Pushkin employs the epithet "miracle-working" (*chudotvornyi*) to describe Peter the Great, a term that is traditionally used with respect to icons or saints (*chudotvorets*). Yet, in each of the variants Pushkin portrays Eugene as "possessed by a dark force" (*obuiannyi siloi chernoi*). The description of the island on which the body of the hero is found is also characteristic: it presents the picture of primeval chaos and takes us back to the beginning of the poem.[20] Once again, now for the last time, Eugene represents a topsy-turvy image of the Bronze Horseman, or Peter the Great: the shore where "*he* stood" (*stoial on*) turns into a threshold where the wretched Eugene lies.

The fate of the hero of *The Bronze Horseman* might be seen as a fine illustration of the anthropological observations of Eliade:

"Not to know or to forget the contents of the 'collective memory' constituted by tradition is equivalent to a retrogression to the 'natural' state (the acultural condition of the child), or to a 'sin,' or to a disaster" (Eliade 1975, 125).

Curiously enough, the theme of initiation, connected with the idea of acquiring the knowledge of "tribal wisdom," is present in a rather altered version in Pushkin's novel *The Blackamoor of Peter the Great*. Like Eugene, Ibragim ponders changing his social status: " 'To marry', mused the African, 'Why not?' " (VIII: I, 27). (Cf. Eugene: "To marry? Shall I? Why not?"). The protagonists' doubts are also similar. Ibragim meditates about his fate in the following way: "Is it that I am destined to spend my life in solitude, never experiencing the greatest pleasures and the most sacred obligations of man, just because I was born below the fifteenth parallel?" (VIII: I, 27) In the main draft of the poem Eugene reflects: "Is it that only the rich can get married . . ." As opposed to Eugene, however, Ibragim complies with the rules of the game, including the main one—the recognition of the "tribal myth"—and he follows the advice of Peter the Great himself to honor the "boyar pride" of his future father-in-law and to observe all the rituals and traditions expected from a member of the boyar class (VIII: I, 27). As a result, the loyal Blackamoor, wishing to join the "community" and not be a "newcomer in his new fatherland," adopts a necessary part of the "tribal myth"—to the great astonishment of his none-too-clever friend: " 'I marvel at your patience,' said Korsakov to Ibragim. 'You have been listening to the ravings about the ancient lineage of the Lykovs' and Rzhevskiis' families for a good hour and still will add to it your own moralistic comments' " (VIII: I, 30).

Clearly, the theme of one's attitude toward the past and toward history tormented Pushkin long before he wrote *The Bronze Horseman*. Yet in 1826, in his article "On the People's Education" ("O narodnom vospitanii"), Pushkin wrote: "The study of Russia should become the chief occupation of the minds of young gentlemen in their final years [of school], who are preparing themselves to serve the fatherland faithfully and with devotion [. . .], and not to lay obstacles to it, senselessly persisting in secret hostility" (XI, 47). At the same time, Pushkin insists on a familial and personal participation in history. It is necessary, he maintains, to know the history not only of one's country but that of one's lineage as well. Pushkin links one's attitude toward ancestors and "the gentry's family chronicles" (*semeistvennye vospominaniia dvorianstva*) with enlightenment and civilization. In 1830 he wrote: "A cultured Frenchman or Englishman values every line of an old chronicle in which his ancestor's name is mentioned, an honest knight who fell in such-and-such a battle or returned from Palestine in such-and-such a year; but the Kalmucks have neither a nobility nor a history. Savagery, baseness, and ignorance do not respect the past; they grovel only before the present" (XI, 162). The same idea is expressed in another article, as well: "Respect for the past is a trait that distinguishes culture from savagery; nomadic tribes have neither a history nor a nobility (XI, 184). These statements echo the beginning of *The Bronze Horseman*. In this work, Pushkin also portrays an unorganized chaos in which a "wretched Finn" (*ubogii chukhonets*) and a "Finnish fisherman, sad step-son of Nature" (*finskii rybolov, pechal'nyi pasynok prirody*) abide and to which Eugene, who has no respect for his genealogical tree, returns.

In contrast, Pushkin identifies knowledge of and respect for the past with wisdom and enlightenment. Moreover, this knowledge is equated with salvation: "To take pride in the glory of one's ancestors is not only permissible but necessary; not to respect it is a shameful faintheartedness. [. . .] The Greeks, even in their humiliation, remembered their glorious ancestry and for that alone deserved their liberation" (XI, 55). Such an attitude toward memory of the past, which is perceived as a pledge for salvation or healing, is characteristic of the mythological consciousness. According to Eliade, "forgetting is equivalent to ignorance, slavery [captivity], and death" (Eliade 1975, 119). Significantly, Pushkin finds even the cause of Radishchev's revolt and ruin in his disrespect for the past, and consequently, in his inability to evaluate the present condition properly: "Ignorant disregard for all of the past; feeble-minded amazement at his own age; blind bias toward novelty; particular, superficial knowledge, applied to everything at random — this is what we see in Radishchev" (XII, 36). Pushkin similarly accuses the "slanderers of Russia" of ignoring or forgetting the past:

> Оставьте нас: вы не читали
> Сии кровавые скрижали;
> Вам непонятна, вам чужда
> Сия семейная вражда (III: I, 269).

> Leave us: you did not read
> These bloody annals;
> You do not understand
> This family enmity; it is alien to you.

In this way history is mythologized. The meaning of the present is identified with the origins of the present. This is why, according to Pushkin, no matter what the past was like, one has to know it and accept it. Pushkin expresses these ideas in his letter to Chaadaev, 1836: "Quoique personnellement attaché de coeur à l'Empereur, je suis loin d'admirer tout ce que je vois autour de moi; comme homme de lettre, je suis aigri; comme homme à préjugés, je suis froissé — mais je vous jure sur mon honneur que pour rien au monde je n'aurais voulu changer de patrie, ni avoir d'autre histoire que celle de nos ancêtres, telle que Dieu nous l'a donnée" (Although personally attached in my heart to the Emperor, I am far from admiring all that I see around me; as a man of letters, I am embittered; as a biased man, I am offended — but I swear to you on my honor that for nothing in the world would I want to change my homeland, or to have any history other than that of our ancestors, such as God has given it to us. XVI, 172) Such an attitude toward history is characteristic of the mythological consciousness. For it is myth that the members of society accept, regardless of a positive or negative evaluation of its heroes and events. Gods and heroes may be good or evil; this fact does not interfere, however, with the sacral nature of myth itself.[21]

In *The Bronze Horseman* there are two clearly definable plot lines in the text of the poem: a "true story" that portrays a cosmogonic myth and a "false story" that describes the failed ritual of initiation. Entering Eugene's plot line, the cosmogonic myth becomes a part of the plot, for it fulfills the role of the "tribal myth," which is recited or staged in front of the initiated. Eugene fails this initiation because he does not recognize the importance of the past. His ignorance of his own genealogy and his inability to understand the history of his country represent merely two sides of the same coin. According to Pushkin, disrespect for the past and history and refusal to accept it "telle que Dieu nous l'a donnée" (that is, regardless of a positive or negative assessment of reality) constitutes a sign of *immaturity* and might lead to ill-grounded revolt and perdition.

Pushkin's ambiguous attitude toward Eugene and his antagonist, Peter/The Bronze Horseman, consists precisely in his mythological perception of history. Pushkin does not condemn Eugene and even arouses a certain degree of sympathy toward his hero. The poet demonstrates, however, that a man who places himself outside the history of his family and his land is doomed to ruin. The genetic ties that connect the Bronze Horseman with Perun emphasize furthermore the ambiguous nature of Pushkin's own attitude toward Peter the Great: he is a god, yet he is merely an idol.

afterword

*An isolated **idea** never expresses anything new, but*

***ideas** may be infinitely diverse.*

—Alexander Pushkin

In his eleventh essay on Pushkin, Vissarion Belinsky enthusias-
tically claimed that *The Bronze Horseman* together with *Poltava*
and such poems as "Stanzas" (1826) and "The Feast of Peter
the Great" form "the greatest Petriad" that a national genius
could create (Belinsky VI, 464). Indeed, it is tempting to consider Pushkin's Peter the Great narratives as a cycle. What
prompted Pushkin to start with a historical novel, to abandon
prose for poetry in *Poltava* and *The Bronze Horseman,* only to
return to prose again, this time in the form of a purely historical project, *History of Peter I?* In short, how do these various
works relate to each other and how could one explain the shifts
in genre that accompany Pushkin's literary treatments of the
Petrine theme?

Pushkin's fictional cycles normally belong to the same genre,
such as the short story (*The Tales of Belkin*) or the drama (*Little
Tragedies*). It is unlikely, therefore, that Pushkin planned these
texts to be considered as a cycle. Yet the discussion of the Peter
the Great narratives in *toto* could be justified by considerations
of convenience for the reader and the critic. We as readers tend
to impose a certain unity on the material, to group and to select
facts in order to advance *our* ideas about the texts. Although
frustrating for a self-conscious critic, this process of fact manipulation represents an inescapable part of any intellectual
endeavor. The ensuing unity, however, is often merely an illusion. Indeed, different versions of Peter represent self-sufficient

portrayals similar to photographs taken from various distances and different perspectives and, therefore, focusing on different aspects of the emperor. If one wishes to have a composite picture, one may put them in the same album and consider them as a group. Yet, seeking the seam, connecting these works into a unifying whole, would be as futile as trying to see when and how a wave becomes a particle in microphysics.

Rather than offer a different interpretation of the same historical period or problem, each work evolves around a *new* issue. Each of the three fictional Petrine narratives portrays a turning point in the political career of Peter and in Russian historical development. Each work is written from a different narrative point of view and includes different participants. In *The Blackamoor of Peter the Great,* the emphasis is on the new type of man emerging during the reign of Peter I, on Peter's social revolution that substituted the privilege of birth with personal merit and brought about, as a consequence, the gradual destruction of the old gentry class. In *Poltava,* Peter is evaluated from the point of view of the interests of the nation. Pushkin focuses on Peter's military and political success as the creator of the Russian empire. Finally, in *The Bronze Horseman,* the point of view shifts again: the poet considers the actual repercussions of the Petrine reforms for an individual and that individual's response to Peter's challenge. On the one hand, St. Petersburg, a glorious and beautiful capital of Russia and the epitome of Peter's successful westernization, represents the might of the new empire. On the other hand, the private individual, Eugene, an heir of the misplaced Russian gentry, finds himself outside of history. Yet Pushkin shows that he is not a passive victim of the tsar or of the historical flux. *The Bronze Horseman* seems to suggest that each individual is a historian of sorts and as such is responsible for his or her own fate and that of the nation. History is what we make of it and so Peter I too is what we make of him. Eugene *chooses* to view Peter as a "proud idol" (*gordelivyi istukan*), who threatens him and gallops after him along the Petersburg streets in vengeance, but Pushkin makes sure to indicate that this vision is, in fact, a mere hallucination. A professional historian, a poet, or a private observer of a historical event makes history by the very fact of its interpreting. Viewed in this way, the past does not fully predetermine the future. Ultimately, the future depends on the way any single individual interprets and responds to the past. It is Eugene's misinterpretation of history that precipitates his doom.

Each work, therefore, suggests a new idea and paints a new face of Peter the Great. By embedding his images of Peter in different contexts and focusing on different speciotemporal units, Pushkin shifts the perspective from which the events are presented. This shift marks the change in *chronotope* and results in differences in genre. How do Pushkin's conceptualizations of various aspects of Peter the Great's reign determine his choice of genre and what kind of historical concept each genre projects?

In his essay "Poetic Genre and the Sense of History in Pushkin," Jurij Striedter shows how Pushkin's preference for certain poetic genres is determined by the poet's changing sense of history. Particularly, Striedter raises an important problem of the chronological distance from the events presented (296). It is the urgent need to represent the historical events as past that ultimately accounts, so his argument goes, for the shift in Pushkin's interests from historical drama to various epic genres (300). For the structure of the dramatic genre presupposes the immediacy of the scenic presence and does not, as a rule, provide the sense of distance from the historical events presented. By contrast, the narrator's presence in the epic genres guarantees a certain degree of epic distance.

Pushkin's choice of one genre over another, however, does not necessarily reflect a significant change in Pushkin's overall sense of history but is rather dictated by his immediate concerns and his awareness of the specifics of the historical material. Although Pushkin chooses the dramatic genre for his portrayal of Boris Godunov, a dramatic rendering of Peter is conspicuously absent from his multigeneric repertoire. As late as 1836, eleven years

after he completed *Boris Godunov*, in his much quoted letter to
Chaadaev, Pushkin refers to the Godunov reign as "le drame sub-
lime," whereas Peter, he claims, is "une histoire universelle." In
other words, even in 1836 Pushkin still conceives Boris Godunov in terms of the drama. Although Pushkin's contemporaries
attempted to represent Peter in drama (cf., for example, *The Historical Tale [Istoricheskaia byl']*] by Nikolai Polevoi or Mikhail Pogodin's tragedy *Peter I*), Pushkin seems to refuse to shape the
subject of Peter the Great in a dramatic form.[1]

Significantly, not only in his fictional works but also in his *History*, Pushkin pays relatively little attention to Peter's personal life,
be it his relationship with Catherine or with his son, Aleksei.[2] It
is clear that Peter intrigued Pushkin not so much as a character
of great psychological complexity, who could be treated in drama
according to the Shakespearean model, but as a historical phenomenon, as the emblem of the whole period of Russian history
that was marked by drastic change and that reflected the complexity and ambiguity of the historical process.[3] Characteristically,
even Pushkin's historical project was intended to cover the entire
Petrine phenomenon that would extend beyond Peter I's biography. Thus, in 1831, he requests permission from the Tsar to work
in the archives "in order to fulfill my old desire—to write a history
of Peter the Great and his successors including the Tsar Peter III"
(Pushkin 1962–66: IX, 544). The awareness of the contradictory
nature of the historical process and of the Petrine phenomenon
specifically leads Pushkin to the understanding of the centrality of
point of view and context to any evaluation of reality. To consider
Peter from various perspectives meant to provide various conceptualizations, which inevitably resulted in the change of genre. The
multigeneric approach to Peter afforded Pushkin with the possibility of rendering the nonhomogeneous nature of history itself.

The notion of distance in Pushkin's historical narratives is not
limited to the sense of actual chronological remoteness and to the
problem of the narration of the historical events as past. Even the

events of one's own times could be viewed from the bird's eye perspective. Moreover, historical events could be represented as past, and they could be characterized by different levels of generalization, depending on the chosen perspective from which they are observed. Distance is a category of historical thinking that puts additional emphasis on the observer and his or her vantage point and influences in this way the level of generalization. In his study *History: The Last Thing Before the Last,* Siegfried Kracauer provides an interesting discussion of the role of distance in historical narratives. "As we ascend progressively higher over the historical terrain," he argues, "events and situations begin to blur and their full particularity is lost; different patterns emerge at different altitudes." Differences in distance result in differences in scope and determine the type of sources and data one selects for a given historical account. The larger the distance the more the viewer depends on his imagination and is, therefore, more subjective.

Interestingly, in 1833, Pushkin complained to Dal' of still standing too close to "this giant," Peter I. As he was contemplating a larger-scale *History of Peter,* he felt the need to step back from the given data in order to broaden his field of vision. It is no coincidence that *The Bronze Horseman* and also *Poltava* contain a rhetorical formula "a century passed," an important distancing device that Pushkin employs to provide a more general evaluation of the events.[4] Both *Poltava* and *The Bronze Horseman* represent Pushkin's attempt to distance himself from Peter and to comprehend him from the bird's eye perspective. As a result, the portraits of Peter in his poems are more subjective and myth-oriented. For myth always narrates about something remote in time and space as do most epic texts.

By contrast, the sense of distance in Pushkin's historical novel, *The Blackamoor of Peter the Great,* significantly differs from that in his two Romantic poems. Even though the presence of the third person narrator allows for the representation of the events as past, Peter is intended to be seen primarily through the eyes of his contemporary, Ibragim (cf. such expressions as "Ibragim looked with curiosity at the newly born capital" or "Ibragim could not stop being surprised at his quick and firm mind"). Ibragim, however, is standing much too close to the Russian emperor to be able to comprehend him in all his magnitude. Thus in place of generalizations, the novel provides a series of isolated and magnified pictures of the emperor, focusing on the particular and often visual details. The Blackamoor's closeness to Peter is emphasized throughout the novel and so is Peter's private personality as opposed to his historical stature. Ibragim could well observe Peter's quotidian occupations, admire the emperor's genius and the success of the unfolding reforms, but he could hardly convey the high-magnitude view of Peter's role in Russian history. This is why when Pushkin wishes to make a comment on Peter's supreme historical role, his narrator recurs to anachronisms and draws conclusions that could be made only from a larger temporal distance inaccessible to Ibragim.

Pushkin's failure to complete *The Blackamoor of Peter the Great* could be explained, at least in part, by his ambivalent feelings in regard to a "close-up" technique that the genre of the historical novel presupposes. The historical novel in the manner of Walter Scott, while dealing with minute circumstances and rendering history in a "domestic manner," tends to ignore a larger historical perspective. It is also no coincidence that such novels rarely introduce kings or other prominent historical figures as central protagonists or as a main force that brings about historical change. The proximity of the observed events does not allow one to exaggerate the impact of an individual's power. Whether in Pushkin's historical novels or in Tolstoy's *War and Peace*, the reader sees historical figures in their daily occupations through the eyes of their contemporaries who stand so close to them that they are utterly unable to recognize a statesman behind a private individual. As Ibragim in *The Blackamoor of Peter the Great* says, "nobody could have suspected this kind and hospitable master of the house of being the hero of Poltava, the powerful and formidable reformer of Russia" (VI, 22).

It is in his long narrative poems *Poltava* and *The Bronze Horseman* that Pushkin introduced Peter as the hero of Poltava or as a bronze idol symbolizing Russia's might and its indeterminate destiny. The poems afforded him with a degree of abstraction and distance that was needed to ascribe more value to the emperor's individual achievements than the genre of the historical novel could tolerate.

Although rather sketchily portrayed, Peter emerges in the novel as a true to life human being. Peter of the novel, therefore, is significantly less mythologized than Peter of *Poltava* and of *The Bronze Horseman*. By contrast, in Pushkin's narrative poems, Peter rises to a mythological dimension of a storm god and becomes a powerful agent in the new cosmology. Merely a "tall man" (*chelovek vysokogo rostu*) in the novel, Peter rises in scale to become a hero, a storm god, a "colossal monument" in *Poltava* and a gigantic equestrian mounting in the "unshakable height" in *The Bronze Horseman*. With the increased distance, Peter's image grows in stature, but becomes more and more generalized, less and less human, so that Peter the man literally turns into the generalization of himself—Peter the statue. Such details as Peter's clay pipe, his green caftan, or his preference for the anise vodka, are no longer visible and no longer relevant for the distanced portrait of the emperor. In his historical poems, one sees fewer details. Instead a more general representation emerges, the one aimed at putting in relief only several most emblematic features of the emperor— his stretched arm and his bronze brow standing out against the darkness of the sky. Individuals are no longer seen from such a distance—only the giants like Peter. Significantly, both in *Poltava* and in *The Bronze Horseman*, the individuals who step against the grain of history are swept away by the historical flux. When Eugene finds himself standing close to the colossal figure of Peter, he perishes. He is literally unable to face the giant. Even though the story of Eugene indicates that Pushkin is trying to consider Peter from the perspective of a "little man," the epic part of the poem that narrates the "cosmological myth" is written from an eagle's eye perspective. The act of Peter's creation is distanced in time by one hundred years, and from this distance Peter emerges as an enigmatic symbol of power and Russian historical destiny. From this perspective, we see only the result of Peter's titanic activity — the imperial city rising from the swamps, whereas the "little man," Eugene, vanishes and leaves no trace in history.

Pushkin seems to be aware of both advantages and disadvantages of the novel's historical "nearsightedness." Although an epic genre, the historical novel avoids sweeping generalizations permissible in the poem. Ironically, the novel's orientation toward immediacy and the small distance from which the events are observed thus endows the novel with a higher degree of objectivity, whereas the more retrospective poem inevitably leads a poet to generalizations and, therefore, subjectivity.

Pushkin, however, considered both the danger of generalization and the risk of being bogged down in details and losing sight of the whole picture. Without trying to correct the "myopic" vision of the novel and the "far-sightedness" of the Romantic poem, Pushkin strove to resolve the problem not by means of mediation, that is, by compromising either the scope or his sense of detail, but diachronically, by focusing on the event from various distances and creating both close-ups and panoramic representations of the historical events.

Not surprisingly, the various fictional genres did not exhaust Pushkin's incessant quest for multiperspectival representation of historical reality. Peter the Great remains at the center of his artistic and historical concerns during his later years, up to his very last days. In his purely historical project, *History of Peter*, Pushkin sought to evaluate the Petrine phenomenon from the distance of "two centuries" in order to "think and judge freely," as he explains it to Dal' (Dal', 262).

Pushkin's refusal to congeal the nonhomogeneity of history into a unifying whole, his multiple generic and stylistic shifts within a single narrative as well as experimentations with different fictional and nonfictional genres reveal his incessant quest for complementarity and coexistence of heterogeneous ideas and interpretations. His multigeneric solution to the problem of representation of historical reality is both modest and realistic. In pursuing historical and imaginative kinds of writing as complementary versions of reality, Pushkin avoids the extremes of idealizing either poetic or scientific consciousness and attempts to reconcile the existence of verifiable facts with the knowledge that the past can never be fully uncovered or explained.

In our own time, when the questions of Russian history, national identity, and the ongoing debate about the Petrine heritage impress themselves upon Russian consciousness with renewed and unprecedented urgency, when the shelves of Russian bookstores heap up with historical novels as well as with newly written and rewritten histories, Pushkin's representations of Russian historical reality become more relevant than ever. Art vs. science, national "elevating illusions" vs. "low truths" of history, chance vs. necessity, East vs. West, the universal vs. particular, the relation of the past to the future, and the options open to an individual confronting the past and the present — these sorts of issues are among those demanding most immediate recognition. And it is these issues that Pushkin's incessant preoccupation with history makes us consider and recognize as our own. Of foremost importance, however, is not only *what* Pushkin has to say about a particular subject but his multifocal approach to the problems of historical reality, his methodological innovativeness and honesty that foster the complementarity of ideas, as well as of forms of representation, question fixed formulas and accommodate difference in context, distance, and point of view. This multifocal approach teaches us how to avoid history's blind spots.

notes

Preface

1. See, for example, Caryl Emerson's monograph *Boris Godunov: Trans-positions of a Russian Theme*, which provides a brilliant interpretation of Pushkin's drama and raises important questions about the treatment of the same tale in various genres: history (Karamzin), drama (Pushkin), and opera (Mussorgsky). Stimulating readings of *Boris Godunov* are also offered by Stephanie Sandler in her book *Distant Pleasures: Alexander Pushkin and the Writers of Exile* and Monika Greenleaf in her *Pushkin and Romantic Fashion: Fragment, Elegy, Orient, Irony*. Various interpretations of *The Captain's Daughter, Poltava* and especially of *The Bronze Horseman* continue to proliferate.

2. Although considerable scholarship has been devoted to the role of Peter the Great in Russian thought (see, for example, Nicholas Riasanovsky's study *The Image of Peter the Great in Russian History and Thought* or Xenia Gasiorowska's book *The Image of Peter the Great in Russian Fiction*), only one book deals directly with the subject of Peter the Great in Pushkin—Victor Arminjon's largely descriptive study, *Pouchkine et Pierre le Grand* (1971). In *An Obsession with History: Russian Writers Confront the Past*, Andrew Wachtel considers Pushkin's approach to the past, but his brief discussion of Pushkin's treatment of history is limited to the comparative analysis of *The Captain's Daughter* and *The History of Pugachev* and is subordinated to a larger goal to identify "the peculiar Russian attitude toward history" (Wachtel, 7).

There are few dissertations that treat the theme of history in Pushkin (Stephanie Sandler) or address Pushkin's treatment of history in connection with one individual work (Virginia M. Burns). Denka Krysteva treats the theme of Peter the Great in Pushkin in terms of its connection to epic genres, but says little about his historical concept ("Epicheskii kharakter temy Petra I i poiski A. S. Pushkina v ee khudozhestvennom osmyslenii").

In Russian scholarship, much has been written on the subject of Pushkin's historicism or his concept of history. Although such prominent Soviet scholars as Tomashevskii, Makagonenko, Feinberg, Eidelman, and Toibin investigated the scope of Pushkin's historical interests, as well as the poet's sources and the way he treated historical material, they generally have relied excessively on extraliterary writings and have left out close examination of Pushkin's fictional texts. As a result, much documentary information has been provided, many generalizations made, but little weight has been given to Pushkin's historical vision as it transpires through his individual works.

3. The term "multi-perspectival" or "poly-perspectival" was used by Mark Poliakov and Caryl Emerson in relation to Pushkin's drama *Boris Godunov* (Poliakov, 106–7; Emerson 1986, 97).

Introduction

1. For analysis of the principal forms of mythic and fabulous literature and the basic plot structures, see Frye, 158–238.

2. See, for example, the collection of essays edited by Stephen C. Behrendt: *History and Myth: Essays on English Romantic Literature.*

3. Moreover, even within historical fictional genres, history is often represented in drastically different ways. Georg Lukács, for example, attempted to demonstrate the different roles kings and other famous historical personages play in a history play and a historical novel, pointing out that in a play they are placed at the center of the narrative, whereas in the novel they remain marginalized. Lukács develops his ideas about the role of history in the historical novel and drama at length in his major study *The Historical Novel* (Lukács 1963, 89–170). Likewise, in his study *Historical Drama: The Relation of Literature and Reality,* Herbert Lindenberger points out that the role of history in historical drama is subordinated to contemporary dramatic conventions and to the audience's knowledge of the historical past (5–6). Still more perceptible is the difference between conventional history and any of the historical fictional genres.

4. For an important discussion of Shakespeare's ambivalences in terms of the principle of complementarity, see Norman Rabkin's study *Shakespeare and the Common Understanding.*

5. " 'The Spirits' of Kiukhelbeker are rubbish; there are only very few good verses there and no invention whatsoever" (XIII, 249).

6. Previously a professor of history at Yena, Schiller did not want to choose between the truth of history and the truth of fiction. His interest in the Thirty Years' War inspired him to write the narrative history (*The History of the Thirty Years' War*) as well as his famous *Wallenstein* trilogy. In the Prologue to *Wallenstein,* Schiller suggests a complementary relationship between history and art and takes pain to delineate the different tasks of history and poetry by reminding his audience that his muse

> [. . .] should thus transform the sombre hues
> Of truth into the realm of art serene,
> Create illusion, then in honesty
> Reveal the trick she plays, and not pretend
> That what she brings us is the stuff of truth.
> Life is in earnest, art serene and free (169).

For good discussions of the genesis of *Wallenstein* and its relation to Schiller's *History of the Thirty Years' War*, see the works of Elfriede Heyer and Lesley Sharpe.

Although not treating the same historical periods in history and fiction, like Pushkin and Schiller, Manzoni is known for his historical novel, *The Betrothed* (*I promessi sposi*), which exhibits great tension between poetry and narrative history. Moreover, along with historical fiction Manzoni was also the author of purely historical and theoretical works, such as *Discorso sopra alcuni punti della storia longobardica* and *On the Historical Novel* among others. His common practice was to supply his historical fiction with additional historical information. Thus, as Sandra Bermann points out in her Introduction to Manzoni's *On the Historical Novel* (*Del romanzo storico*), the *Discorso* would serve as the "historical supplement" to his historical tragedy *Adelchi* (Manzoni, 20).

7. Although Lindenberger argues that in the nineteenth century "the division between history and myth was only an apparent one — the product, surely, of that new scientific mentality which limited historical research to what 'really' was and relegated less real phenomena to some realm of the imagination," it is clear that the structure of fictional works has more affinities with myth than purely historical narratives (Lindenberger 1990, 9).

Chapter 1 The Impediments of Russian History

1. Cf. Barante: "I did not believe that events followed one another in succession [. . .] without being destined by Providence to accomplish some great end" (Cit. in Gossman, 119).

2. In his differentiation between autocracy and despotism, Pushkin follows Karamzin. See Vatsuro, 1968. Another and probably more direct source of influence on Pushkin's political ideas was Professor A. P. Kunitsyn who taught at the Lycée of Tsarskoe Selo. For a brief survey of Kunitsyn's political ideas and their impact on Pushkin, see Leonard Schapiro's *Rationalism and Nationalism in Russian Nineteenth-Century Political Thought*, 48–58.

3. For a detailed discussion of Pushkin's views of the Russian nobility (*boiarstvo*), see Gerald Mikkelson's dissertation "Pushkin and the History of the Russian Nobility" (1971, 114–273). Sam Driver's *Pushkin: Literature and Social Ideas* provides a well researched and thorough examination of Pushkin's aristocratism (Driver 1989, 21–51).

4. The concept of history as a biography of personalities characterized romantic historiography and dominated Karamzin's mode of narrating the past. For an illuminating discussion of Karamzin's *History*, see Emerson 1986, 31–87. In his treatment of the Boris Godunov tale, Emerson maintains, Karamzin constructs a "distinctive chronotope that denies, in essence, any developmental potential to time" (Emerson 1986, 61).

5. Quoted by Leonard Schapiro, 53.

6. In his discussion of Russian nineteenth-century political thought, Leonard Schapiro argues that, according to Pushkin, "the attacks by the monarchy on the privilege, and therefore independence, of the nobility in favor of promotion by service paved the way for that alliance between autocrat and mass which is everywhere and always a first step toward tyranny" (Schapiro, 58).

Chapter 2 Chance and Historical Necessity

1. Pushkin's criticism of Polevoi and Guizot curiously coincides with Alexis de Tocqueville's definition of "historians in democratic times." Tocqueville writes:

> Historians who live in democratic ages, then, not only deny that the few have any power of acting upon the destiny of a people, but deprive the people themselves of the power of modifying their own condition, and they subject them either to an inflexible Providence or to some blind necessity. According to them, each nation is indissolubly bound by its position, its origin, its antecedents, and its character to a certain lot that no efforts can ever change. They involve generation in generation, and thus, going back from age to age, and from necessity to necessity, up to the origin of the world, they forge a close and enormous chain, which girds and binds the human race. To their minds it is not enough to show what events have occurred: they wish to show that events could not have occurred otherwise. They take a nation arrived at a certain stage of its history and affirm that it could not but follow the track that brought it thither. It is easier to make such an assertion than to show how the nation might have adopted a better course (Tocqueville, 92–93).

2. Curiously, the historians of the positivistic mold, who regarded historical theories of chance as unscholarly and based on emotion rather than analysis, also observed the connection between faith in chance and a specific historical situation. Thus, for example, Edward H. Carr, a twentieth-century positivist historian, contended that "in a group or a nation which is riding in the trough, not on the crest, of historical events, theories that stress the role of chance or accident in history will be found to prevail. The view that examination results are all a lottery will always be popular among those who have been placed in the third class" (Carr, 101). Although insightful, this observation does not fully account for the reasons that might generate theories of chance. An obvious implication of Carr's distinction between the "trough" and "crest" theories is that theories of chance are considered not as adequate and sophisticated as the positivistic theories of deterministic causality. Finding himself on the "crest of historical events," Carr seems to ignore that the larger part of mankind is in the trough. It may well have been that theories of the accidental attract those who feel themselves unable to accept painful reality in some other terms, as Carr implies. Carr, however, seems not to realize that not only certain nations which are not "on the crest of historical events" develop theories of chance, but that there are, in fact, certain societies in which chance plays a larger role than, for instance, in democracies.

3. According to Jurij Striedter, Boris's failure is the result of his inability "to master the irrational in politics and history — the irrational manifesting itself no less in the persistence of tradition than in the power of blind coincidence" (Striedter, 298). Likewise, Caryl Emerson points out that "Tsar Boris is victim of a most unfortunate combination of fates" (Emerson 1986, 104).

4. Boris Godunov's psychological conflict anticipates that of Pushkin's Salieri in many respects. While Salieri is trying to resolve the problem of the compatibility of *genii* and *zlodeistvo* by isolating the aesthetic and ethical categories, Boris attempts to rationalize the connection between politics and ethics by separating the political good from personal morality and by isolating the goal from the means. The problem of the relationship between politics and ethics is at the center of Pushkin's historical drama, just as the relationship between ethics and aesthetics is one of his governing concerns in *Mozart and Salieri*.

5. The volatility of glory and of popular opinion is a recurrent motif in Pushkin's poetry. Consider, for example, the epigraph to "Poltava" or his poem "Hero" ("Geroi," 1830).

6. See, for example, Rassadin, 55.

7. See, for example, Gershenzon, 42–49; Eikhenbaum 1937, 349–57. Boris
   Gasparov departs from the traditional interpretation of the tale as representing Pushkin's meditations on the paradoxes of history and argues
   instead that the comic poem is an "Apocalyptic prophecy" disguised as a
   joke (Gasparov 1987, 23).
8. The fates of his Decembrist friends definitely could not leave Pushkin
   indifferent and forced him to think about the whims of chance. One of
   Pushkin's unfinished plans, "Notes of a Young Man" ("Zapiski molo-
   dogo cheloveka"), was connected with the fate of a young man who had
   graduated from military school (*Kadetskii korpus*). Nina Petrunina draws
   the following conclusion about this fragment: "The form of these notes
   with their confidential confessional tone, with the rather distinct image of
   the hero-narrator in the completed part of the work, and the shadow of
   impending historical events—all that makes one conclude that Pushkin
   conceived a narrative about a young man who enters real life in 1825,
   under the circumstances of the Chernigovskii regiment's revolt" (70–
   71). Oksman links this fragment and its plan with the well-known episode
   related to the uprising of the Chernigovskii regiment. This is the story
   of the nineteen-year-old Ippolit Muraviov-Apostol, who participated in
   the revolt almost by chance. He had been recently promoted to the rank
   of an ensign and, in the winter of 1825, he left Petersburg for Tulchin,
   the destination of his appointment. On his way to Tulchin he decided to
   stop by in Vasilkov to see his brother. Accidentally, he came there in the
   heat of the revolt, joined the revolting army, was wounded during the
   confrontation with the government troops and committed suicide (shot
   himself) to avoid surviving the defeat. (See: *Vosstanie dekabristov: materialy i issledovaniia*, VI, 318; Oksman, 769; *Memuary dekabristov. Iuzhnoe
   obshchestvo;* Eidelman 1975, 220–21; Eidelman 1984, 120).
9. For details concerning this argument, see Carr's *What Is History?*
10. See Lotman 1992: II, 407; Toibin 1880, 23.
11. Predictably, Soviet Marxist scholars refused to acknowledge the promi-
    nent role of chance in Pushkin's historical vision. Interpreting *Count
    Nulin*, Gukovskii stresses the role of historical laws and underestimates
    the metahistorical significance of the poem. *Count Nulin*, according to
    Gukovskii, demonstrates Pushkin's predilection for realist depiction of
    local morals.
12. Cf. for example, the conclusion of Mikhail Gershenzon: "As a result of
    this tiny deviation, the later unfolding of the event gives in both cases two
    widely diverging paths: in one case [the story of Lucrece and Tarquin],
    a tragedy, at first only a personal one, but in its consequences a global

one; in the other case [Pushkin's *Count Nulin*], an anecdote resulting in laughter. Thus, not the event itself, but only one microscopic part of it served as a cause of historical events. This tiny part of this one event is not at all organic, but accidental; it happened, but it might not have. For it is pure chance that what occurred to empty-headed Nataliia Pavlovna, i. e. to slap the rapist, did not occur to Lucrece" (45).

13. For a brief discussion of *Count Nulin* as compared to Shakespeare's *The Rape of Lucrece*, see Briggs, 103–6.

14. Cf., for example, the discussions of the historicity of *Eugene Onegin*.

15. It is difficult to agree with Abram Tertz's assertion that "blind chance, raised to a law, suited Pushkin" and that for Pushkin, "everything in the world is accidental" (Tertz, 358, 360). Pushkin undoubtedly believed in the power of chance to liberate history from complete determinism, or *lois fatale*. Pushkin's attitude toward chance, however, is far more complex than a simple opposition "chaos vs. order" or "chance vs. determinism." As Lotman argues in his article " 'Pikovaia dama' i tema kart i kartochnoi igry v russkoi literature nachala XIX veka," chance has a profoundly ambivalent nature in Pushkin's oeuvre: "The world in which everything is chaotically accidental and the world in which everything became so deadened that there is no place left for an 'event,' these two worlds can be seen through each other" (1992: II, 412).

16. For an important discussion of the phenomenon of pretendership in Russia, see Boris Uspenskii's article "Tsar and Pretender: Samozvančestvo or Royal Imposture in Russia as a Cultural-Historical Phenomenon." Uspenskii argues that the frequency of various pretenders in Russia was rooted in a "specifically Russian concept of royal power, i.e., in the distinction between true and false Tsars," a distinction that ironically had no "clear-cut criteria on how to distinguish between a true and a false Tsar" (Uspenskii, 265, 277).

17. See, for example, M. I. Osipova's memoirs (in *Pushkin v vospominaniiakh sovremennikov*, 459). See also Gasparov 1992, 253–4, and a bibliography on the subject in *Pushkin v vospominaniiakh sovremennikov*, 538.

Chapter 3 The Historian as Contextualist: Pushkin's Polemic with Radishchev

1. White differentiates four paradigms of the forms that a historical explanation may take: Formist, Organicist, Mechanistic, and Contextualist. According to White, "The Formist theory of truth aims at the identification of the unique characteristics of objects inhabiting the historical

field." Thus, White continues, "the Formist considers an explanation to be complete when a given set of objects has been properly identified, its class, generic, and specific attributes assigned, and labels attesting to its particularity attached to it" (13–14). Curiously, Pushkin seems to accuse Polevoi of being too "Formist" in his narratives: "After honestly narrating the events, a historian draws the conclusion, you might draw another one, but Mr. Polevoi draws no conclusion at all. [. . .] We judge not by Mr. Polevoi's own words, as one cannot derive from them any positive conclusion, but by the spirit in which *The History of the Russian People* is, on the whole, written, by Mr. Polevoi's effort to preserve the precious colors of the past, and by his frequent borrowing from the chronicles" (XI, 121). In fact, a Formist historian can make generalizations about the nature of the historical process as a whole, but, as White contends, their generalizations "are so extensive that they bear very little weight as propositions that can be confirmed or disconfirmed by appeal to empirical data" (White, 15). Such is Karamzin's *History,* and Polevoi's *History* in parts where, according to Pushkin, Polevoi simply "parodies" his great predecessor (XI, 121).

An Organicist historian in White's definition "attempts to depict the particulars discerned in the historical field as components of synthetic process. At the heart of the Organicist strategy is a metaphysical commitment to the paradigm of the microcosmic-macrocosmic relationship." These historians, White continues, "tend to structure their narratives in such a way as to depict the consolidation or crystallization, out of a set of apparently dispersed events, of some integrated entity whose importance is greater than that of any of the individual entities analyzed or described in the course of the narrative" (15). "Moreover, history written in this mode tends to be oriented toward the determination of the end or goal toward which all the processes found in the historical field are presumed to be tending" (White, 16). It is not hard to notice that Guizot's and Thierry's attempt to explain the historical development of the European countries as that culminating in the French Revolution falls very neatly into the Organicist category. Hence their inclination to talk about the "principles" of the historical processes.

The Mechanistic historians, on the other hand, are "integrative in their aim, but they are inclined to be reductive rather than synthetic" (White, 16). "The Mechanistic theory of explanation turns upon the search for the causal laws that determine the outcomes of processes discovered in the historical field" (17). "Ultimately, for the Mechanist, an explanation is considered complete only when he has discovered the laws that are presumed to govern nature" (17).

2. The title *Puteshestvie iz Moskvy v Peterburg* was attributed to this fragment by Pushkin's editors.

3. Makagonenko is inconsistent: he arbitrarily links some views expressed by the narrator with those of Pushkin. Ultimately, he arrives at the conclusion that Pushkin was compelled to terminate his work on *A Journey from Moscow to Petersburg* because he felt that his narrator could not refute Radishchev.

4. Pushkin expressed a similar idea in his early ode "Freedom" ("Vol'nost,' " 1817):

> Лишь там над царскою главой
> Народов не легло страданье,
> Где крепко с Вольностью святой
> Законов мощных сочетанье (II: I, 46).

> Only there the people's suffering does not weigh
> Upon the Tsar's head
> Where the powerful laws
> Are tightly bound to holy Freedom.

About the tension between freedom and law in Pushkin's writing, see an article by G. M. Fridlender, "Vol'nost' i Zakon (Pushkin i Velikaia Frantsuzskaia revoliutsiia)." See also Efim Etkind, "L'idée de la révolution dans l'oeuvre de Pouchkine."

5. It is no coincidence that Pushkin's ideal character, Tatiana, according to William Todd learns that life's choices should be governed by a moral law. In the end of the novel, she emerges as a triumphant master of conventionality, the only kind of freedom accessible to a woman of her status (Todd 1986, 129–30).

6. For an elegant outline of the "ideology of polite society" and institutions of literature see Todd 1986, 10–105. Significantly, Pushkin's narrator's belief in the enlightened censorship is not as utopian as it might seem. As Todd points out, censorship, in itself, was not "necessarily a principal retarding force. Much of the censoring was performed [. . .] by professor-littérateurs who shared the best aspirations of writers and public. The central problem was surely the unpredictability, arbitrariness, and vindictiveness of the government" (Todd 1986, 75).

Chapter 4   History in the Service and Disservice of Life: "The Hero"

1. Earlier versions of this Chapter were read as a paper at the annual AAT-SEEL Convention in Chicago in December 1990, as well as presented in lectures at Yale University, Stanford University, University of Michigan, University of Chicago, and Brown University in 1989–91.

2. *Bourrienne et ses Erreurs, ou Observations sur ses Mémoires.* Later referred to as *Erreurs.* Concerning the Jaffa episode we read: "M. de Bourrienne prétend qu'il a suivi le général Bonaparte dans la visite qu'il fit à l'hôpital de Jaffa, que celui-ci parcourut rapidement les salles et ne toucha aucun pestiféré. Le contraire cependant résulte d'une foule de documents, comme du récit du médecin en chèf de l'armée d'Orient, d'un rapport fait à l'institut par le général Andréossi, etc. Il y a plus, c'est que la visite n'eut pas lieu à l'époque où il la place, c'est-à-dire au retour, mais lorsque l'armée entrait en Syrie. Comment le sécretaire intime a-t-il pu faire un anachronisme semblable? Comment la date d'une visite si périlleuse a-t-elle pu sortir de sa mémoire?" (Monsieur de Bourrienne pretends that he followed General Bonaparte during the visit he made to the hospital in Jaffa, and that the General made his way rapidly through the rooms and did not touch a single plague victim. Contrary evidence, however, can be found in an abundance of documents, such as the account of the head doctor of the Oriental army, the report made to the institute by General Andréossi, etc. Moreover, the visit did not take place at the time he states, that is during the return, but rather when the army was entering Syria. How could the intimate secretary have committed such an anachronism? How could the date of such a perilous visit have escaped his memory?" Erreurs 5)

3. Hans Blumenberg observes that Goethe here, as elsewhere, seeks to compare himself to Napoleon (Blumenberg, 467).

4. See, for example, Marilyn Gaull's account of Napoleon's representations in English Romanticism: "To the English poets and writers, Napoleon represented all that was excessively great and excessively wicked, a Satanic figure for Wordsworth and Coleridge, and a Promethean one for Blake, Shelley, and Byron" (Gaull, 167). For an insightful discussion of Promethean myth and Napoleon, see, Blumenberg 465–521.

5. Goethe, it should be noted, will sometimes juxtapose Christ with Napoleon as well. Even in these cases, however, he is interested in Christ's "demonic" power to exert influence over the elements, not in the redeeming aspect of the Christian Savior (Blumenberg 480). Heine too was one of the few writers who linked Napoleon to Christ. Heine, however, viewed

Napoleon as a Savior primarily because of Bonaparte's favorable politics toward Jews.

6. On the interpretation of the poem as Pushkin's appeal to Nicholas I to "have heart" and to pardon the Decembrists, see the works of such scholars as Fridman, 123–29; Tomashevskii, 256; Gorodetskii, 323; Blagoi, 506–7. For the analysis of the paradox of the "elevating illusion," see also Gukasova, *Boldinskii period v tvorchestve A. S. Pushkina;* Mikkelson, "Pushkin's 'Geroj': A Verse Dialogue on Truth,"; Krasnov, " 'Apokalipsicheskaia pesn' A. S. Pushkina (K sporam o stikhotvorenii 'Geroi')."

7. Pushkin's own tribute to the traditional Napoleonic iconography of his time is apparent in such poems as "Recollections in Tsarskoe Selo" ("Vospominaniia v Tsarskom Sele," 1814), "Napoleon on Elba" ("Napoleon na El'be," 1815), "Napoleon" ("Napoleon," 1821), "A motionless guard was in slumber . . ." ("Nedvizhnyi strazh dremal na tsarstvennom poroge," 1824), and "To the Sea" ("K moriu," 1824). For an excellent analysis of the Napoleonic theme in Pushkin, see the article by Olga S. Murav'iova "Pushkin i Napoleon."

8. The Greek word for "truth" in John's Gospel is αληθεια. See *Theological Dictionary of the New Testament:* "In John αληθεια denotes 'divine reality' with reference to the fact 1. that this is different from the reality in which man first finds himself, and by which he is controlled, and 2. that it discloses itself and is thus revelation" (245).

9. I do not fully agree with Mikkelson's interpretation of the epigraph and its role in the poem. His understanding of Pilate's words and the meaning of "truth" as it is used in John's Gospel is supported by the biblical text. Mikkelson suggests that the Gospel presents two concepts of truth:

> Jesus speaks of the truth which it is his mission to propagate: 'For this I was born, and for this I have come into the world, to bear the witness to the truth. Everyone who is of the truth hears my voice.' (The Russian and Church Slavonic word here is *istina.*) Even as Pilate listens his ears are bombarded by the harsh clamor of the Jewish leaders advocating a more mundane truth, the truth of political expedience ('If you release this man, you are not Caesar's friend'). Pilate's query has had lasting significance; it eloquently poses two of humanity's most persistent quandaries: how to determine, in the case of a dispute, what is the truth, and how to mediate between conflicting truths. These are the issues which Pushkin raised by supplying the poem with this epigraph (Mikkelson, 1974, 368).

A historian definitely has a choice to perceive the Jewish leaders' opposition to Jesus as "truth," but this would be an extratextual interpretation
of the Gospel, since the context of the Gospel does not provide grounds
for such a reading. The word "truth" is never used in the Gospel in reference to the claims of the Jewish leaders. In Mikkelson's interpretation
Pilate's question is practically reduced to the question of who is right.
However, this is not the issue. Pilate's question is related not to the dispute between the two truths (that of Jesus and of the Pharisees) but to
Christ's teaching of the truth. His question has a philosophical focus;
skepticism on the part of a representative of pagan antiquity, not the
hesitation of a person unable "to mediate between the conflicting truths,"
is at the root of Pilate's question. Pilate's question immediately follows
Jesus' words about truth, "For this I was born, and for this I have come
into the world, to bear witness to the truth. Everyone who is of the truth
hears my voice." There is no evidence in the Gospel's text that while listening to Christ, Pilate's "ears are bombarded by the harsh clamor of the
Jewish leaders advocating a more mundane truth." Moreover, the conversation between Pilate and Jesus takes place *inside* the palace and between
the two men alone. The clamor of the Jews "If you release this man, you
are not Caesar's friend" occurs much later, after Jesus' flagellation (John
19: 12).

Mikkelson's interpretation of this Gospel's text and, in turn, of the
role of the biblical epigraph in Pushkin's poem as "mediation between
conflicting truths" seems to be a projection of a modern post-Nietzschean
consciousness not only onto Pushkin's time but also onto that of early
Christianity when the Gospel of John was written. Pushkin's consciousness, however, was shaped by the Christian tradition. His thinking is
closer to the traditional interpretation of the biblical text. See, for example, *The Interpreter's Bible* account of Pilate's interview with Jesus:
"Jesus does not deny his **kingship,** but shows that it is not of earthly origin or political in character. Earthly kings have servants to fight for them.
But the kingship of Jesus belongs to the realm of **truth.** Those who recognize the royal authority of **the truth** acknowledge him. To this Pilate can
reply only with a shrug, **What is truth?** The **truth** of which the Johannine
Jesus speaks is the true knowledge of God" (*The Interpreter's Bible,* 769).

Concerning the use of the word "truth," or $\alpha\lambda\eta\theta\epsilon\iota\alpha$ in Pilate's question, see also *Theological Dictionary of the New Testament:* "Pilate's ques-
tion gives emphasis to the word, and the continuation shows again that
$\alpha\lambda\eta\theta\epsilon\iota\alpha$ is the self-revealing divine reality, and that its comprehension

is not a free act of existence, but is grounded in the determination of existence by divine reality" (246).

10. Cf. Eliade's analysis of the structure of "popular memory": "If certain epic poems preserve what is called 'historical truth,' this truth almost never has to do with definite persons and events, but with institutions, customs, landscapes. [. . .] But such 'historical truths' are not concerned with personalities or events, but with traditional forms of social and political life (the 'becoming' of which is slower than 'becoming' of the individual)—in a word, with archetypes" (Eliade 1974, 43–44).

11. As has been demonstrated by Eliade, the transformation of the exploits of a historical personage in accordance with his archetype and reconstruction of his biography according to the norms of myth were typical of what he calls "popular memory" or "archaic mentality" (Eliade 1974, 38–40). "This mythicization of the historical prototypes who gave the popular epic songs their heroes takes place in accordance with an exemplary standard; they are 'formed after the image' of the heroes of ancient myth" (Eliade 1974, 42).

12. See Eliade, *Myth and Reality,* 166–67.

13. It is important to point out that while refusing to synthesize the oppositions, Pushkin is far from the relativist acceptance of two or more positions as equally true. Rather he demonstrates here, as elsewhere (especially in his *Journey from Moscow to Petersburg*), the pattern of thought that privileges context and perspective over ultimate claims. The notion of truth(s) emerges as inseparable from a multiplicity of viewpoints.

14. For a stimulating discussion of Pushkin's vision of divine justice in *Mozart and Salieri,* see Vladimir Golstein's article "Pushkin's *Mozart and Salieri* as a Parable of Salvation."

15. Cf. White's critique of Nietzsche's aesthetic theory: "In separating art from science, religion, and philosophy, Nietzsche thought that he was returning it to union with 'life.' Actually he provided the grounds for turning it against *human* life, for, since he regarded life as nothing but the will to power, he wedded the artistic sensibility to that will and turned life itself away from that knowledge of the world without which it can not produce anything of practical benefit to anyone" (White, 374).

16. Virtually every major Russian writer participated in the polemic on the "elevating illusion" and "low truths," either claiming the supremacy of one over another or, like Turgenev, trying to balance these two types of historical and philosophical vision. (See, Turgenev's essay "Hamlet and Don Quixote.")

Chapter 5 Forging Russian History: *The Blackamoor* *of Peter the Great*

1. The question central to most studies is why Pushkin abandoned the work. For a detailed analysis see Lapkina, "K istorii sozdaniia 'Arapa Petra Velikogo' "; Blagoi, *Tvorcheskii put' Pushkina*, 243–44; Abramovich, "K voprosu o stanovlenii povestvovatel'noi prozy Pushkina (Pochemu ostalsia nezavershennym 'Arap Petra Velikogo'?"; Bocharov, *Poetika Pushkina*, 114–26. Paul Debreczeny provides a good summary of possible causes that prevented Pushkin from completing his novel (1983, 33). Debreczeny suggests that Pushkin had difficulty with a suitable narratorial perspective: "Pushkin's attempt to develop an omniscient mode of narration was a pioneering venture, but it involved—because of its very novelty—enormous technical difficulties. These difficulties may well have contributed to his decision to abandon his novel, though there may have been other factors as well" (1983, 33). Pushkin, according to Debreczeny, could not find a right angle to view either Peter or Ibragim: "At the time he was writing *The Blackamoor* he still stood too close to Peter to be able to portray him as a hero, yet too far to be able to depict him as an ordinary human being. [. . .] As it turned out, Pushkin was not able to find the right angle from which to view his central character, any more than he was able to establish the right approach to Peter" (Debreczeny 1983, 37). Petrunina arrives at an analogous conclusion: "In *The Blackamoor of Peter the Great*, the distance between an author-narrator and various spheres of the depicted historical reality, various heroes of his narrative is not established yet, it vacillates in front of the reader's eyes" (Petrunina, 55). This "switching of the foreshortening and the tempo of the narration" (*smena rakursov i tempa povestvovaniia*) puzzled many critics. Bocharov pointed out a stylistic inconsistency of *The Blackamoor:* "Pushkin's prose style is clearly revealed within the limits of particular areas of the text; however, the *narrative* in a large prose form as conceived by Pushkin remains an unsolved problem" (Bocharov 1974, 116).

I maintain, however, that the combination of different styles was precisely the main purpose of Pushkin's narrative, because it was a variety of behavioral styles that represented the object of his portrayal.

Bocharov continues: "To correlate *in prose* the great and the tiny, the historical and the domestic—this is a problem, it seems, that Pushkin could not have solved in his novel about Gannibal" (Bocharov 1974, 123).

It is not so obvious, however, that Pushkin's goal was to compare "the historical with the domestic" (*istoricheskoe s domashnim*). Pushkin's purpose seems different: not to compare the historical and the domestic, not just to treat history in a domestic manner, but to treat the domestic as historical. In so doing Pushkin is truly innovative and anticipates a historical method of Tolstoy.

2. Pushkin was very happy with what he had written and did not consider the completed chapters a failure. In 1833, he confessed to Dal': "You would not believe how much I long to write a novel, yet I cannot. I have begun three of them. I start off perfectly well, but then I run out of patience and cannot manage" (Dal' 262). Even though there had to be reasons for Pushkin not to finish the novel, these reasons are not necessarily rooted in the imperfections of the existing text.

Consider, for example, the novel's fragmentary status in the context of Romantic fascination with the fragmentariness of human experience. As Viktor M. Zhirmunskii points out in his classical study *Byron and Pushkin*, fragmentariness is characteristic of the structure of Romantic poems of both Byron and Pushkin and represents part and parcel of the Romanticist outlook (Zhirmunskii, 54–68). In her book *Pushkin and Romantic Fashion*, Monika Greenleaf discusses the Romantic cult of the fragment and offers a deeper understanding of what she calls "Pushkin's idiosyncratic penchant for fragmentary structures" (14). Both Zhirmunskii and Greenleaf, however, focus on poetic fragment and—probably justifiably so—do not consider *The Blackamoor of Peter the Great* as an example of a Romantic fragment.

3. Pushkin allows himself several historical inaccuracies. For details concerning Pushkin's use of, and deviation from, historical facts, see: Levkovich, "Printsipy dokumental'nogo povestvovaniia v istoricheskoi proze pushkinskoi pory"; Iakubovich, "Arap Petra Velikogo." Along with other scholars Debreczeny observes Pushkin's distortion of facts, but does not provide a satisfying interpretation of Pushkin's treatment of historical materials. Among the most important inaccuracies he states the following: "He made Peter propose to the Rzhevskiis on Ibrahim's behalf, though the real Hannibal did not marry until well after Peter's death; he made Ibrahim's bride a member of Russian ancient nobility in order to sharpen the social contrast with Peter's black officer; and he brought together such historical personalities as I. F. Kopievich and Feofan Prokopovich, who could not have been at Peter's court at the same time" (Debreczeny 1983, 27).

As I will show later, Pushkin's reasons for making Ibragim marry a member of an ancient Russian nobility might be more complex than "to sharpen the social contrast." Pushkin needed to arrange this marriage not for the sake of the contrast itself, but in order to put in relief his idea of mediation between the conservatives and the reformers.

4. Coincidentally, discussing two possible types of behavior in eighteenth century Russia ("the one being neutral or 'natural' and the other specifically gentlemanly and at the same time consciously theatricalized"), Lotman observes that "it was typical of Peter that for himself he preferred the former, and even when he did take part in the ritualized performances, he would reserve for himself the role of producer, the person who organized the game. He would demand that his courtiers take part, but personally he kept out of it" (Lotman 1984, 235). In *The Blackamoor of Peter the Great* Pushkin captured Peter the Great precisely in the moment of being a "producer"; Pushkin depicts gatherings and activities associated with his epoch, but keeps Peter in the background.

5. For a discussion of the historicity of *Eugene Onegin* see: Toibin, " 'Evgenii Onegin': poeziia i istoriia." See also: Todd, "*Eugene Onegin:* 'Life's Novel,' " *Literature and Society in Imperial Russia, 1800–1914,* 122–3.

6. The disparity between the old gentry's life style of the Larins and that of Petersburg's aristocrats may be traced back to the social conflict depicted in *The Blackamoor of Peter the Great:* the opposition of the old Russian nobility and a new type of men represented by Peter the Great's supporters. An early eighteenth-century social situation, portrayed in *The Blackamoor of Peter the Great,* reminds one of the heterogeneous aspects of an early nineteenth-century Russian culture, depicted in *Eugene Onegin* in the scenes of Russian country life, and in contrast, westernized Petersburg high society. The tenor of country life in *Eugene Onegin* is strongly reminiscent of the boyars in *The Blackamoor.*

7. The importance of coordination between the two types of probability was suggested to me by Harry E. Shaw. Shaw discusses these two kinds of fictional probability in his study *The Forms of Historical Fiction: Sir Walter Scott and His Successors,* 20–21. See also Harvey, *Character and the Novel,* 11–13.

8. Debreczeny suggests instead that "It is not clear why Pushkin decided in the end to switch to fiction. Possibly he simply came across some unflattering details about Hannibal and thought he could handle them more easily in fiction than in a conscientious historical account" (Debreczeny 1983, 26–27); "The most noticeable trace of Pushkin's original nonfictional approach to the story is the novel's detached mode of narration" (Debreczeny 1983, 27).

Debreczeny's explanation of the reasons that induced Pushkin to depict the times of Peter the Great in fiction implies a certain dishonesty on
the part of Pushkin who was trying, as it were, to hide the truth behind
the fiction. The very opposition of fiction to a "conscientious historical
account" seems to be tenuous, however, for fiction and history are simply
two different modes of cognition.

9. The relationship between Pushkin's prose and a genre of anecdote
   is briefly discussed by Odinokov. See his book *"I dal' svobodnogo romana . . . ,"* 5–6. For the role of anecdote in Pushkin's poetics, see especially Grossman, 45–75.

10. Harry Shaw in his analysis of Scott's novels calls such protagonists "con-
    junctive" as opposed to "disjunctive" protagonists, whose "successes
    and failures do not translate into propositions concerning the course of
    history" (Shaw 1983, 155).

11. Cf. Todd, *"Eugene Onegin:* 'Life's Novel,' " 113.

12. The mere fact that the poetics of contrast is a main formative device of
    the novel had been noted by Pushkin scholars. See, for example, Petru-
    nina, 54. However, the way Pushkin employs this device requires further
    consideration.

13. Pushkin employs many other negative locutions in the novel in order
    to afford the reader with a sense of the opposite perspective. While por-
    traying Peter in an unthreatening and "domestic manner" the narrator
    observes, as if en passant: "Nobody could have suspected this warm and
    cordial host of being the hero of Poltava, of being the powerful and for-
    midable reformer of Russia" (VIII: I, 11). Although brief, this comment
    establishes a counter-perspective on Peter the Great.

14. For a classical analysis of different styles of speech in *The Blackamoor
    of Peter the Great*, see Vinogradov, *O iazyke khudozhestvennoi literatury,*
    586–90; Bogorodskii, "O iazyke i stile romana Pushkina 'Arap Petra
    Velikogo.' "

15. Russian conservatives view the new customs as a masquerade; this is why
    a boyars' fool, Ekimovna, wears a European dress in order to parody new
    fashions. The boyars perceive the European outfit not as normal dress,
    but as a costume: "Just at that moment an old woman with a whitened
    and rouged face, decorated with flowers and tinsel and wearing a low-
    necked damask robe, danced into the room humming a tune" (VIII: I,
    20).

16. Lapkina suggests that this epigraph suits better the first part of Chap-
    ter 3, rather than Chapter 1: "Judging by literary associations it evoked,
    this epigraph suited better the first part of Chapter Three, in which ap-

peared Korsakov, who had just returned from Paris and was outraged by the 'barbaric' way of life in Russia" (Lapkina, 298).

17. In this connection it is interesting to note Gogol's architectural cravings that expressed his own urge to "slyly coalesce" different styles: "A city should consist of different styles of building, if we wish it to be pleasing to the eye. Let as many different tastes combine there as possible. Let the somber Gothic and burdened with the luxury of embellishments Eastern buildings, the colossal Egyptian and buildings of Greek style, which is impregnated with harmonious dimensions, arise in the same street. Let us see there the gently bulbous milky cupola and the ecclesiastic, endless steeple; the Eastern miter and the Italian flat roof; the tall, Dutch-figured quadrilateral pyramid, the cylindrical column and the tapered obelisk. Let the houses fuse into a single, even, monotonous wall as seldom as possible, but let them lean upwards or downwards" (Gogol, 1937–1952 VIII, 71).

18. Some critics insist that "the best parts of the novel are those in which Pushkin succeeds in maintaining a consistent point of view" (Debreczeny 1983, 39). I believe, however, that Pushkin might have consciously avoided a "consistent point of view," for he wanted to show the eclecticism and inconsistencies of the age of Peter the Great. The oscillating point of view could facilitate the depiction of the multifarious elements of everyday life.

Chapter 6 Poltava: The Myth of Holy War

1. Summarizing the ideas of the most authoritative scholars on the subject of Poltava (such as Gukovskii, Vinogradov, Blagoi, Izmailov, Zhirmunskii, Aronson), Iurii Lotman concludes: "The complex and multileveled conflict that defines the semantic structure of Poltava manifests itself as a confrontation between ode-like and Romanticist textual organizations [. . .], as a juxtaposition of Mazeppa's egoism and a profound connection with historical laws that was typical of Peter. (It is difficult to find any other examples of such an unambiguously negative evaluation of a personage as that of Mazeppa in Pushkin's oeuvre, an evaluation lacking even any attempt to characterize the protagonist from 'inside'; it could be compared only to the evaluation of Onegin in Chapter VII of the novel, written approximately at the same time)" (Lotman 1975, 46).

Virginia M. Burns in her dissertation "Pushkin's Poltava: A Literary Interpretation" and her article "The Narrative Structure of Pushkin's

Poltava: Toward a Literary Interpretation" attempts to prove the opposite: "Pushkin created a character of unprecedented psychological depth
and complexity which goes beyond romanticism to the psychological
realism of the later nineteenth century" (Burns 1977, 175–76). Thus
she arrives at the odd conclusion that Mazeppa "persisted honorably in
the pursuit of his duties as seen by himself" (Burns 1977, 321). This
conclusion is achieved through discovery of Pushkin's "dynamic polyphonic mode of characterization," which leads the author, in her attempt
to define the poem's genre, to a leap from "psychological realism" to
"a symbolic novel in verse": "In point of fact, the double function of
many of the poem's motifs, as both narrative elements and symbols,
make of 'Poltava' a symbolic novel in verse virtually a century ahead of
its time" (Burns 1977, 184). Burns attempts to transform Pushkin into a
"modern" writer; as a result she projects modern literary theories onto
a text which does not conform to them. The author even goes so far as
to assume that only a "modern" reader can "decipher the semantics of
the narrative": "Thus, as with the symbolic poetic novels of the moder-
nity (which *Poltava* resembles in its complexity and intensity), the poem
requires a modern synthesizing reader. If this is true, it would go far
toward explaining the puzzlement of nineteenth-century readers; but
the post-Bely, post-Joyce reader, attuned to finding meaning in structure
and symbol, including the 'realistic' symbol, should be able to find the
meaningful connections in the text and decipher the semantics of the
narrative" (Burns 1980, 19).

In his article "Narrative Voices in Poltava," Debreczeny explains the
contradictory nature of Mazeppa by the different points of view introduced by Pushkin in the text. This is definitely correct. But the question
remains: why does Pushkin introduce these different points of view
into his narrative? Why is the characterization of Mazeppa so complex
and marked by narratorial multivoicedness, whereas Peter is so mono-
logical? My goal is to find the roots of some of the inconsistencies and
contradictions in Pushkin's text.
2. See Pauls and Pauls, "Maria in Pushkin's *Poltava* (The Character and the
Person)."
3. In his commentary to the poem, Walter Arndt tries to explain, somewhat
confusingly, Pushkin's choice of title. First he claims that the title *Poltava* "would seem plausible enough had the poem been an account of the
climactic period of the war and Peter I's political and strategic role in it."
"Such is far from being the case, though," he concludes (Arndt, 312).

He suggests instead that Mazeppa, "despite contrary appearances or even intentions on the part of his creator, became or remained the protagonist by default, the residual (anti-)hero as it were" (Arndt, 313).

4. Paul Ricoeur, in his book *The Symbolism of Evil*, distinguishes three more types of the origin of evil in addition to the first one. The second type he identifies with myths of the "fall" of a man in already completed and perfect creation. The third type is attributed to Greek tragedy and therefore is called "tragic": "here the fault appears to be indistinguishable from the very existence of the tragic hero; he does not commit fault, he is guilty" (Ricoeur 173). The fourth type is the "myth of the exiled soul."

5. Cf. Zhivov and Uspenskii: "Glorification of the monarch is realized first of all through religious elements; by elevating the emperor over the people, our panegyrists place him next to God. These religious elements may go back both to Christian and to pagan traditions of antiquity that may be freely combined here in accordance with the laws of semantic multilevelness characteristic of Baroque culture in general" (Zhivov and Uspenskii 1987, 121).

Chapter 7 History as Myth: *The Bronze Horseman*

1. See, for example: Aronson, "K istorii sozdaniia 'Mednogo vsadnika,'" *Vremennik Pushkinskoi komissii*, 4–5; Pumpianskii, " 'Mednyi vsadnik' i poeticheskaia traditsiia XVIII veka," *Vremennik Pushkinskoi komissii*, 4–5; Lednicki, *Pushkin's "Bronze Horseman".*

2. See Pumpianskii, op. cit.

3. Cf. the observations of Richard Gregg: "As for the question, why then does Pushkin insert the proviso *byt' mozhet*, the answer is that it reflects a very fundamental fact about Eugene, namely, that he is *obscure*—so obscure, indeed, that the narrator himself claims himself to be uncertain about the lineage" (Gregg 1977, 177).

4. See Lotman, "Proiskhozhdenie siuzheta v tipologicheskom osveshchenii," *Stat'i po tipologii kul'tury.*

5. A remarkable description of the Petersburg myth and *The Bronze Horseman* may be found in Antsyferov, *Dusha Peterburga*, (1922, 62–72). See also an analysis of this motif in the article by Gregg, (168).

6. See Toporov, "Drevo mirovoe," *Mify narodov mira*, (1980).

7. I leave aside the interesting question of the transposition of the myth into a "text" of sculpture, and of the sculptural "text" into a poetic one.

8. Significantly, the Bronze Horseman was commonly referred to as a "thunder-stone" (*grom-kamen'*).

9. Cf. Ivanov and Toporov, "Perun," in *Mify narodov mira*, vol. 2 (1982, 307). The motif of George the Victorious (Georgii Pobedonosets) could be seen as one more variant of the myth.

10. In his use of the epithet *groznyi* in relation to Peter the Great, Pushkin follows the tradition according to which first Ivan III, then Ivan IV, and later Peter I were all called *groznyi*. This tradition is connected with the concept of a "threatening power" (*groznaia vlast'*), a notion that first found its fictional representation in *The Tale of Magmet Saltan* (*Povest' o Magmet Saltane*) by Ivan Peresvetov. The concept of the "threatening" or "terrible" power represents in essence a contamination of the Christian idea of the tsar as the Lord's Anointed one and a pagan view of the supreme deity as a storm-god.

11. Another curious coincidence is a phonetical similarity of the names: Petr-Perun. According to the myth, Perun throws *peruny* (lightning) and stones (Petr etymologically means "stone"). In *The Bronze Horseman*, children cast stones at the mad Eugene.

12. See an article by Ivanov and Toporov, "Slavianskaia mifologiia," *Mify narodov mira*, vol. 2. See also Ivanov and Toporov, *Issledovaniia v oblasti slavianskikh drevnostei. (Leksicheskie i frazeologicheskie voprosy rekonstruktsii tekstov)*, Moscow, 1974.

13. In the 1937–59 edition, these lines read slightly differently. Instead of the first person pronoun "I" a third person pronoun "he" is used: "Somehow he will make / A humble and simple refuge for himself / And will settle down Parasha there" (V, 139). I believe, however, that the first person is more consistent with the rest of Eugene's inner monologue and accept, therefore, Tomashevskii's version in the 1962–66 edition.

14. Curiously enough, the etymology of the name "Parasha" in this case coincides with the image of the literary character associated with this name since the eighteenth century (cf. Aleksendr Izmailov's poem "Prostodushnaia"). In the literature of the first half of the nineteenth century a character bearing the name Parasha was already perceived as a literary cliché (Cf., for example, *Count Nulin* or Lermontov's poem *Sashka*). Concerning this name, Belinsky wrote the following: "Parasha is a type of those Russian chambermaids serving young ladies who received the new, that is, a boarding-school education" (Belinsky 1953–9, VIII, 429). Obviously, any chambermaid serves in a sense as a "means." Precisely in these terms Pushkin describes the maid, Parasha, in *Count Nulin:*

> Друзья мои! Параша эта
> Наперсница ее затей:
> Шьет, моет, вести переносит [...] (V, 8)

> My dear friends! This Parasha
> Is a confidante of her [the mistress'] fancies:
> She sews, she washes, and she spreads news [. . .]

15. See Meletinskii, 266.

16. See Izmailov's article "K istorii zamysla i sozdaniia 'Mednogo vsadnika.'"

17. Lednicki interprets Pushkin's description of Eugene's social status as a "stylization into a pathetic complaint and even into a protest of the unjustly and thoughtlessly ill-treated elite." I see in this description merely Pushkin's irony and his condemnation of those members of the elite who themselves forget their noble lineage.

18. Pushkin formulates the same idea in prose in his "Refutation of the Critics" ("Oproverzhenie na kritiki"), 1830: "No matter what my way of thinking is, I would never share a democratic hatred of the nobility with anyone. It had always seemed to me to be an essential and natural class for a great, cultured people. Looking around myself and reading our old chronicles, I was sorry to see how the ancient noble families have been destroyed, how the remaining ones are falling into decline and vanishing, how new families, new historical names which have taken the place of the former ones, are already falling, unprotected by anything, and how a nobleman's name, humbled more and more by the hour, has finally become a subject of gossip and the laughing-stock of the *raznochintsy* who have become nobility, and even of idle buffoons! (XI, 161–62).

19. In this case I refer not to the historical Peter the Great, who drove the ancient Russian nobility to misery and decline, but to Peter as a central protagonist of the Petersburg cosmogonic myth, in which he plays the role of the forefather.

20. Cf. Gregg, op. cit., 175.

21. I believe that the essence of Pushkin's polemic with Mickiewicz consists in their different attitudes toward history. This dispute is present not only in Pushkin's explicitly polemical Introduction but in the character and the fate of the poem's main protagonist. It is no coincidence that Eugene's actions recall in many ways the behavior of Gustav-Konrad, the hero of *Dziady*. The typological affinity between Eugene and Gustav is supported by several parallels; among these similarities is the fact that both protagonists go mad and that both lose their fiancées. Mickiewicz's description of a Polish pilgrim in Petersburg strikingly recalls Pushkin's portrayal of Eugene's "revolt" in front of the Bronze Horseman:

Dumali — poszli — został z jedenastu
Pielgrzym sam jeden, zaśmiał się złośliwie,
Wzniósł rękę, ścisnął i uderzył mściwie
W głaz, jakby groził temu głazów miastu.
Potem na piersiach założył ramiona
I stał dumając, i w cesarskim dworze
Utkwił źrenice dwie jako dwa noże;
I był podobny wtenczas do Samsona,
Gdy zdradą wzięty i skuty więzami
Pod Filistynów dumał kolumnami.
Na czoło jego nieruchome, dumne
Nagły cień opadł, jak całun na trumnę,
Twarz blada strasznie zaczęła się mroczyc [. . .]

They stood, lost in thought for a while, then left.
Out of the eleven, only one pilgrim stayed. He laughed angrily,
Lifted his arm, clenched his fist, and vengefully struck
The stone, as if threatening this city of stone.
Then he crossed his arms on his chest
And stopped, lost in thought. Upon the Tsar's palace,
He fixed his eyes like two knife blades.
At this moment he looked like Samson
When, treacherously captured and tied,
He stood in thought beneath the columns of the Philistines.
Upon his immobile, proud brow
A sudden shadow fell, like a shroud upon the grave.
His pale face began to darken terribly [. . .]

There is no need here to bring in all the textual parallels related to the
madness of Eugene and his revolt; these correspondences are obvious.
Pushkin retains even such motifs as the columns (cf. "He [Eugene]
found himself under the columns / Of a large mansion" / *On ochutilsia
pod stolbami / Bol'shogo doma*). If one accepts the traditional view that
Konrad represents, to some extent, a "double" of Mickiewicz, then one
may assume that Eugene, in turn, is a double of this double. Significantly,
in those years Pushkin viewed Mickiewicz as a double-faced figure (see
Pushkin's poem "On mezhdu nami zhil", 1834). It is no coincidence
that precisely the epithet *zlobnyi* (Polish "złośliwie") unites Eugene, the
pilgrim from *Dziady*, and a "spiteful poet" (*zlobnyi poet*) from the poem
dedicated to Mickiewicz. Pushkin often employs this epithet in reference

to "the enemies of Russia" (Cf. *ozloblennye syny* from his poem "Klevet-nikam Rossii"; "Davno goriu stesnennoi zloboi" — Mazeppa's words in *Poltava; gor'koe zlorechie* of Radishchev from Pushkin's article "Alexander Radishchev"; and, of course, the *tshchetnaia zloba* of the enraged Neva in *The Bronze Horseman*). If Mickiewicz perceived history historically, for Pushkin it is a myth that has to be accepted "tel, que Dieu nous l'a donné."

Afterword

1. Some critics suggest that censorship was also partially responsible for a very limited representation of Peter I on stage (cf. Vatsuro, "Istoricheskaia tragediia i romanticheskaia drama nachala 1830-kh godov," 365).

2. In his study of Pushkin's *History of Peter*, Il'ia Feinberg indicates that Pushkin, in fact, was very much interested in, and conducted a thorough research on, the case of tsarevich Aleksei and the circumstances of the execution of Catherine's alleged lover, Mons (Feinberg, 36–9). This is true, but Pushkin's narrative as a whole is very reserved and brief when it touches on these sensitive issues. Pushkin does not avoid important aspects of Peter's personal life, but he does not structure his *History* around them.

3. Feinberg emphasizes that Pushkin attempts to portray the emperor in development and strives to comprehend his character (60). This may be correct, but Pushkin seems to be more interested in the contradictory nature of Peter's reforms, in his political activity and its repercussions for Russian history than in the chronological development of his character.

4. "A century has passed" is a common rhetorical cliché characteristic of the genre of the ode.

selected bibliography

Editions and Translations of A. S. Pushkin's Works

Collected Narratives and Lyrical Poetry, ed. and tr. W. Arndt. Ann Arbor: Ardis, 1984.

Eugene Onegin, tr. Charles Johnston. New York: Penguin Books, 1979.

Perepiska A. S. Pushkina v dvukh tomakh. Moscow: Khudozhestvennaia literatura, 1982.

Polnoe sobranie sochinenii, ed. B.V. Tomashevskii. 10 vols. Moscow: Nauka, 1962–66.

Polnoe sobranie sochinenii, ed. V. D. Bonch-Bruevich et al. 17 vols. Moscow: Akademiia nauk SSSR, 1937–59.

Pushkin on Literature, ed. and tr. Tatiana Wolff. London: Methuen, 1971.

Other Works

Abramovich, S. L. "K voprosu o stanovlenii povestvovatel'noi prozy Pushkina (Pochemu ostalsia nezavershennym 'Arap Petra Velikogo?')" *Russkaia Literatura*, 17, No. 2, 1974, 54–73.

Alekseev, M. P. *Pushkin: Sravnitel'no-istoricheskie issledovaniia*. Leningrad: Nauka, 1984, 221–52.

Antsyferov, A. *Dusha Peterburga*. Petrograd: Brokgauz-Efron, 1922.

Arminjon, Victor. *Pouchkine et Pierre le Grand*, Paris: Cinq Continents, 1971.

Arndt, W., ed. *Alexander Pushkin: Collected Narrative and Lyrical Poetry*. Ann Arbor: Ardis, 1984.

Aronson, M. "K istorii sozdaniia 'Mednogo vsadnika'," *Vremennik Pushkinskoi komissii*, 4–5, Moscow-Leningrad: Akademiia nauk, 1939.

———. "'Konrad Vallenrod' i 'Poltava'," *Pushkin. Vremmennik Pushkinskoi komissii*, 2, Moscow-Leningrad: Akademiia Nauk, 1936, 43–56.

Babinski, Hubert F. *The Mazeppa Legend in European Romanticism*. New York: Columbia University Press, 1974.

Bachelard, Gaston. *The New Scientific Spirit*. Tr. by A. Goldhammer. Boston: Beacon Press, 1984.

Bakhtin, Mikhail M. "K metodologii gumanitarnykh nauk," *Estetika slovesnogo tvorchestva*. Moscow: Iskusstvo, 1986.

———. "Formy vremeni i chronotopa v romane," *Literaturno-kriticheskie stat'i*. Moscow: Khudozhestvennaia literatura, 1986.

Barthes, Ronald. "Science versus Literature," in K. M. Newton ed., *Twentieth-Century Literary Theory*. New York: St. Martin's Press, 1988: 140–44.

Bayley, John. *Pushkin: A Comparative Commentary*. Cambridge: Cambridge University Press, 1971.

Behrendt, Stephen, ed. *History and Myth: Essays on English Romantic Literature*. Detroit: Wayne State University Press, 1990.

Belinsky, V. G. *Sobranie sochinenii*, 9 vols. Moscow: Khudozhestvennaia literatura, 1976–82.

———. Polnoe sobranie sochinenii, 13 vols. Moscow: Akademiia Nauk SSSR, 1953–59.

Berdiaev, N. *Smysl istorii*. Paris: YMCA–Press, 1969.

Bethea, David. "The Role of the *Eques* in Pushkin's *Bronze Horseman*," in David M. Bethea, ed., *Pushkin Today*, Bloomington, Ind.: Indiana University Press, 1993.

Bethea, David M., and Davydov, Sergei. "The [Hi]story of the Village Gorjuxino: In Praise of Pushkin's Folly," *Slavic and East European Journal*, 28, No. 3, 1984: 291–309.

———. "Pushkin's Saturnine Cupid: The Poetics of Parody in *The Tales of Belkin*," *PMLA*, 96, No. 1, 1981: 8–21.

Black, J. L. *Nicholas Karamzin and Russian Society in the Nineteenth Century: A Study in Russian Political and Historical Thought*. Toronto: University of Toronto Press, 1975.

Blagoi, D. D. *Tvorcheskii put' Pushkina (1826–1830)*. Moscow: Sovetskii pisatel', 1967.

Blumenberg, Hans. *Work on Myth*. Tr. by Robert M. Wallace. Cambridge, Mass.: MIT Press, 1985.

Bocharov, S. G. *Poetika Pushkina: Ocherki*. Moscow: Nauka, 1974.

Bogorodskii, B. L. "O iazyke i stile romana A. S. Pushkina 'Arap Petra Velokogo'," *Uchenye zapiski LGPU imeni A. I. Gertsena*, 122, 1956: 201–39.

Bourrienne, Louis-Antoine Fauvelet De. *Mémoires sur Napoléon*, 10 vols. Paris: Ladvocat, 1829.

Bourrienne et ses Erreurs, ou Observations sur ses Mémoirs, recueillés par A. B., tome I, Paris, 1830.

Briggs, A. *Alexander Pushkin: A Critical Study*. London: Croom Helm, 1983.

Budgen, David. "Pushkin and Chaadaev: The History of a Friendship," in *Ideology in Russian Literature*, ed. by Richard Freeborn and Jane Grayson. New York: St. Martin's Press, 1990.

———. "Pushkin and the Novel," in *From Pushkin to Palisandriia: Essays on the Russian Novel in Honor of Richard Freeborn*, ed. by Arnold McMillin. New York: St. Martin's Press, 1990.

Burns, Virginia. "The Narrative Structure of Pushkin's *Poltava:* Toward a Literary Interpretation," *Canadian Slavonic Papers*, 22, No. 1, 1980.

———. "Pushkin's *Poltava:* A Literary Interpretation" (Dissertation, University of Toronto, 1977).

Carr, Edward H. *What Is History?* New York: Knopf, 1961.

Chaadaev, Peter Yakovlevich. *Philosophical Letters and Apology of a Madman.* Tr. by Mary-Barbara Zeldin. Knoxville: University of Tennessee Press, 1969.

Conversations of Goethe with Eckermann and Soret. Tr. by John Oxenford. London: George Bell & Sons, 1906.

Dal', V. "Vospominaniia o Pushkine," in *A. S. Pushkin v vospominaniiakh sovremenikov*, vol. 2. Moscow: Khudozhestvennaia literatura, 1985: 260-4.

Debreczeny, Paul. "*The Blackamoor of Peter the Great:* Pushkin's Experiment with a Detached Mode of Narration," *Slavic and East European Journal*, 18, No. 21, 1974, 119-31.

———. "Narrative Voices in *Poltava*," *Russian Literature*, No. XXIV-III, North-Holland—Amsterdam: Elsevier Science B. V., 1988.

———. *The Other Pushkin: A Study of Alexander Pushkin's Prose Fiction.* Stanford, Calif.: Stanford University Press, 1983.

Dolinin, Aleksandr. *Istoriia, odetaia v roman: Val'ter Skott i ego chitateli.* Moscow: Kniga, 1988.

Dostoevskii, Fiodor. *Polnoe sobranie sochinenii*, 30 vols. Leningrad: Nauka, 1973-1990.

Driver, Sam. "Chénier and Pushkin: The Problem of the 'Lofty-Spirited Gaul'," in *For Henry Kucera: Studies in Slavic Philology and Computational Linguistics.* Ed. by Andrew W. Mackie et al. Ann Arbor: Michigan Slavic Studies, 1992.

———. *Pushkin: Literature and Social Ideas.* New York: Columbia University Press, 1989.

Eckermann, Johann Peter. *Gesprache mit Goethe.* Wiesbaden: F. A. Brockhaus, 1959.

Eidelman. N. *Apostol Sergei: Povest' o Sergee Murav'iove-Apostole.* Moscow: Politizdat, 1975.

———. *Pushkin i dekabristy: Iz istorii vzaimootnoshenii.* Moscow: Khudozhestvennaia literatura, 1979.

—. *Pushkin: Istoriia i sovremennost' v khudozhestvennom soznanii poeta.* Moscow: Sovetskii pisatel', 1984.

Eikhenbaum, Boris M. "Geroi nashego vremeni," *O proze. O poezii.* Leningrad: Khudozhestvennaia literatura, 1986, 269–338.

—. "O zamysle 'Grafa Nulina,'" *Vremenik Pushkinskoi komissii,* v. 3. Moscow-Leningrad, 1937, 349–57.

Eliade, Mircea. *Myth and Reality.* New York: Harper & Row Books, 1975.

—. *The Myth of the Eternal Return, or Cosmos and History.* Princeton: Princeton University Press, 1974.

Emerson, Caryl. *Boris Godunov: Transpositions of a Russian Theme.* Bloomington, Ind.: Indiana University Press, 1986.

—. "Grinev's Dream: *The Captain's Daughter* and a Father's Blessing," *Slavic Review,* 40, No. 1, 1981: 60–76.

—. " 'The Queen of Spades' and the Open End," in David M. Bethea, ed., *Pushkin Today,* Bloomington, Ind.: Indiana University Press, 1993.

Engelgardt, B. *Istorizm Pushkina: K voprosu o kharaktere pushkinskogo ob'ektivizma.* Petrograd: Tipografiia A. F. Dresslera, 1916.

Eremin, M. *Pushkin-publitsist.* Moscow: Khudozhestvennaia literatura, 1976.

Etkind, Efim. "L'ideé de la révolution dans l'oeuvre de Pouchkine," *Canadian Slavonic Papers: An Interdisciplinary Quarterly Devoted to the Soviet Union and Eastern Europe.* V. 29 (23), 1987: 131–51.

Evdokimova, Svetlana. "History and Myth in the Works of Aleksander Pushkin" (Ph.D. Dissertation, Yale University, 1991).

—. "*Mednyi vsadnik:* istoriia kak mif," *Russian Literature,* XXVIII-IV, North-Holland—Amsterdam: Elsevier Science B. V., 1990.

Feinberg, I. *Nezavershennye raboty Pushkina.* Moscow: Sovetskii pisatel', 1962.

—. *Chitaia tetradi Pushkina.* Moscow: Sovetskii pisatel', 1985.

Foucault, Michel. *The Order of Things: An Archeology of the Human Sciences.* New York: Pantheon Books, 1971.

Frank, S. L. *Etiudy o Pushkine.* Paris: YMCA Press, 1987.

Fridlender, G. M. "Volnost' i zakon (Pushkin i Velikaia frantsuzskaia revoliutsiia)," *Izvestiia Akademii Nauk SSSR,* 48, No. 6, 1989: 536–42.

Fridman, N. V. "Geroicheskii romantizm 'posledekabr'skogo' Pushkina (K voprosu o proiskhozhdenii malen'kikh tragedii)," *Uchenye zapiski MGU,* issue 110, vol. 1, Moscow, 1946.

Frye, Northrop. *The Anatomy of Criticism: Four Essays.* Princeton: Princeton University Press, 1957.

Gallie, W. B. *Philosophy and the Historical Understanding.* New York: Schoken Books, 1964.

Gasiorowska, Xenia. *The Image of Peter the Great in Russian Fiction.* Madison: University of Wisconsin Press, 1979.

Gasparov, Boris. *Poetika "Slova o polku Igoreve."* (*Wiener Slawistischer Almanach,* 12), Wien: Kubon & Sagher, 1984.

————. *Poeticheskii iazyk Pushkina kak fakt istorii russkogo literaturnogo iazyka.* (*Wiener Slawistischer Almanach,* 27). Wien: Kubon & Sagher, 1992.

————. "The Apocalyptic Theme in Pushkin's 'Count Nulin,' " in Peter Alberg Jensen, ed., *Text and Context: Essays to Honor Nils Åke Nilsson.* Stockholm: Almqvist & Wiksell International, 1987: 16–25.

Gaull, Marilyn. *English Romanticism: The Human Context.* New York: W. W. Norton, 1988.

Gearhart, Suzanne. *The Open Boundary of History and Fiction: A Critical Approach to the French Enlightenment.* Princeton: Princeton University Press, 1984.

Gershenzon, M. O. *Stat'i o Pushkine.* Moscow: Academia, 1926.

Gibian, George. "Pushkin's Parody on The Rape of Lucrece." *Shakespeare Quarterly* 1, 1950: 264–66.

Gifford, Henry. "Shakespearean Elements in Boris Godunov," *The Slavonic (and East European) Review,* 26 (1947–48).

————. "Tolstoy and Historical Truth," in *Russian Thought and Society, 1800–1917: Essays in Honour Of Eugene Lampert,* ed. Roger Bartlett. Keele: University of Keele Press, 1984: 114–27.

Gogol, Nikolai. *Arabesques.* Tr. by Alexander Tulloch and intr. by Carl R. Proffer. Ann Arbor, Mich.: Ardis, 1982.

————. *Polnoe sobranie sochinenii,* 14 vols. Moscow: Akademiia Nauk SSSR, 1937–1952.

Golstein, Vladimir. "Pushkin's *Mozart and Salieri* as a Parable of Salvation," *Russian Literature* XXIX, Amsterdam, North-Holland: Elsevier Science B. V., 1990: 155–76.

Gombrich, Ernst Hans. *Art and Illusion: A Study in the Psychology of Pictorial Representation.* Princeton: Princeton University Press, 1972.

Gooch, George P. *History and Historians in the Nineteenth Century.* London: Longmans, Green, 1913.

Gorodetskii, B. P. *Lirika Pushkina.* Moscow, Leningrad: Akademiia nauk SSSR, 1962.

————. *Tragediia A. S. Pushkina "Boris Godunov." Kommentarii.* Leningrad: Prosveshchenie, 1969.

Gossman, Lionel. *Between History and Literature.* Cambridge, Mass.: Harvard University Press, 1990.

Greenleaf, Monika. *Pushkin and Romantic Fashion: Fragment, Elegy, Orient, Irony.* Stanford, Calif.: Stanford University Press, 1994.

Gregg, Richard. "The Nature of Nature and the Nature of Eugene in 'The Bronze Horseman'," *Slavic and East European Journal,* 21, No. 2, 1977.

Grossman, Leonid. *Etiudy o Pushkine.* Moscow: L. D. Frenkel', 1923.

Guizot, François. *Historical Essays and Lectures.* Ed. and intr. by Stanley Mellon. Chicago: University of Chicago Press, 1972.

———. *The History of Civilization,* vol. I. London: George Bell and Sons, 1878.

Gukasova, A. G. *Boldinskii period v tvorchestve A. S. Pushkina.* Moscow: Prosveshchenie, 1973.

Gukovskii, G. A. *Pushkin i problemy realisticheskogo stilia.* Moscow: GIKhL, 1957.

Gurevich, A. M. "Sokrovennyi smysl 'Poltavy.' " *Izvestiia Akademii Nauk SSSR,* tom, 47, No. 3, 1988: 228–35.

Gustafson, Richard F. *Leo Tolstoy, Resident and Stranger: A Study in Fiction and Theology.* Princeton: Princeton University Press, 1986.

Gutsche, George J. "Pushkin and Nicholas: The Problem of 'Stanzas'," *Pushkin Today,* ed. by David M. Bethea. Bloomington: Indiana University Press, 1993.

———. "Pushkin's *The Bronze Horseman,*" *Moral Apostasy in Russian Literature.* Dekalb, Ill.: Northern Illinois University Press, 1986.

Harvey, W. J. *Character and the Novel.* Ithaca: Cornell University Press, 1968.

Hegel, Georg Wilhelm Friedrick. *The Philosophy of History.* New York: Dover Publications, 1956.

Heisenberg, Werner. *Physics and Philosophy: The Revolution in Modern Science.* New York: Harper, 1958.

Heyer, Elfriede A. "The Genesis of *Wallenstein:* From History to Drama," in Alexej Ugrinsky ed., *Friedrich Von Schiller and the Drama of Human Existence.* New York: Greenwood Press, 1988.

Hutcheon, Linda. " 'The Pastime of Past Time': Fiction, History, Historiographic Metafiction," in Marjorie Perloff, ed., *Postmodern Genres.* Norman: University of Oklahoma Press, 1988: 54–74.

Iakubovich, D. P. " 'Arap Petra Velikogo'," *Pushkin: Issledovaniia i materialy,* 9, Leningrad: AN SSSR, Nauka, 1979.

The Interpreter's Bible, vol. VIII. New York: Abingdon-Cokesbury Press, 1952.

Ivanov, V. V., and Toporov, V. N. *Issledovaniia v oblasti slavianskikh drevnostei. (Leksicheskie i frazeologicheskie voprosy rekonstrukthii tekstov).* Moscow: Nauka, 1974.

———. "Perun," *Mify narodov mira,* vol. 2. Moscow: Sovetskaia entsiclopediia, 1982.

Izmailov, N. V. "K istorii zamysla i sozdaniia 'Mednogo vsadnika," *Pushkin i ego sovremenniki,* 38–39, Leningrad: AN SSSR, 1930.

———. "K voprosu ob istoricheskikh istochnikakh 'Poltavy'," *Pushkin: Vremennik Pushkinskoi komissii,* vols. 4–5. Leningrad: AN SSSR, 1939.

———. *Ocherki tvorchestva Pushkina.* Leningrad: Nauka, 1975.

Jackson, Robert Louis. *Dostoevsky's Quest for Form: A Study of his Philosophy of Art.* Bloomington, Ind.: Physsardt, 1978.

Jakobson, Roman. "The Statue in Pushkin's Poetic Mythology," in *Selected Writings,* vol. 5. New York: Mouton Publishers, 1979.

Karamzin, N. M. *Istoriia Gosudarstva Rossiiskogo.* 5th edition. 4 vols. St. Petersburg, 1842–44. Reprint, Moscow: Kniga, 1988–89.

———. "O sluchaiakh i kharakterakh v Rossiiskoi istorii, kotorye mogut byt' predmetom khudozhestv," *Izbrannye stati'i i pis'ma.* Moscow: Sovremennik, 1982.

———. *Pis'ma russkogo puteshestvennika.* Leningrad: Nauka, 1984.

Kerr, James. *Fiction against History: Scott as Storyteller.* Cambridge: Cambridge University Press, 1989.

Kibal'nik, Sergei. "Istoricheskaia tema v poezii A. S. Pushkina," *Literatura i istoriia (Istoricheskii protsess v tvorcheskom soznanii russkikh pisatelei XVIII–XX vv.).* St. Petersburg: Nauka, 1992: 57–77.

———. *Khudozhestvennaia filosofiia Pushkina: Uchebnoe posobie po spetskursu.* St. Petersburg: Poleks, 1993.

Kireevskii, I. N. *Izbrannye stat'i.* Moscow: Sovremennik, 1984.

Kornilovich, A. O. *Russkaia starina: Karmannaia knizhka dlia liubitelei otechestvennogo na 1825 god.* St. Petersburg, 1825.

Kracauer, Siegfried. *History: The Last Things Before the Last.* New York: Oxford University Press, 1969.

Krasnov, G. N. " 'Apokalipsicheskaia pesn' A. S. Pushkina (K sporam o stikhotvorenii 'Geroi')", *Problemy Pushkinovedeniia: Sbornik nauchnykh trudov,* Leningrad, 1975.

———. "Dialektika khudozhestvennoi mysli ('Strannye sblizheniia' Pushkina)," *Bodinskie chteniia.* Gor'kii, 1976: 4–16.

Krysteva, Denka. "Epicheskii kharakter temy Petra I i poiski A. S. Pushkina v ee khudozhestvennom osmyslenii," in *Problemy sovremennogo
pushkinovedeniia: Mezhvuzovskii sbornik nauchnykh trudov*. Leningrad:
LGPI. 1986.

Lapkina, G. A. "K istorii sozdaniia 'Arapa Petra Velikogo'," *Pushkin:
Issledovaniia i materialy*, 2, Moscow-Leningrad: AN SSSR, Nauka,
1958: 293–309.

Lednicki, Waclaw. *Pushkin's "Bronze Horseman": The Story of a Master-
piece*. Berkeley: University of California Press, 1955.

Lévi-Strauss, Claude. *The Savage Mind*. Chicago: University of Chicago
Press, 1966.

Levkovich, Ia l. "Printsipy dokumental'nogo povestvovaniia v istoricheskoi proze pushkinskoi pory," *Pushkin: Issledovaniia i materialy*, 6,
Leningrad: AN SSSR, Nauka, 1969: 171–96.

Lindenberger, Herbert. *Historical Drama: The Relation of Literature and
Reality*. Chicago: University of Chicago Press, 1975.

——. *The History in Literature: On Value, Genre, Institutions*. New York:
Columbia University Press, 1990.

Lotman Iu. M. *Izbrannye stat'i*. 3 vols. Tallinn: Aleksandra, 1992.

——. "The Poetics of Everyday Behavior in Russian Eighteenth-
Century Culture," in Ann Shukman, ed., *The Semiotics of Russian
Culture*, Ann Arbor: Michigan Slavic Contributions, 1984.

——. "Posviashchenie 'Poltavy'," *Problemy pushkinovedeniia: Sbornik
nauchnykh trudov*. Leningrad, 1975.

——. "Proiskhozhdenie siuzheta v tipologicheskom osveshchenii,"
Stat'i po tipologii kul'tury. Tartu: TGU, 1973: 9–41.

——. *Roman Pushkina "Evgenii Onegin."* Leningrad: Prosveshchenie,
1983.

——. *V shkole poeticheskogo slova: Pushkin, Lermontov, Gogol*. Moscow:
Prosveshchenie, 1988.

——. "Tri zametki k pushkinskim tekstam," *Vremenik Pushkinskoi
komissii*, Leningrad: AN SSSR, 1977.

Lukács, Georg. *The Historical Novel*, tr. by Hannah and Stanley Mitchell.
Boston: Beacon Press, 1963.

Makogonenko, G. P. *Tvorchestvo A. S. Pushkina v 1830-e gody (1833–
1836)*. Leningrad: Khudozhestvennaia literatura, 1982.

Manzoni, Alessandro. *On the Historical Novel*. Lincoln: University of
Nebraska Press, 1984.

Markovich, Vladimir M. " 'Povesti Belkina' i literaturnyi kontekst,"

Pushkin: Issledovaniia i materialy, 8. Leningrad: AN SSSR, Nauka, 1989.

Mazour, Anatole G. *The First Russian Revolution, 1825.* Stanford, Calif.: Stanford University Press, 1977.

McKeon, Richard, ed. *Introduction to Aristotle.* New York: Random House, 1947.

Meletinskii, E. M. *Poetika mifa.* Moscow: Nauka, 1976.

Memuary dekabristov: Iuzhnoe obshchestvo. Moscow: Izdatel'stvo Moskovskogo universiteta, 1982.

Mickiewicz, Adam. *Dziady: Czesc II, IV i I,* Warszawa: Czytelnik, 1968.

Mify narodov mira, 2 vols. Moscow: Sovetskaia entsiklopediia, 1980–82.

Mikkelson, Gerald E. "Pushkin and the History of the Russian Nobility" (Ph.D. Dissertation, University of Wisconsin, 1971).

―――. "Pushkin's 'Geroj': A Verse Dialogue on Truth," *Slavic and East European Journal,* vol. 18, No. 4, 1974.

―――. "Pushkin's *History of Pugachev:* The Littérateur as Historian," in Gutsche, George J., Leighton, Lauren G., eds. *New Perspectives on Nineteenth-Century Prose.* Columbus, Oh.: Slavica, 1982: 36–40.

―――. "The Mythopoetic Element in Pushkin's novel *The Captain's Daughter,*" *Canadian-American Slavic Studies,* vol. 7, No. 3, 1973: 296–313.

Mirsky, D. S. *Uncollected Writings on Russian Literature.* Berkeley: Berkeley Slavic Specialties, 1989.

Monnier, André. "Puskin et Napoléon," *Cahiers du monde russe et soviétique,* 32 (2), avril-juin 1991: 209–16.

Morson, Gary Saul. *Hidden in Plain View: Narrative and Creative Potentials in* War and Peace. Stanford, Calif.: Stanford University Press, 1988.

Munhall, Edgar. "Portraits of Napoleon," *Yale French Studies,* 26 (Fall–Winter), 1960–61: 3–20.

Murav'iova, O. C. "Pushkin i Napoleon," *Pushkin: Issledovaniia i materialy,* 14, Leningrad: AN SSSR, Nauka, 1991, 5–32.

Nemoianu, Virgil. *The Taming of Romanticism: European Literature and the Age of Biedermeier.* Cambridge, Mass.: Harvard University Press, 1984.

Nietzsche, Friedrich. *Beyond Good and Evil.* Tr. by R. J. Hollingdale. New York: Penguin Books, 1988.

―――. *The Use and Abuse of History,* tr. by Adrian Collins. New York: Liberal Arts Press, 1957.

————. *Unmodern Observations*. Ed. by William Arrowsmith. New Haven: Yale University Press, 1990.

Odinokov, V. G. *"I dal' svobodnogo romana . . .".* Novosibirsk, 1983.

Odoevskii, V. F. *Sochineniia*, 2 vols. Moscow: Khudozhestvennaia literatura, 1981.

Oksman, Iu. G. "Pushkin v rabote nad romanom 'Kapitanskaia dochka,'" in A. S. Pushkin, *Kapitanskaia dochka*. Moscow: Nauka, 1984: 145–99.

Ovchinnikov, P. V. *Pushkin v rabote nad arkhivnymi dokumentami ("Istoriia Pugacheva").* Leningrad: Nauka, 1969.

Panchenko, M. M., Uspenkii B. A. "Ivan Groznyi i Piotr Velikii: kontseptsii pervogo monarkha," *Trudy otdela drevne russkoi literatury*, 37, Leningrad: AN SSSR, 1983.

Pauls, John P., and Pauls, La Verne R. "Maria in Pushkin's *Poltava* (The Character and the Person)," *Festschrift für Nikola R. Pribic*. Munchen: Hierenymus Verlag Neuried, 1983.

Peirce, Charles S. *Philosophical Writings of Peirce*. Ed. by Justus Buchler. New York: Dover Publications, 1955.

Petrov, S. *Istoricheskii roman Pushkina*. Moscow: Akademiia nauk SSSR, 1953.

Petrunina, N. N. *Proza Pushkina*. Leningrad: Nauka, 1987.

Poliakov, Mark Ia. *Voprosy poetiki i khudohestvennoi semantiki*. Moscow: Sovetskii pisatel', 1986.

Pumpianskii, L. V. " 'Mednyi vsadnik' i poeticheskaia traditsiia XVIII veka," *Pushkin: Vremennik Pushkinskoi komissii*, 4–5. Leningrad: AN SSSR, 1939: 91–124.

Pushkin v vospominaniiakh sovremennikov, 2 vols. Moscow: Khudozhestvennaia literatura, 1985.

Rabkin, Norman. *Shakespeare and the Common Understanding*. New York: Free Press, 1967.

Radishchev, A. N. *Izbrannye sochineniia*. Moskva: Khudozhestvennaia literatura, 1952.

Rassadin, Stanislav. *Dramaturg Pushkin*. Moscow: Iskusstvo, 1977.

Reizov, B. G. *Frantsuzskaia romanticheskaia istoriografiia*. Leningrad: LGU, 1956.

————. "Pushkin, Tatsit i 'Boris Godunov,'" *Iz istorii evropeiskikh literatur*. Leningrad, 1970.

Riasanovsky, Nicholas V. *The Image of Peter the Great in Russian History and Thought*. New York: Oxford University Press, 1985.

Ricoeur, Paul. *The Symbolism of Evil*. Boston: Beacon Press, 1969.

Rossiia v period reform Petra I. Sbornik statei pod redaktsiei N. I. Pavlenko. Moscow: Nauka, 1973.

Rousseau, Jean Jacques. *The Social Contract.* Tr. and intr. by Willmoore Kendall, Chicago, Illinois: Henry Regnery Company, 1954.

Sandler, Stephanie. *Distant Pleasures: Alexander Pushkin and the Writers of Exile.* Stanford, Calif.: Stanford University Press, 1989.

———. "The Problem of History in Pushkin: Poet, Pretender, Tsar" (Ph.D. Dissertation, Yale University, 1982).

Schapiro, Leonard. *Rationalism and Nationalism in Russian Nineteenth-Century Political Thought.* New Haven: Yale University Press, 1967.

Schiller, Friedrich. *The Robbers and Wallenstein.* London: Penguin Books, 1979.

Serman, I. Z. "Khudozhestvennaia problematika i kompozitsiia poemy 'Poltava,' " *A. S. Pushkin: Stat'i i materialy,* Gor'kii, 1971.

———. "Pushkin i russkaia istoricheskaia drama 1830kh godov," in *Pushkin: Issledovaniia i materialy,* 6, Leningrad: Nauka, 1969.

Shakespeare, William. *The Poems.* London: Methuen, 1978.

Sharpe, Lesley. *Schiller and the Historical Character: Presentation and Interpretation in the Historiographical Works and in the Historical Dramas.* London: Oxford University Press, 1982.

Shaw, Harry E. *The Forms of Historical Fiction: Sir Walter Scott and His Successors.* Ithaca: Cornell University Press, 1983.

Shmurlo, E. *Petr Velikii v otsenke sovremenikov i potomstva.* St. Petersburg: Senatskaia Tipografiia, 1912.

———. *Petr Velikii v ruskoi literature.* St. Petersburg: Tipografiia V. S. Balasheva, 1889.

Sidiakov, L. S. " 'Arap Petra Velikogo' i 'Polatava'," *Pushkin: Issledovaniia i materialy,* 12, Leningrad: AN SSSR, Nauka, 1986.

Slonimskii, A. L. *Masterstvo Pushkina.* Moscow: GIKhL, 1963.

Sokolov, A. N. " 'Poltava' Pushkina i 'Petriady' " *Pushkin: Vremennik Pushkinskoi komissii,* 4–5. Moscow, Leningrad: AN SSSR, 1939: 57–90.

Sovremennik, 5. St. Petersburg: Guttenbergova Tipografiia, 1837.

Stennik, Iu. V. "Kontseptsiia XVIII veka v tvotcheskikh iskaniiakh Pushkina," *Pushkin: Issledovaniia i materialy,* 11. Leningrad: Nauka, 1983.

Striedter, Jurij. "Poetic Genre and the Sense of History in Pushkin," *New Literary History,* 8, No. 2 (Winter 1977): 295–309.

Tertz, Abram. *Sobranie sochinenii v dvukh tomakh,* tom 1. Moscow: SP Start, 1992.

Theological Dictionary of the New Testament. Ed. by Gerhard Kittel, tr. and ed. Geoffrey W. Bromiley. Grand Rapids, Mich.: Eerdmans, 1964–1976.

Tocqueville, Alexis de. *Democracy in America,* vol. 2. Ed. by Phillips Bradley, New York: Vintage Books, 1945.

Todd, William Mills III. "Eugene Onegin: 'Life's Novel,'" *Literature and Society in Imperial Russia, 1800–1914.* Stanford, Calif.: Stanford University Press, 1978.

———. *Fiction and Society in the Age of Pushkin: Ideology, Institutions, and Narrative.* Cambridge, Mass.: Harvard University Press, 1986.

Toibin, I. M. " 'Evgenii Onegin': poeziia i istoriia," *Pushkin: Issledovaniia i materialy.* Leningrad: AN SSSR, Nauka, 1979: 83–99.

———. *Pushkin i filosofsko-istoricheskaia mysl' v Rossii na rubezhe 1820 i 1830 godov.* Voronezh: Izdatel'stvo voronezhskogo universiteta, 1980.

———. "Voprosy istorizma i khudozhestvennaia sistema Pushkina 1830-kh godov," *Pushkin: Issledovaniia i materialy,* 6. Leningrad: AN SSSR, Nauka, 1969: 35–59.

Tolstoy, Lev N. *Sobranie sochinenii v dvadtsati dvukh tomakh,* Moscow: Khudozhestvennaia literatura, 1978–85.

Tomashevskii, B. V. *Pushkin: Kniga vtoraia.* Moscow: Akademiia nauk SSSR, 1961.

———. *Pushkin i Frantsiia.* Leningrad: Sovetskii pisatel', 1960.

Toporov, V. N. "Drevo mirivoe," *Mify narodov mira,* vol. 1. Moscow, 1980.

Tsvetaeva, Marina. "Pushkin i Pugachev," in *Sochineniia,* vol. 2. Moscow: Khudozhestvennaia literatura, 1980: 368–96.

Turgenev, I. *Sobranie sochinenii v desiati tomakh,* 10. Moscow: Pravda, 1962.

Uspenskii, Boris A. "Tsar and Pretender: Samozvančestvo or Royal Imposture in Russia as a Cultural-Historical Phenomenon," in Lotman Ju. M. and Uspenskij B. A. *The Semiotics of Russian Culture.* Ed. by Ann Shukman, Ann Arbor: Ardis, 1984.

Vatsuro, Vadim. "Istoricheskaia tragediia i romanticheskaia drama nachala 1830-kh godov," in *Istoriia russkoi dramaturgii: XVII—pervaia polovina XIX veka.* Leningrad: Nauka, 1982: 327–67.

———. " 'Podvig chestnogo cheloveka,'" *Prometei,* 5. Moscow, 1968.

Vetlovskaia, V. E. "Pushkin: Problemy istorii i formirivanie russkogo realizma," *Literatura i istoriia (Istoricheskii protsess v tvorcheskom soznanii russkikh pisatelei XVIII–XX vv.).* St. Petersburg: Nauka, 1992.

Viazemskii, P. A. *Polnoe sobranie sochinenii.* Ed. S. D. Sheremetev. 12 vols. St. Petersburg: M. M. Stasiulevich, 1878–86.

Vinogradov, V. V. *O iazyke khudozhestvennoi literatury.* Moscow: GIKhL, 1959.

Vinokur, G. O. "Kommentarii k *Borisu Godunovu,*" *Polnoe sobranie sochinenii A. S. Pushkina,* vol. 7, Moscow: AN SSSR, 1935: 430–31.

Voltaire. *Russia Under Peter the Great.* Tr. by M. F. O. Jenkins. Rutherford, N.J.: Fairleigh Dickinson University Press, 1983.

Wachtel, Andrew. *An Obsession with History: Russian Writers Confront the Past.* Stanford, Calif.: Stanford University Press, 1994.

Weinstein, Mark. "The Creative Imagination in Fiction and History," *Genre,* 9, 3, 1976: 263–77.

White, Hayden. *Metahistory: The Historical Imagination in Nineteenth-Century Europe.* Baltimore: Johns Hopkins University Press, 1987.

Zhirmunskii, V. M. *Bairon i Pushkin.* Leningrad: Nauka, 1978.

Zhivov, V. M., and Uspenskii, B. A. "Tsar' i Bog. Semioticheskie aspecty oaoralizatoii monarkha v Rossii." *Iazyki kul'tury i problemy perevodimosti.* Moscow: Nauka, 1987: 47–154.

index

Page numbers followed by "n" or "nn" refer to information in notes.

russian literature and thought

Rereading Russian Poetry
Edited by Stephanie Sandler

Liberty, Equality, and the Market: Essays by B. N. Chicherin
Edited and translated by G. M. Hamburg

Toward Another Shore: Russian Thinkers Between Necessity and Chance
Aileen M. Kelly

Dostoevsky and Soloviev: The Art of Integral Vision
Marina Kostalevsky

Abram Tertz and the Poetics of Crime
Catharine Theimer Nepomnyashchy

Untimely Thoughts: Essays on Revolution, Culture, and the Bolsheviks, 1917–1918
Maxim Gorky

A Voice from the Chorus
Abram Tertz (Andrei Sinyavsky)

Strolls with Pushkin
Abram Tertz (Andrei Sinyavsky)

1920 Diary
Isaac Babel